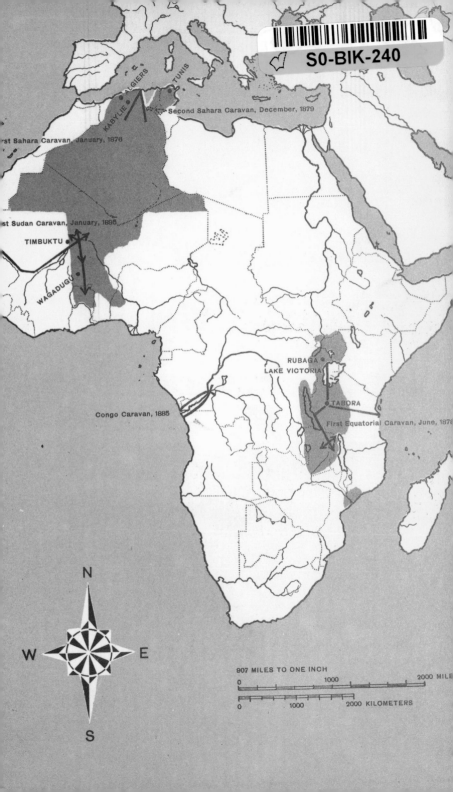

SO-BIK-240

Second Sahara Caravan, December, 1879

First Sahara Caravan, January, 1876

First Sudan Caravan, January, 1895

TIMBUKTU

WAGADUGU

RUBAGA
LAKE VICTORIA

TABORA

Congo Caravan, 1885

First Equatorial Caravan, June, 1878

N
W   E
S

907 MILES TO ONE INCH

0   1000   2000 MILES

0   1000   2000 KILOMETERS

THE WHITE FATHERS

His Eminence Cardinal Lavigerie (1825-1892),
Founder of the White Fathers.

THE

WHITE
FATHERS

BY
GLENN D. KITTLER

INTRODUCTION BY BISHOP LAURIAN RUGAMBWA

HARPER & BROTHERS, PUBLISHERS
NEW YORK

THE WHITE FATHERS
Copyright © 1957 by Glenn D. Kittler
Printed in the United States of America

Library of Congress catalog card number: 57-6134

TO
MY MOTHER AND FATHER

A WHITE FATHERS MAP OF AFRICA

Total Number of White Fathers in Africa: 2,253
Total Number of White Sisters in Africa: 1,200
Number of Mission Stations, White Fathers: 468 } Total 577
Number of Mission Stations, African Clergy: 109 }
Dioceses: 37

First Sahara Caravan, January, 1878

Second Sahara Caravan, December, 1879

KABYLIE
ALGIERS
TUNIS

First Sudan Caravan, January, 1895

TIMBUKTU

WAGADUGU

Congo Caravan, 1885

RUBAGA
LAKE VICTORIA

TABORA

First Equatorial Caravan, June, 1878

N
W   E
S

907 MILES TO ONE INCH
0   1000   2000 MILES
0   1500   2000 KILOMETERS

"THE cries of anguish arising from afar where Africa has for centuries lain stricken in the agonies of slavery, the ruins nearer home of a bygone Christian age, and the memory of her famous men and of her saints will move your hearts with love for Africa. The very stones of Sion, symbols of such great hopes, were treasures to the hearts of the Patriarchs of old, and I have learned to love my Africa as they their Sion, its distant past, its glories yet to come; its mountains and its limpid sky; its radiant sun, the vast expanses of its desert sands, the azure waves that gently wash its shores."

—CARDINAL LAVIGERIE *to the first White Fathers*

A sixteen-page section of illustrations will be found following page 174.

ACKNOWLEDGMENTS

IT is rare for a layman to observe the Catholic Church and one of its religious societies as intimately as I did during the preparation of this book. All my questions were answered; any documents I wanted to see were provided without hesitation. The structure of the Catholic Church and its position in world affairs require a certain prudence: at all times during the work on this book, prudence was left to my discretion. For their co-operation and assistance, I am indebted to a score of White Fathers in Rome and Washington, D.C. Despite the constant pressures upon them, they generously gave me the benefit of their time, talent and experience, all of which I borrowed with a presumptuous enthusiasm which I hope is now forgiven. The bishops, priests, nuns, and brothers throughout Africa who made my journey a pleasure and an education will always have my deepest appreciation. Special thanks must go to Miss Iris Gabriel, who one day in Washington introduced me to the White Fathers without realizing what she was starting. And—long overdue—I want to declare my admiration and my debt to an outstanding member of the limbo of the literary profession—my agent, Miss Evelyn Singer, whose wisdom and perception, patience and understanding have fulfilled her ancient prophecy when we first began to work together: "You won't get rich, but you'll have a lot of fun." I hope that together we have also managed to do some good.

G.D.K.

A WORD FROM AFRICA

It is the custom of my people always to accept gifts with both hands in order to show that we consider the gift so precious that we want to hold it carefully and with a great love. For sixty-five years now, we have had among us a gift so precious that we hold it best when our hands are clasped in prayer. It is the gift of Christianity, first given to us by the White Fathers in 1892, and it has changed our lives in many ways.

With Christianity came all the riches inherent in it. The White Fathers gave us our first schools, and we learned to read and write our own language, something we could not do before. Learning this, we were equipped to learn other languages, to read the books of many lands, to discover the world which we never knew existed and to absorb from that world the things we felt would be best for us. Moreover, the White Fathers built hospitals for us, rescuing us from diseases which at one time had killed entire villages and then teaching us how to defend ourselves against new attacks of sickness. And they instructed us in their trades and skills so that we could make our lives easier and better.

But material progress would be meaningless if it did not have a spiritual parallel, and I have been in an excellent position in the past few years to observe that the spiritual parallel among my people has been steadfast. My family became Christian about thirty-five years ago, when my parents and their children were baptized by the White Fathers at the Kagonodo Mission in northwest Tanganyika. I was eight years old then, and just beginning to attend the mission school. For the next five years, I watched all that the African Fathers were doing for my people, and when I was thirteen I decided to enter the minor seminary which the missionaries had built at Rubya so that I might one day, sharing the priesthood with them, work with them in the good they were accomplishing. It was in 1943 that I became a priest, and for five years I worked side by side with the White Fathers. In 1948 I was chosen to study canon law in Rome for three years. Shortly after I returned to Tanganyika, I was consecrated the first bishop of the newly created Rutabo Diocese, and I made my home at the mission where I had first learned to say my prayers.

Now, as is proper in the Church, the future of the Faith became the responsibility of those who claimed to be Christians, and quickly my people showed that they wanted to share this responsibility. One day a committee came from a distant village and asked me to build a church there so that the people could have priests always with them. I was forced to tell them that my budget did not permit me to build the church at the present time, so the people themselves donated the materials and built the church and a rectory with their own hands. Surely I could not have asked for stronger evidence of devotion to the Faith which the White Fathers had brought to us.

When the White Fathers relinquished the diocese to me, they gave me the seventeen primary schools they had established. In five years, we have built two parishes and twenty more schools, and again with mostly volunteer assistance from the people. We have also opened two middle schools, and a trade school where boys can learn skills to help them earn a living in our fast-growing country. Almost all our teachers are trained in institutions founded and maintained by the White Fathers, returning to us equipped to help our people to improve themselves.

The opportunity for self-improvement is all the African asks. We have learned from Christianity that we have a place of dignity and self-respect in the brotherhood of mankind and we are anxious to assume it. In some parts of Africa, this has already been achieved. It is reasonable to believe that it will also be achieved throughout Africa as more of our people develop the requisites of leadership.

That we have progressed as far as we have is due directly to the missionaries who came to us almost a hundred years ago. What they have done for the material progress of the African can only be surpassed in importance by what they have done for his soul. And what they have done for his soul has stirred a nobility of the mind and purity of the heart which will produce a continent of just men dedicated to God and the welfare of all.

Materially, much remains to be done in Africa, but these days more and more Africans are appearing who are properly trained, spiritually and intellectually, for the task ahead. For the present—and perhaps for a little while to come, Africa must rely upon the Christians of other continents for the assistance and guidance necessary to conquer our remaining problems, but history shows that the time inevitably comes when new lands are able to stand alone. When I visited the United States in 1956, Bishop Fulton J. Sheen expressed the opinion to me that in another century African countries will be among the world leaders and the time may well be when Christians of other nations turn to Africa for the aid which we are now obliged to seek from them. If this should come to pass, they will find here a Christianity that is strong and deep in the hearts of the people, a Faith planted and nurtured by missionaries who sacrificed, suffered and died, like the White Fathers, in order to lead the African to his place in the unity of the Mystical Body of Christ and the fraternity of men. Then perhaps we shall be able to reciprocate the cherished gift of Christianity, but gratitude for it will remain distinctly and eternally ours.

✚ LAURIAN RUGAMBWA
Bishop of the Rutabo Diocese
P. O. Box 33 Kamachumu
Tanganyika Territory
British East Africa

THE WHITE FATHERS

I

THE morning was surprisingly cold for September. There was a brisk
wind at the windows. The high Atlas Mountains held back the sun,
making the morning dark blue. At ten minutes to five came the usual
tap at the door and the soft, *"Benedicamus Domino."* The priest in the
bed replied with a muffled, *"Deo gratias,"* then threw back the
covers and sat up. Footsteps outside moved to the next door; again
the gentle knock, again the greeting, "Let us praise the Lord,"
and the response, "Thanks be to God." The morning coldness
wrapped itself around Father Jean Tabart, and he shuddered. His
eyes accustomed to the gloom, he did not bother to put a match
to the oil lamp on his night table. With a step he was across the
room at the pan of water he had poured the night before to take
the chill off it. He splashed his face and reached for a towel in the
same moment, sent a dry brush darting over his teeth, rinsed his
mouth, went to his clothes, and dressed quickly: white socks and
black shoes, a blousey white robe that hung loosely to the ankles,
a white capelike burnoose that slipped over the head, a red fez, a
large black-and-white rosary double-looped around the neck. He
picked up his breviary and stepped outside. The sudden wind
stopped him at his door.

Even after a dozen years in Algeria, Father Tabart could not get used to the idea that African nights could be so cold. With a move of his shoulder he let his burnoose fold warmly around him and he hurried across the garden to the small room at the end of the house which the three priests of the mission used as their private chapel. The others were already there. Father Superior waited until he heard Tabart kneel at his *prie-dieu,* then slowly and solemly made the sign of the cross upon himself and began to lead morning prayers. At that same moment in six hundred missions from the Mediterranean to the Rhodesias, from the Atlantic to the Indian Ocean, some two thousand other priests, dressed exactly the same, were beginning the same prayers. They were men who were known throughout Africa as the White Fathers.

There was great need for prayers that September, 1956, morning. Algerian Arabs were in revolt against France and there was fighting in the hills everyday. A French contingent had settled in a valley twenty miles from the village of Géryville, where Father Tabart knelt at his prayers, and there was talk of a big battle soon. French settlers had moved out, abandoning the farms they had spent years carving from the rugged mountainsides, and Arab forces had moved in. Certainly the fight would be a terrible one. Father Tabart prayed for the men on both sides who would die. The prayers finished, the three priests sat back in their chairs, lowered their heads, and began their forty-five minutes of morning meditation.

Father Tabart had always looked upon meditation as a vital part of each day and he was happy the White Fathers rule prescribed it. His head bowed, his eyes closed, he could become lost in God for forty-five minutes, choosing some moment of Christ's life, studying it, analyzing it, comparing himself to it, discovering from each meditation some new way to make himself more like Christ. On this particular morning, Father Tabart concentrated on the Crucifixion—not all of it, of course: there was too much to it to encompass in one meditation, so he fixed his thoughts on the idea of how much love Christ must have had for mankind that He should permit Himself to be put to such a horrible death in order that Heaven could be opened. Father Tabart examined his days for new channels by which he could love to the same extent the Arabs who

2

surrounded him, in the village, on their mountain farms, on the plains beyond where they drove their flocks. He remembered that just a few days ago the French commander had come to the mission and told the priests they had better make arrangements to leave the area as soon as possible.

"We can't leave," Father Tabart had said. "Our work is here."

"You can come back someday," the commander said, "but there's going to be a lot of trouble around here for the next few weeks and this will be no place for a Frenchman."

"But the White Fathers aren't French any more," Tabart said. "We're Arabs now."

The commander shook his head. "I'll bet the Arabs don't feel that way."

Tabart said: "They certainly won't if we leave."

Simply remaining, however, would not be enough in itself to convince Arabs that the White Fathers considered themselves part of the people. Much more had to be done, and the White Fathers had been doing it for almost a hundred years. The society had been founded on the principle—Be all things to all men. In North Africa, that meant becoming Arabs to the fullest degree the priesthood would allow. It meant dressing like Arabs and speaking like Arabs, it meant eating Arab food and living in an Arab house, and it meant something more. It meant injecting into Arab life the kind of service and charity that was not Arabic at all. It meant crowded hours every day of demonstrating the brotherhood of Christianity to people who for more than a thousand years had looked upon Christians as dogs. This was the Moslem attitude the White Fathers were determined to overcome. Chances of converting any of the Arabs were so utterly slim that a successful missionary to North Africa had to be a man of strong and patient faith. Father Tabart had spent two years developing that spiritual defense in special White Fathers' training centers, then went to the missions fully aware that as long as he remained in North Africa he could never expect to enjoy the consolation so rewarding to a priest: a fervent congregation. Islam and its inherent hatred of Christians were so deep in the Arabs that Father Tabart knew he might never baptize anyone, would probably never give Communion to a layman, and

3

the only confessions he would most likely hear would be those of other missionaries. His contacts with Arabs were, therefore, limited to acts of friendship—better still, Christian charity—with the hope that sometime in the future, perhaps decades away, the people might change their attitudes and that the Koranic prerogative of killing any Moslem who became a Christian would not be so readily applied.

After the French commander had left, Father Tabart hurried across town to an illiterate merchant who wanted a letter written to his son in Tunis. Tabart took the dictation, read it back to be sure he had it right, then posted the letter. Next he went out to a hut at the edge of the village to give another antibiotic injection to a baby that had been bitten by a rat a few days before. The baby's mother had offered him a cup of thick black coffee, but he could not pause because he had promised a young Arab to call on the parents of his sweetheart to see if the required dowry payment by the youth could be cut down so that the couple might marry sooner. He also knew that waiting for him at the mission was a backwoods farmer whose mountain-side vineyard had been swept away by heavy rains, and Tabart had asked the man to come in so that he could explain to him how to terrace his land against similar troubles in the next torrents.

Mental notations of such incidents passed through Tabart's mind as he sat at meditation, and he told himself he was not doing enough. He would have to do more. He searched the day ahead for opportunities, lined up a schedule, then dedicated each deed to God, offering it as an effort to bring the Arabs closer to Christ, however indirect the route.

From the wall clock in the refectory across the garden came six sharp pings. The priests in the chapel knelt for the prayers con-cluding meditation, then Father Superior went into the sacristy to vest for Mass. Tabart followed him to pick up the Mass kit he had packed the day before, and then he went outside. Since the French troops had moved into the area, Tabart had made a point of going to their camp at least twice a week to say Mass for the men. The visits were important to Tabart; each time he went there he learned that one or the other man had been killed in action, and it meant a lot to the priest—and undoubtedly to the man—to know that he

4

had received the sacraments before he died. Father Tabart strapped the Mass kit to his bicycle and started off.

At the same moment throughout Africa, hundreds of other White Fathers were also starting out to say Mass, in a bush village, a distant hospital, a school perhaps. Knowing this always filled Father Tabart with a sense of fraternity he greatly enjoyed. There, of course, were other societies of missionaries in Africa, but the White Fathers were the largest, and they were the only society dedicated exclusively to Africa. A love for Africa was practically a prerequisite for the society, yet an unnecessary one, for the men who joined the White Fathers had that love from boyhood, a love they couldn't explain but had felt all their lives as vividly as they felt the desire to become priests. It was perhaps a spiritual inheritance from the man who had started the society—Charles Martial Allemand Lavigerie, who had come to Africa as a bishop at the age of forty-one—Tabart's age now—and who had almost single-handedly changed the face of the continent. Lavigerie had been a tornado of a man, big and powerful, who tackled every problem as if it were a living enemy. He had been one of the first men to maintain that Africa should be for the Africans—a form of political heresy a century ago, and he had organized the White Fathers as a step in that direction. It had seemed an unattainable goal in 1856; even in 1956 it was not much closer, but now the Africans—both the brown man of the Sahara and the black man of the Equator—were better equipped for the job, and the White Fathers were greatly responsible. There had been many obstacles, but Lavigerie was a man who thrived on obstacles, and so were the priests who followed him. The hardships, even deaths, had served to unify the White Fathers, to crystallize their aim: to help the African to help himself.

This unique crusade had created a deep brotherhood among the White Fathers, strengthened them, and gave their efforts greater impact upon the people. True, progress had been slowest in the north, but if Lavigerie had been correct in predicting that by example and acts of charity the priests would inevitably break down the Moslem resistance to Christianity and the social advancement implicit in it, then the only thing to do, Tabart told himself, was to keep hard at the job, just as others that moment were doing all over Africa.

5

Tabart's road took him high into the mountains, and as he hurried along he saw in distant fields the smoke rising from what he deduced to be insurgent camps. Once or twice he thought he heard sudden movement in the roadside bushes; a lookout probably. Tabart pretended to hear nothing and continued toward the French camp. As a White Father dedicated to Africa, he found his sentiments in the war were with the Arabs. He disapproved of what they were doing, but he could understand why they felt they must. Yet as a priest there was nothing he could do about it, one way or the other; under the circumstances he could only go on with the regular work, as normally as possible. Arabs in Géryville had tried to sound him out, but he had replied merely: "You people should know me well after all these years. Judge me in that light." All he could hope was that they understood.

It was seven-thirty when Tabart arrived at the camp. Men were waiting for him. He vested quickly and said his Mass. After it, several men accompanied him to the mess hall where they had breakfast of coffee and bread. It was almost nine when they finished and drifted out to Tabart's bicycle for a cigarette and a bit of chat before he headed back to town. One of the men said: "This must be a terrible trip for you to make on a bicycle. Why don't you use a car?"

"I don't have one," Tabart said. "There's a pickup at the mission, but Father Superior often needs it unexpectedly and I don't like to take it."

"A motorcycle then," suggested the man.

Tabart laughed. "On these roads? It would be like riding a wild horse. The trip's not bad, though. See that hill?" Tabart pointed. "That's the only rough part. Full of holes. You have to walk it both ways. One spot"—he pointed again—"looks like it's been hit by an H-bomb. But once you get to the top"—again he pointed—"you can coast practically all the way to town."

"Well," said the soldier, "I still wouldn't want to make the trip twice a week. Maybe we can make arrangements to pick you up."

"I don't mind it," Tabart said. "It gives me some exercise. Besides, it's something I can offer up to God in penance for your black souls."

They all laughed easily. Tabart got on his bicycle.

"See you Sunday, Father?"

"Yes. I'll be here." Then solemnly: "Be careful, friends."

6

He rode across the valley to the foot of the big hill, got off his bicycle, and walked up it. At the top, he mounted again for the long downhill ride. He had gone part way when he saw several Arabs rush from the bushes and block his path. He skidded to a stop at their feet. He was about to ask them what was wrong when they jumped him. Before he could speak, one man struck him brutally across the face. Dazed, he felt himself being pulled from his bicycle and dragged off the road. He spoke, and his voice sounded distant, hollow. He tried to free himself, but the Arabs held him fast. They carried him into the thick bush and threw him to the ground, and when he attempted to get up, they straddled him. One man took out a dagger with one hand and with the other ripped Tabart's rosary off his neck. The morning sun caught the dagger as the man raised it.

Tabart had time to say: "God!"

His body was found five days later. The ground was still black moist from his blood. His throat had been cut almost clean through. He was lying face down, his arm outstretched. There were blood on his fingers and markings in the dust, as if he had put his hand to his wound for blood to write a message. His rosary was missing; so were the bicycle and the Mass kit.

He was brought back to the mission and prepared for burial, and that night the village of Géryville was unusually quiet. Very late, there was a knock on the mission door, and Father Superior went to answer it. Standing in the darkness were several men of the village.

One of them said: "We have come to tell you how sorry we are that this has happened."

"Thank you," Father Superior replied.

"And we want you to know we had nothing to do with it."

"Thank you. I believe you."

"The men who did it were not from around here and they did not know him."

"I'm sure that's understandable," the priest said. "There are many strangers in the hills these days."

"We are going to find out who killed him," the man said, "and we are going to avenge his death."

7

"Oh, no," Father Superior said quickly. "No vengeance. He would not want that. Vengeance would be against everything he believed in."

The men were silent a moment, thinking, then said: "In the hills they say Father was killed because he showed the French where the men were hiding."

Father Superior was surprised. "What do you mean?"

"They say they saw him with the French, pointing to where the lookouts were and where the camps were. He pointed many times. They say that was why he was killed."

"There must be some mistake," the priest said. "Father would never do a thing like that, no matter what he knew."

"That was what we told them in the hills. We knew Father was going to the French for the Mass, but we were sure he would not do anything against us."

Another man asked: "Will you close the mission because of this?"

"I hope not," answered Father Superior. "That depends on the French, but I will do everything to keep it open."

"We want you to stay."

And still another man queried: "Have you chosen those who will lower him into the ground?"

"No," said Father Superior. "I will probably do it myself with the other priest here with me, and perhaps a couple of the French soldiers."

"Would it be possible for us to do it?"

"You mean you want to be his pallbearers?"

"If it is possible. Among our people it is a special honor. It is the greatest tribute of friendship we have."

"Very well," said Father Superior. "You may do it. I'm sure nothing could please Father Tabart more than knowing you considered him your friend."

Next morning, the Arabs were there in the courtyard next to the mission, and when Father Superior gave the signal, they gently lowered Father Tabart into his grave. The illiterate merchant was there, too, and the woman with the sick child, and the young man who wanted to get married, and many others Father Tabart had befriended. The scene proved many things, but above all it proved that no matter what Moslems had been taught to believe about

8

Christians, they could still have no defense against men who loved them. This Lavigerie had predicted a century before when, as Bishop of Algiers, he had founded the White Fathers. And he had predicted much more.

II

WITHIN a few days after Lavigerie had been invited to assume the prelate's throne in Algiers, the offer was withdrawn. He was then Bishop of Nancy, an important post for a man who was only forty-one years old. Already he was famous throughout France. He had taught at the Sorbonne, he had raised thousands of francs to aid the persecuted Christians of Lebanon, he had held a high position at the Vatican and, at thirty-seven, had been made a bishop. To be so successful at so young an age indicated a great future in the Church in France, but Lavigerie threw it all aside when the invitation came to go to Algiers. His friends were puzzled, particularly when he insisted on going even after the Governor of Algeria, who had originally extended the invitation, dropped the idea.

"I was asked to go to Africa," Lavigerie said firmly, "and I am going."

It was this same type of firmness that had discouraged Governor MacMahon. A brilliant young bishop like Lavigerie would have attracted much attention to Algeria and to the Governor himself, and this MacMahon wanted. But he did not want a bishop who threatened to walk off with the spotlight, which Lavigerie appeared to be doing even before he set foot in Africa. Since the French conquest of Algeria in 1830, there had been two bishops in the country, both sadly ineffectual, hamstrung by taut government control. The second of them, Bishop Pavy, struggled for years to make the Church in Algeria something more than a social center for visiting dignitaries, but his requests to the government in Paris for authority to proceed unhampered by the local administrations went unheeded and unanswered. At the time, Catholicism was the state religion of France, a relationship which supposedly involved certain benefits for the Church, but historically this rarely proved to be the fact. In Algeria, Pavy was forbidden to make contact with the Arabs, and it was illegal for Arabs even to enter a Catholic church. Lavigerie was aware of this when, soon after Pavy's death in 1866, he received a glowing letter from Governor MacMahon:

I have just heard the sad news of the death of Bishop Pavy. Foreseeing that in all probability the Emperor will consult me with regard to his successor in the See, I have after careful consideration come to the conclusion that there is no one so pre-eminently fitted to be Archbishop of Algiers as the Bishop of Nancy. Of this I am intimately convinced, but before naming you, I must know your wishes regarding this matter. I beg of you, therefore, to let me know if you will accept the position—in my opinion one of the most important which could be given to a priest of France. True, it is one of considerable difficulty. But I know your zeal for religion, and I am confident that the difficulties will not frighten a man of your character. Let me have your answer as soon as possible.

The answer, affirmative and equally glowing, was on its way to MacMahon in twenty-four hours, and the same day the news was all over France. With it went a remarkable statement from Lavigerie:

The sad sight of blindness and impotence that we have seen for thirty years in Africa is only explained by the calculated absence of all Christian thought in the administrations of Algeria, which instead of assimilating these Berber populations by leading them to our civilization keep them in their barbary and their Koran. Well, it is necessary to react at last by a virile word and example against these prejudices. There are two means of assimilation which are at the present right, even more—prudent, efficacious, possible and practicable: works of charity for all and European-type schools for the children. Algeria is only the door, opened by Providence on a barbaric continent of two hundred million souls. It is especially there that we must bring the Catholic apostolate. That is

11

what I believe the clergy of Algeria will be called upon to attempt one day. And that is what they can attempt tomorrow, even at the risk of their lives.

It was not what Governor MacMahon had in mind. His attitude, and that of his predecessors, was that it was better to leave the Arab alone. That way, in his poverty, sickness and ignorance, the Arab was easier to manage. If from his Koran the Arab could find solace for his misery, why stir things up by handing him a Bible and letting him learn he should have a better world?

Because Lavigerie had so widely publicized his acceptance of MacMahon's offer, the Governor could not very well withdraw it himself. However, through the private channels of the Church and government, MacMahon let Lavigerie know that this was exactly what he wanted to do. But Lavigerie was adamant. MacMahon went to Paris, to Emperor Napoleon III, for help. Napoleon offered to appoint Lavigerie coadjutor bishop of Lyons, with the right of succession someday to the archbishopric and eventually the cardinalate. Lyons was the finest French archdiocese outside of Paris and a less dedicated man would have grabbed at the opportunity. Lavigerie's close friends, more anxious about his future than he, urged him to accept the proposition. But Lavigerie remained adamant.

"The opportunity [of Africa] without my seeking it has been unexpectedly presented to me," he wrote to one of them. "What motive could I have before God to refuse such a call? It would be nicer to live at Lyons, but it would be easier to die in Algiers."

To seal this matter, Lavigerie had his friends in Rome encourage Pope Pius IX to give his prompt approval of the transfer, and this made it too official for even the Emperor of France to do anything about.

Lavigerie had not asked for the Algiers appointment and he had never sought any of the positions assigned to him. From boyhood, he had wanted nothing else but to be a priest. As a child, he often played at saying Mass and hearing the confessions of his two brothers and sister. His favorite pastime was baptizing his Jewish friends by forcibly placing them under the spigot of a public faucet —prophetic evidence of his subsequent missionary zeal.

The Lavigeries were not a particularly religious family. The children were baptized at birth and later educated at Catholic schools, but family spiritual manifestations went little further than that. Léon Lavigerie worked as a customs officer at Bayonne, where Charles was born on October 31, 1825. Though the family was by no means rich, they had enough money to keep two servants and to spend summers at the seashore. Léon Lavigerie hoped young Charles would become a lawyer. The boy's interest in the priesthood struck his father as merely a childish whim.

The whim persisted. Contributing to it were the two family servants—Jeanette and Marianne—from whom, Lavigerie attested sixty years later, he had learned his prayers, catechism, and Christian charity. On the day Charles was eleven, he received his First Communion. The same day, he told his family quite definitely that he was going to become a priest. Still his father was not impressed, and it took the boy four more years, plus the intervention of the Bishop of Bayonne, to convince Léon Lavigerie that Charles should have the opportunity of testing his vocation at least to the extent of entering a seminary. The influence of Bishop LaCroix, to whom Charles had made a direct appeal, was more than Léon Lavigerie could withstand.

"All right," he told his son hotly, "go to the seminary, but I warn you that you'll be home in six weeks telling me how right I've been all along."

But Charles did not come home. He was delighted with the seminary at Laressore. From the first day, he was both head of his class and ringleader of the students. His spiritual zeal at moments soared to such displays of austerity that he startled his friends. But there were also moments of devilment that shocked the faculty. One day he would break so many rules that he was on the verge of expulsion; next day the superior of the seminary would have to order him to spend less time at prayers and more time at study. His mother was a victim of these extremes. It was the custom of the era for priests to wear their hair long, and Charles already presumed himself a priest. Visiting her son one weekend, Laure Lavigerie took one look at the locks curling down the back of his neck and gasped. Convinced, like her husband, that Charles's vocation would not endure, she said: "I will not have you coming home looking like a barbarian. Get a scissors." She cut his hair herself. When she

13

returned a month later, she discovered he had gone to the opposite extreme. He looked like a shorn goat and he had shaved the back of his head, giving himself a homemade and somewhat crude tonsure.

To his family's dismay, Charles not only finished the minor seminary with honors and praise, but he rushed off directly to the major seminary in Paris to continue his studies. He soon found how different life was in a major seminary. Again he stood at the head of his class, but now he studied diligently only because that he wanted to take his mind off his surroundings. The spiritual exercises were more severe, student life much more subdued. Also, the building itself was big and dark, cold and damp. Charles admitted that at times he felt he was living in a tomb. His stubborn determination for the priesthood mellowed. He wrote home: "It is possible I will become a priest, but it is for God to decide." Reassured, his family, when he was eighteen, began to make arrangements for him to marry a distant cousin in Paris.

Charles remained in the seminary; the marriage plans faded and at last were discarded. At twenty-two, he had finished all his preliminary studies, but he was still two years too young for ordination. Archbishop Affre of Paris suggested that Lavigerie occupy the waiting years by working to earn his bachelor and licentiate degrees at the Carmelite university in the Rue Vaugirard. Ordinarily, it would have taken at least two years to prepare for the examinations. Lavigerie won both degrees within ten months. There was nothing left for the Archbishop to do but obtain a special dispensation from Rome to ordain Lavigerie at the age of twenty-three.

While he awaited the dispensation, a Socialist revolution burst in Paris. Many revolutionists, aware of the union of Church and State, erroneously concluded that the Church actually had influence on the government and was therefore equally guilty of the injustices which existed. They turned their guns on the clergy as well as government officials. Archbishop Affre was shot as he approached a street barricade in an effort to speak to the rioters. The seminary was closed. Lavigerie and the other students disguised themselves in lay clothes and hid out with friends or relatives until King Louis Philippe was dethroned and the revolution subsided.

Despite the papal dispensation, Lavigerie's superiors felt he was still too young to begin his priestly work in Paris and they urged

14

him to return to the university to acquire higher degrees. In less than a year, he took his doctorate in Church history. This was a remarkable achievement. Officials of the university were overhelmed, as were educators throughout France. Offers came from everywhere for him to join university staffs. As a priest, he would have had to accept in obedience any appointment his superiors—the bishops of Paris— decided for him. However, instead of making an assignment they asked him what he wanted to do.

He did not know. He was quite sure he did not want to teach. He had attained the priesthood, which was his lifelong ambition, and he remembered his boyhood desire to work in a country parish. There was small chance of that in Paris. For that matter, Lavigerie wasn't especially eager to remain in Paris. From time to time, he felt inexplicable urges to go somewhere, but he had no idea where he wanted to go, or what he would do when he got there. Paris stifled him. It was one of the biggest cities in the world, and yet it seemed too small for him. It made him feel awkward. He had grown into a tall man, well over six feet. His bones were big and his body was heavy and solid. He had a rich, deep voice which could fill a cathedral without effort. He was handsome in a formidable way, as a battleship is handsome, or a mountain. Strangers admired him quickly, but out of respect for what seemed potential in him. Nevertheless, he had a boy's capacity for arousing deep affections even in those who came to know him only slightly. He was, by ordination and personality, a father; people confided in him easily and often. His size, his knowledge, his air of quiet confidence made him seem older than he was, more mature. References to his youth, which his superiors frequently voiced, annoyed him. Because of his natural faculty to learn easily, he was unimpressed by the portentous solemnity of universities. The deep spirituality which seminary life had inculcated in him made him somewhat impatient with more ambitious priests who were too often at their desks, too seldom at their prayers. Something about Paris hemmed him in. He needed a place where he could stretch, mentally, physically, spiritually. He needed a continent.

What he got was a high school. Concerned about this tense, somber young man, his superiors decided that a couple of years as a chaplain might relax him enough to unwind. Then, with a clearer view of him, they could determine where and how he could best serve the Church.

He moved into a school supervised by the Benedictine Sisters, became chaplain, and acted as spiritual director to the nuns. In search of more to do, he gave spiritual instructions to Augustinian nuns in a convent nearby. Subsequently, he began returning to the Carmelite university to give conferences in Latin literature. Such was his life for almost four years.

Vicar General Maret, sort of executive officer of the archdiocese, had watched Lavigerie for a long time, and was disturbed by what seemed to him the waste of genius. He went to the young priest one day and suggested that he try for a seat as canon in the Chapter of the Panthéon. The Chapter's prime responsibility, as with chapters in all major cathedrals, was to perform each day the full liturgy of the Church. But at the Panthéon, the Chapter was also the breeding grounds of bright young men destined for high places. To be a member of the Chapter was a great honor, and there was severe competition whenever an opening occurred. Applicants had to present discourses on Church doctrine, usually some obscure and controversial principle, then defend their theses orally before a board of brilliant examiners who appeared to be bitterly determined to reject everybody who came in front of them.

More out of obedience to Maret than anything else, Lavigerie submitted his paper and eventually went before the Chapter board. His defense was magnificent. For hours, the board thrust its piercing questions and tenacious arguments at him; his replies were as clear and sharp as lightning. Suddenly the examiners rose to their feet and applauded the young priest: out of a score of applicants Lavigerie was the only man admitted to the Chapter.

His new position brought new tasks, yet he continued his spiritual directions for the nuns at the hospital and the convent. But Maret had further plans for him. Catholic educators were becoming increasingly aware that standards at the Sorbonne were not so high as they once were. St. Thomas Aquinas had taught there; at one time the university was the center of Catholic education in the world. Those concerned realized that something had to be done to restore the school to its former prominence. Surely one way was to staff it with the finest teachers available. Maret was appointed dean, and the first man to whom he turned was Lavigerie. Teaching was the furthest from Lavigerie's aspirations, but again in obedience to Maret he went to the Sorbonne as a professor of Church history.

It was 1854. Lavigerie received word that his mother was dying at Bayonne. He rushed home just in time for her death. In her last moments, she looked at him, still unable to believe he had actually become a priest, still worried about his future. "I do hope," she managed, "that you amount to something."

He thought of his new post at Sorbonne. "I don't think I will," he said.

He underestimated himself. From the beginning, his classes were packed with eager students, hypnotized by his brilliant discourses. His lectures on heresies brought wide attention to the university. He defined Protestantism with an outspoken clarity that aroused resentment and complaints throughout the Protestant world. Some Catholic leaders were apprehensive when he began on Jansenism, a seventeenth-century heresy springing from extreme scruples toward the Eucharist and a strong advocacy for predestination. Both attitudes still held some appeal to Catholics—the young who were over-scrupulously religious and the old who were afraid to face death. Lavigerie cautiously guided his arguments between the two extremes and exposed the fallacies of the heresy as neatly as if he had dissected it with a scalpel. Again there was some uneasiness when he approached the subject of papal infallibility, demonstrating the logic of it so vividly that he won supporters for the doctrine thirteen years before it was enounced as Catholic dogma by the Vatican Council of 1870.

At this time, there existed in Paris an organization known as *L'Oeuvre d'Orient*, a philanthropy created for the purpose of erecting Christian schools in the Middle East. It had grown out of the Crimean War. Implicit in its aims was the hope of returning Oriental Christians to Rome, in spirit if not in fact. Unfortunately, *L'Oeuvre d'Orient* made very little headway. What limited success it achieved sprang from the personality of its founder, Baron Cauchey, and when the Baron died, the organization began its slow but steady movement toward extinction. Its directors knew that the goal they sought was too important to be allowed to fade. The campaign had been entirely a lay movement, and it occurred to the directors that one of their mistakes might be in trying to achieve their end without the benefit of clergy. If, then, they needed a priest to guide them, there was only one man in France they wanted. The problem was how to get to him, to offer him the leadership of the organization in a way he could not refuse.

Lavigerie's confessor was Father de Ravignan, a saintly man, an old friend, a fellow native of Bayonne. As his confessor, de Ravignan knew Lavigerie as well as the young professor knew himself, perhaps a little better. Not only was de Ravignan aware of Lavigerie's restlessness, but he felt it was time that Lavigerie face a test that could truly challenge his full capacities. One night, de Ravignan called on Lavigerie and suggested they go for a walk. They strolled silently for several minutes before de Ravignan spoke.

"Do you know Gagarin?" he asked.

"Father Gagarin? Of course." Gagarin was active in educational circles.

"And *L'Oeuvre d'Orient?* Do you know it?"

"Yes."

"The directors of *L'Oeuvre d'Orient* are looking for a new man to be their chairman. They have gone to Gagarin about it."

"Really?"

"Yes," de Ravignan said. "They have in mind a certain professor of the Sorbonne whom they are most anxious to have at the head of affairs." He took a few steps before he added: "I am here as their representative. What is your answer to their request?"

Lavigerie looked straight ahead. He seemed neither surprised nor flurried by the proposal. He said: "If you think, Father, that it is the will of God, I am ready."

"I do think so," said de Ravignan.

No time was wasted. Early the next morning, a delighted Gagarin arrived at Lavigerie's house to take him to *L'Ouevre d'Orient* offices in Paris. The directors were there, and they welcomed Lavigerie warmly. Then they handed him the organization's account books and the cash box. The cash box was empty.

Father Gagarin looked at Lavigerie with a droll smile and said: "You are launched upon the waters, my dear Father. What you have to do now is keep afloat."

It is possible with some men to pinpoint the moment which

18

changed their lives. This was such a moment for Lavigerie. He recognized this himself many years later. "I was smothering at Sorbonne," he confessed long afterwards. "While working with *L'Oeuvre d'Orient*, I found my road to Damascus; it was probably the major factor of my life."

It took him out of himself, away from the libraries of the university, from the nuns at the hospital and the convent, even away from the Panthéon. It gave him his first room to stretch. He traveled on a speaking tour throughout France, setting up committees wherever he went, organizing groups to expand the work while he continued on his way. He succeeded phenomenally. In 1857, he raised 16,000 francs for *L'Oeuvre d'Orient*; 46,000 in the next year, and in 1859, more than 60,000. These were enormous sums for the time.

He recognized the power of the daily press and he called news conferences on the slightest provocation. Most often, reporters were waiting for him when he arrived in a new city, but if they were not there, he did not hesitate to send for them. When he was out of Paris for any length of time, he kept his work before the public by writing articles for the Paris newspapers. Certainly such efforts added to his own popularity, but Lavigerie was not concerned about that; the publicity made it easier for him to attract crowds wherever he spoke, and it was from the crowds that he got the money needed. He frequently referred to himself as a mere front-man for the work, a work to which he dedicated himself because he considered it an important facet of the Church. It was the Church Lavigerie loved. The Church was his whole life. It was the instrument of God on earth, and in serving the Church he was serving God. From such an attitude he derived an ocean of energy and thus crammed more deeds into one day than most men perform in their lifetime.

In May of 1860 two Arab tribes—the Druses and the Metualis—organized a plot against the Christian villages of Lebanon. Ottoman pashas of large cities aided the clans by giving them men and money. Christian villages were ransacked; twenty thousand people were massacred. Most churches were destroyed and houses were robbed and burned. A half million Christians were homeless overnight.

The Western world was stunned by the attack. France sent troops, but troops were not enough. The homeless, the sick, the orphans had to be cared for. As head of *L'Oeuvre d'Orient*, Lavigerie felt that such care was the responsibility of his organization. He rushed through France on a broadside appeal for funds. He appealed to England, Ireland, Spain, and Germany. In a few months he raised over a million francs, and he decided to go to Beyrouth himself to supervise the reconstruction program.

The misery he saw cracked his heart. It was his first direct encounter with the terror Moslems could stir in a country, with the calculated fiendishness with which they could inflict the greatest horrors upon the Christians whom they inherently hated, and he never forgot what he saw. He worked day and night, distributing food and clothes, assisting doctors in makeshift clinics, supervising the construction of barracks where people might live temporarily and of orphanages for the thousands of destitute children. He crisscrossed the country continually, ignoring his personal needs even though his own health deteriorated. He was rushing ahead on horseback one day when the horse slipped and he was thrown. He broke an arm, but he rested only long enough for it to be set in a cast, and he was on his way again. The committees he had previously organized in France continued to raise money. Funds arrived at the rate of a hundred thousand francs a month, but so great were the needs that it was spent as fast as it appeared. After three months in the Middle East, Lavigerie decided he should go home and exert his own influences to raise more cash. En route to France, he stopped at Rome to give a personal report to the Pope about what had happened in Lebanon, what was being done, and what must be done. Pius IX was deeply impressed by the zeal and vigor of the young priest, and it occurred to him that it would be a good idea to have such a man at the Vatican.

Back in France, Lavigerie again plunged into fund-raising. In three months, he had over three million francs. In March, 1861, he was about to return to Beyrouth when he received word that he had been appointed French auditor to the Rota at Rome. The appointment, certainly important, was an unhappy one for Lavigerie. He knew he could not refuse it; it had come, he learned, from the Pope. It meant that he would now mingle in high diplomatic circles as representative of both the French government and Church at the Vatican, but it also meant he would have to give up the work he was doing in Lebanon. This he was reluctant to do. He wrote Rome, asking if he might retain his position as head of *L'Oeuvre d'Orient*. The Vatican replied that by all means he could and suggested that he set up a similar program in Rome. Further, because of his experience along that line, he was appointed consultant to the new Congregation for Oriental Rites, the papal office concerned with the Eastern groups whose liturgy varied somewhat from those of the Latin Rite. Also, he was named a domestic prelate.

His many tasks kept him busy at Rome. When the French ambassador was out of the country, Lavigerie took his place at conferences and social functions. His work sent him frequently to Paris, where he had many private consultations with Napoleon III. His mother would have been pleased: unquestionably her son had amounted to something. But quite plainly Lavigerie was bored in Rome.

He told the Pope: "I suffer too much here, Holy Father, I wasn't born a diplomat nor a political arbitrator. I was born a priest."

Keeping Lavigerie in Rome in that frame of mind would have been a great mistake, and the Pope realized it. On March 22, 1863, he was consecrated bishop and appointed to the diocese of Nancy. At thirty-seven, he was the youngest bishop in France. For his coat of arms, he chose the symbol of the pelican, the bird which, according to old legends, took blood from itself to nourish its young. On the seal, Lavigerie put one word: *caritas*—charity; more accurately, love.

At first, the people of Nancy were happy that the famous Lavigerie was going to be their bishop, but after a while they were not so sure that this was a good thing. He arrived with a storm of ideas. He let people know that he expected them to display more charity toward the poor, adding: "If you haven't the time, then I shall expect you to provide the money for others who have." He inspected hospitals and prisons and made sweeping improvements to alleviate the lives of those who were unfortunate enough to be in either place. He reorganized teaching methods, from primary schools through the seminary, and he did so with firm steps that left staffs trembling in his wake.

Nor was he satisfied with the staffs. Teachers who themselves hadn't studied for years received written instructions to trot off to Paris for higher degrees. Priests, comfortable in their parishes, found themselves uprooted and on their way to Paris or Rome for specialized studies that would make them more valuable to the diocese. A year, and occasionally more, was added to the major seminary training; brighter students were sent on to universities. When pastors complained that the extra training meant they had to wait longer for needed curates, Lavigerie replied: "Never mind; you will get better men."

In three years, fifteen new priests had earned their doctorates; the city was becoming overrun with intellectuals.

Lavigerie's pressures on nuns verged on the revolutionary. Most of them who were teaching had scarcely finished school themselves. He pointed out that the time was coming when more and more children would be attending school. "They will never be able to achieve the top of education unless they learn more at the bottom," he said. "Therefore, *you* will have to learn more. Go to school."

Mother superiors bombarded his office with complaints. They did not like having their calm convent lives disrupted. Lavigerie heard them out, then said easily: "As long as I am the bishop here, you will do what I say. Come to think of it, it might be a good idea for you, too, to go back to school and learn something about the obedience of the religious life."

No prelate had ever talked like that to nuns before, probably out of man's natural fear of women, but Lavigerie was keenly aware of the importance of nuns to the Church and he was determined to make those in his city worthier of their responsibilities. He began making surprise visits to convents throughout Nancy, inspecting them, offering suggestions that would make the houses and the nuns more effective and modern. A few weeks later, he would again appear unannounced to see if his suggestions were being carried out. If they weren't, the halls shook with his strong assurances that he was not making these visits because he had nothing to do at his office.

At one convent, Lavigerie waited fifteen minutes at the door before anyone answered his ring. Deducing that all the nuns were busy, he said nothing when he was finally admitted. On his next visit, he again stood outside, pulling repeatedly at the bell cord, minutes dragging by, until a nun finally opened the door. Again he said nothing, but this time he looked around for whatever it might be that kept the nuns so intently occupied. There seemed no reason for

22

it. The house was just badly organized, and there was no one appointed to answer the door. He left, but he was back in an hour.

He pulled the bell cord and waited. After a few minutes, he pulled the cord again. No one came. Then he gave the cord a hard pull and yanked it right off the wall. He heard the bells inside crash to the floor. Still no one came. He backed off, threw his huge hulk against the door, and broke the lock. Startled nuns came running from the convent's dark hallways. He waited until they were all assembled, then handed the superior the broken bell cord and spoke to her in exaggerated sweetness.

"Maybe you will understand now what I mean by having a well-organized house," he said. "In the future, have the door answered immediately so no one will be kept waiting there. The next caller may be the Emperor—or worse, it may be your bishop again."

Obedience and humility, Lavigerie believed, were absolutely essential in those in the religious life. He insisted on these traits in himself as well as those under his direction. At the height of his career, he said to those closest to him: "You will find me making many mistakes, but you will never be able to accuse me of being disobedient to the Pope." It was this obedience that eventually brought on his greatest heartache and led to his death.

He stopped at nothing to instill obedience and humility in those around him. Pride, ambition, concern for one's whims and wants were, Lavigerie felt, serious detriments in a man who had given himself to serve God and the Church, and he would not put such a man in a position of authority no matter what qualifications he might have. Moreover, he did whatever he could to puncture such a man. At conferences or large dinners, Lavigerie would turn suddenly on a self-content clergyman and ask airily, "What was that stupid remark you made to me the other day?" If the victim appeared to wither, Lavigerie knew he had pricked the man where it hurt most—in his pride of his intellect. After that, he gave him no peace. Despite the value he placed on higher education, Lavigerie was aware that the Holy Ghost notoriously granted Divine Guidance to men who appeared the least capable of executing it, and so he prized submissiveness far more than brilliance.

Always Lavigerie emphasized the spiritual side of a man. "Saints! I want saints!" he declared when, years later, he was asked what

23

kind of men he wanted for the missionary society he was founding. In Nancy, he stressed spiritual exercises as the sole source of a priest's strength, whatever his job in the diocese. After heaping enough chores on his priests to keep them rushing every waking moment, he then ordered them to spend twenty minutes a day in meditation. Priests wilted under the additional duty. Few spiritual exercises can exhaust a man as thoroughly as intensive meditation, however brief the period of it. To concentrate utterly on a moment of Christ's life, to analyze His reactions during it, to compare oneself to Him under the same circumstances and thus recognize one's shortcomings, and then guard against these failings the rest of the day is a wholly consuming and weakening adventure.

Because of the dedication he demanded of his clergy, it was inevitable that complaints should arise against Lavigerie. The complaints spread. They reached Lavigerie, but he ignored them. In a pastoral letter, he told his clergy: "My mission is to teach you three things—the most sacred, the most important, the most indispensable which can be taught on earth: to know God, to love Him, and to serve Him. All else is but a dream which passes away." Whatever people thought of him in the process of fulfilling this mission made little difference to Lavigerie. But the complaints spread further. Lavigerie was startled and infuriated to receive one day a letter from the Vatican which indicated that the Pope was ordering him to relax his pressures on his clergy. He went immediately to Rome, made his way to Pius IX, and put the letter on his desk.

"I will do anything you say, Holy Father," he said, "but I have one question: on what grounds did you send me this letter?"

The Pope examined the letter. He said: "I know nothing about all this, my son. I had nothing to do with this letter. In fact, I have been extremely pleased by reports I have received from Nancy, and I encourage you to continue as you are."

Lavigerie returned to his diocese. Instead of bothering to track down the persons responsible for what amounted to a fraud, he merely pursued the program he had laid down for his city. As so often happens, the people who once resented the perfection demanded of them eventually were happily surprised to find themselves achieving it. Substandard efforts were replaced by wholehearted application. Diocesan morale soared. People began to suspect that maybe Lavigerie was not such a ruthless overseer after all. To keep the Church in the forefront, Lavigerie ordered a surge of ecclesiastical pomp. Novenas, processions, Solemn High Masses, even Pontifical High Masses were held regularly throughout the city. Scarcely a day passed but the people witnessed evidence to remind them that they were Catholics, and soon they began to act accordingly. The city was never in better spiritual condition. The clergy still shook its head at Lavigerie's demands, but it was a different kind of headshake because at last they understood him, at last they loved him.

Then the invitation to Algiers arrived from Governor MacMahon. Lavigerie arrived at Algiers on May 15, 1867. From the thunderous greeting from guns at the forts and battleships in the harbor, no one could imagine that the Governor would have been happier had Lavigerie remained in France. A huge crowd waited on the quay to welcome him. He made his way slowly through the city to the cathedral, formerly a Moslem mosque, and there went through the ceremony of formally accepting its throne. A large procession then accompanied him to his official residence, a beautiful building once the home of the Bey of Algiers. Approaching the house, he saw that the windows and balconies were crowded with elegantly dressed women.

He stopped. "Who are those people?" he asked.

"They are the wives of the military officers and city officials walking in the procession," he was told.

Lavigerie had already learned that too many prominent Catholics in Algiers limited the practice of their religion to attendance at gala social functions held from time to time at the episcopal residence. This was not in his plans for the city, and he decided that his first hour there was as good a time as any to let everyone know.

He said: "Gentlemen, when all these people have left my house, I shall enter it—but not until then."

After the surprised women had been ushered from the house, Lavigerie went inside and closed the door behind him. In the garden, men and women looked at one another, stunned and puzzled, wondering just who this young upstart thought he was. It did not take them very long to find out.

III

RARELY had a bishop ascended a throne with as much knowledge of his new diocese as Lavigerie brought with him to Algiers. He had, after all, been a professor of Church history at the Sorbonne, and there was not much he didn't know about the Church anywhere in the world. At the Panthéon and in Rome he became intimately acquainted with the conduct of the government of France toward the Church, conduct which seemed co-operative enough on the surface but which underneath was fast rotting from a steadily growing anticlericism. Feelings against the Church had been nurtured over many years by a succession of radicals who were under the impression that the Church and the government were partners in a plot against the people. Anticlerics who were not of this deluded ilk came from the ranks of the rapidly strengthening Freemasonry or from Protestant circles—both with firm reasons for opposing the prominence of the Church in France. From his studies of history and his personal experiences, Lavigerie was fully aware that antagonism against the Church was not completely without foundation. The Vatican agreement with France had placed under Church jurisdiction such matters as the religion itself, education, marriage laws, the care of orphans, the sick, the aged. The government was to con-

26

tribute to the support of Church institutions and to have the right of approval in appointments among the hierarchy. As long as everybody stayed where he was supposed to, things went well enough, but the moment either side invaded the sphere of the other, there was trouble. Confusing matters even more was the fact that many prelates were members of royal familes. Lavigerie was an exception to this, and not by far the only one, but there were nevertheless in prominent Church positions men who by the accident of their birth were more concerned with the matters of Versailles than with matters of the Vatican. Such men frequently had difficulty deciding between their divided allegiances, and often the positions they took as noblemen reflected against them as prelates, and always it was the Church that suffered. Lavigerie was completely cognizant of the dangers in the Church-royalty alliance, he foresaw the pitfalls in it, and to curb the rush of resentment among the middle class he had, while Bishop of Nancy, appointed more and more commoners to influential positions in Church affairs. He was yet to do something far more significant, but that moment did not arrive for almost forty years.

His background prepared Lavigerie for the situation that faced him in Algiers. As always the case in crises, the problem in Algiers had not sprouted overnight. Severe restrictions against the Church had been imposed since the first moment of French influence in North Africa—not only to prevent the Church from recapturing the ancient glory she had enjoyed there long before there ever was a France but particularly to preclude any chance of priests getting at the Arab and enlightening him to the fact that he need not be a slave to the people who ruled him. As it was, Islam had kept North Africa intellectually stagnant for more than a thousand years, and it was to the advantage of France that it stay that way. But the French overlooked an important fact. The Arab prayed. And he suspected that other people prayed as well. Whatever else Islam had done to the Arab, it alerted him to his duty to pray with certain regularity. That the French did not feel similarly duty-bound was perhaps evidence of the new-found freedom they thought they had in their anticlericism. In any event, the neglect of God did not escape the Arab eye.

The reason given by the French for the occupation of North Africa in 1830 was the need to subdue Arab pirates who were attacking

27

European shipping in the Mediterranean and the Atlantic. A sizable military force was assigned to make the occupation effective. From the beginning there were uprisings, some of them serious, and the French commanders could not understand why the natives seemed unwilling to adjust to the situation and thereby let the occupation proceed peaceably. After eight years of constant skirmishes, the French thought of putting the question to the Moorish leader, Emir Abd El Khader, who told them: "Make haste and build your church, for not until we see it shall we believe that there is a God you worship, and that we can put faith in your word."

Thus the French brought Christianity to North Africa on the advice of a Moslem, not particularly to provide spiritual solace for the ninety-five thousand French settlers and troops then in the country but to make a favorable impression on the conquered people. The impression did not go very deep because the effort behind it was so weak. Finally embarrassed by Moslems into admitting the clergy into the country, the government approved the appointment of the first prelate, Bishop Dupuch, and allowed five priests to come from France. The first cathedral was an abandoned mosque; a dozen decrepit shops and warehouses throughout the vast country were converted into chapels. The French population in Algeria certainly provided enough work for the priest; however, implict in Christianity since its first days had been the missionary factor commanded by Christ and initiated by the apostles. Busy though they were, the priests felt they should devote some part of their efforts to that end. The government strictly forbade it. The government even ordered the removal of all crucifixes from hospitals managed by nuns who later came to Algiers. Christianity was being permitted into the country, to be sure, but in disguise.

The basic reason for the government's attitude was, quite evidently, the anticleric trends of the day. Openly, the government said it opposed evangelizing among Arabs because conversion might rob them of their best qualities. They were odd qualities to admire: feudal government by beys and sheiks, local rule based on despotic paternalism, the virtual enslavement of women, court justice favorable only to the rich, business transactions with the fairness of armed robbery. Nevertheless, the government remained adamant, and millions of impoverished Arabs were not only deprived of what

28

spiritual rewards they might have found in Christianity, they were also denied education, guidance in agriculture, even medical care.

Under the circumstances, Bishop Dupuch could obviously achieve very little during his eight years in Algeria. His successor, Bishop Pavy, achieved little more. An orphanage he opened for Arab boys was closed by the government. His attempt to establish a mission at Laghouat, on the edge of the Sahara, was thwarted by the government, which ordered the station shut down on the grounds that the Bishop was using it to spread dangerous propaganda.

Such was the Christian realm Lavigerie inherited when he arrived at Algiers in 1887. He knew all about it before he first set eyes on Africa, and he did not intend to let things remain that way for long. Above all, he wanted freedom for the Church in Africa, and he believed that this freedom would involve responsibility for the material progress as well as the spiritual enlightenment of the African people. But he felt, too, that these responsibilities should be not only upon the Church, but also upon the Christian countries which had taken on the colonization of Africa. With remarkable vision Lavigerie foresaw the day when Africans would want to be their own rulers, and it was his conviction that Christian nations assuming authority in Africa had a moral obligation to contribute to the development toward that end. Doing so would have guaranteed a lasting friendship with European countries and an enduring preference for Western culture. Lavigerie believed that even the early European settlers should be forerunners of that achievement. Many of the settlers agreed with Lavigerie, but unfortunately most of the European leaders who benefited from empire expansions felt quite differently, and in that was the seed of the troublesome decades that followed.

On the French throne was Emperor Napoleon III, a man of fluctuating religious fervor, but around him were men, leaders of the 1830 and 1848 radical uprisings, whose anticleric sentiments were well known. From experience, Lavigerie knew that possible success could come only by frontal attack. Soon after settling in Algiers, he wrote his first pastoral letter to his people, a letter which was widely publicized and in which he said:

In His Providence, God now allows France the opportunity to make of Algeria the cradle of a great and Christian nation. He is calling upon us to use those gifts which He has given us to shed around us the light of that true civilization which has its source and its spring in the Gospel, to carry that Light beyond the desert to the center of the Continent which is still enshrouded in the densest darkness. And it is to my weak hands that God has entrusted the direction of this work. By my teaching and example I am to lead my brothers to believe, respect and love the precepts and commandments of His holy religion. Like the great bishops whose names make illustrious the early history of this country I am to make myself all things to all men, shrinking neither from toil nor from suffering in order to prepare the way for the complete resurrection of a land still sitting in the shadow of death. This is what, with the help of God, I must succeed in accomplishing.

And to the Arabs, he said: "I claim the privilege of loving you as my sons, even though you would not acknowledge me for your father."

The statement was heavy with the dramatics the French loved and at which Lavigerie was a master. But couched quite plainly amid the sweeping gestures was a clear statement of intentions. As far as Lavigerie was concerned, the Church had now ceased marking time in Africa and was ready to move ahead. His reference to Arabs and to the whole of Africa let everyone know he was putting no boundaries on his expansion program. Governor MacMahon was furious. He sent lengthy reports to Paris, complaining that Lavigerie threatened to disrupt completely the status quo he had been struggling to maintain. Rumors of the astonishment in Paris seeped back to Lavigerie, but he decided the best thing to do was to ignore them and keep going. His predecessors, both fine prelates, had allowed themselves to be blocked by the strong-arm methods of the government; Lavigerie was determined that this would not happen to him.

In three months, he made a thorough study of what he felt were the needs of the country, then he headed for Rome. There he told Pope Pius IX his plans and warned him of the opposition likely to come from the colonial government. The same opposition need not come from the government in Paris. To curry Catholic favor in France during his long and stormy career, Napoleon III had, despite the anticleric latecomers, always supported the Pope. A test of this occurred in 1848 when the extreme radical forces of Italy were struggling for unification of the country. In doing so, they wanted to absorb the Pope's own temporal realm at Rome. This, had it succeeded, would have reduced the Pope to being something less than a chaplain to the ruler of Italy. To Catholics, the Pope as head of the Church was the vicar—the representative—of Christ among those who adhered to the Faith, and since the Church was international in nature, the Pope must be free of subjugation to any specific political sovereign. To achieve this, the Pope should be a sovereign himself, however small his realm. The unifiers of Italy did not want that realm within the country they were in the process of forming, particularly since Pius IX, though he favored unification, would not openly support the Italians against the Austrians who occupied northern sections of the country. Italy turned against the Pope, and he was forced to flee. Napoleon III, either out of political expediency or personal conviction, sent troops to Rome and restored the Pope. It was an unsteady triumph because the troops had to remain there some twenty years to protect the Pope.

The troops were in Rome when Lavigerie arrived to discuss his plans for Algiers. Because of the opposition sure to come from MacMahon, Lavigerie, after receiving the Pope's approval, decided that he would go next to the Emperor himself for endorsement. In Paris, Lavigerie told Napoleon III of his program to open schools, orphanages, and hospitals throughout Algeria, to improve the lot of the Arab woman, the Arab farmer, the Arab himself.

"I'm not asking you for any money," Lavigerie said. "I will raise the money myself. But I know that I need government approval to do what I want, and that's what I ask of you."

"You have it," the Emperor said. "I think you have a splendid program. Tell Governor MacMahon to forward to me through the regular channels the usual request for official permission and I will see that you get it immediately."

So opposed was MacMahon to the program that he ignored the Emperor's instructions and refused to send through the official request. In turn, Lavigerie ignored MacMahon.

En route back to Algiers, an incident occurred which further strengthened Lavigerie's position. Ordinarily the voyage from Marseilles took thirty-six hours, but shortly after leaving France a storm broke. The *Hermus* took on water, her fires went out, the violent sea ripped off the ship's rudder. The terrified seven hundred passengers were convinced they would never live to see land. Lavigerie called them all together.

"Let us submit ourselves to the protection of the Blessed Virgin," he said, "and promise her that when we reach Algiers we will go directly to the basilica and dedicate ourselves to her, ourselves and all travelers on the Mediterranean."

The storm raged on, and yet there seemed to be an unusual calm about the ship. The crew managed to start the fires. Six days after leaving Marseilles, the rudderless *Hermus* limped into Algiers. A huge crowd was at the quay, waiting anxiously with food, clothes, doctors. To its astonishment, the passengers and crew of the *Hermus* left the ship, fell in behind Lavigerie and walked slowly through the rain, praying and singing hymns, passing westward through the city to a hilltop where workers were putting the finishing touches to the magnificent basilica of Our Lady of Africa which Bishop Pavy had started and Lavigerie was completing. There everyone fulfilled the promise made at sea. Later, Lavigerie raised an obelisk on the hilltop, overlooking the Mediterranean, and every Sunday afternoon since then a ceremony has been held, both commemorating the *Hermus* voyage and invoking protection for those at sea.

The French on the quay had been deeply impressed by the display of piety they deduced Lavigerie had inspired in the travelers. The travelers, on the other hand, were deeply impressed by the beautiful church they saw, and they took this as evidence of the piety they suspected Lavigerie must have aroused in the people since becoming their bishop. As a result, each tried to live up to the impression the other had made, and out of it grew a new and vital support of the Church. Lavigerie vowed to do all he could to keep the fervor alive.

IV

The rain that had welcomed Lavigerie back to Algiers seemed even a greater miracle than the safety of the *Hermus* passengers. It was the first rain in months, and even then there was not enough of it. In a few days, the parched earth was sand again, as it had been for more than a year. The previous winter it had scarcely rained at all, and the crops were stunted and withered. What managed to grow was destroyed in summer when grasshoppers descended from the mountains. Again the farmers tried, but the lack of rain had virtually turned the soil to concrete, and by September there was nothing for the people to eat. Lavigerie exhausted his diocesan funds to import food from France to feed the thousands who crowded into the city, shipping what could be spared to villages in the south. Then cholera broke out. Hundreds died every day. Lavigerie rushed to Paris to beg from every pulpit money to buy food, clothes, and medicine. He managed to raise several hundred thousand francs, but when he returned to Algiers, he realized that this was far from enough. Pleas for help came from priests he had appointed to distant regions. One man wrote:

My house is besieged by crowds of beggars who are literally nothing but skin and bone, and are living on roots and thistles. I have seen troops

33

of men and women driving the cattle out of the ditches so as to seize the scanty weeds on which they had trampled.

From Mahelma, another priest reported:

The country is littered with hosts of starving wanderers clothed in rags, resembling skeletons rather than human beings, and they can be seen rooting up the very weeds of the fields to stay the pangs of hunger. No offal or refuse is too filthy to be greedily devoured, and even the carcasses of animals that have died of disease are being disinterred to serve as human food. The roadside is daily strewn with the corpses of those who perish from want and exhaustion. In the course of a few months, thousands of unhappy children have been left orphans by the death or abandonment of their parents, and are found straying from house to house in search of food, or dying of fever and starvation in desolate huts.

Even at Lebanon, Lavigerie had never seen such misery. He demanded an explanation why the Algiers government was not helping, but he received no direct reply. All he could learn was that the first evidences of the catastrophe had been ignored, and then when all hell had broken loose, the situation seemed too far out of hand for the government to do anything. This disinterest in the Arabs was the very thing that would keep peace out of the country, Lavigerie warned, and he went to work on his own.

Despite his own need for personnel, Lavigerie realized he needed money more. He sent teams of his priests to Europe, to England and Ireland, to Canada and the United States to raise funds. To Rome, he sent an urgent cry for trained people to help at hospitals and orphanages. The Vatican sent money, then turned to the superiors of various religious societies for the personnel. Soon Sisters from the Congregation of Perpetual Help were on their way to Algiers; from France came a group of Christian Brothers. Desperate, Lavigerie ordered his seminarians to give up their studies and help out wherever they could, and to the Europeans in the city he challenged: "Now is the time for you to show the Moslems what it means to be a Christian." The Europeans, too, had suffered, but not so badly, for they had a little money and they had provisions they had stored away. Immediately they responded to Lavigerie; they gave food, clothes, money; they worked among the sick and the orphans.

On November 1, 1867, Lavigerie had taken in his first orphan. Within a month, the house was full of them. Additional housing space he found was quickly filled, and by the following March he had two thousand children in his care. He did all he could for them, but even so, sick and weary, they were dying at the rate of ten and twenty a day. Death also struck many of the people who had come from Europe: within a week in the spring of 1868 five Sisters of Charity, a Sister of the Good Shepherd, a Sister of Christian Education, and a Brother of the Society of Jesus had all died. And the children kept pouring in.

News of the tragedy spread, and soon all of Europe knew what Lavigerie was doing. Reporters rushed to Algiers for firsthand stories. The Paris government began to wonder why none of the colonial officials in Algiers were making the headlines, and started to make inquiries. Aware of them, Governor MacMahon finally announced that he personally endorsed Lavigerie's work and said he would take steps to participate in the program. Lavigerie's reaction was crisp; he instructed his staff: "Tell that man to stay out of my sight."

There occurred, however, an event of too public importance to exclude local officials from it. Lavigerie was convinced that the famine had been partly caused by the fact that the Arabs were bad farmers, and he made up his mind that he was going to teach them how to farm properly. Furthermore, with thousands of orphans to feed, he needed a source of large quantities of food, so much food that he could store enough of it away in the event of another famine. With this in mind, he purchased a vast stretch of wasteland near the Arab village of Maison Carrée, eight miles from the city on the Bay of Algiers. To assure modern agriculture techniques, he ordered two steam-powered plows from France. They were the first such equipment to reach Africa, and there was great interest in them. On the day work was to begin and the farm was to be blessed, a big crowd appeared, Arab and European. The reporters were there, and so were government officials. Lavigerie used the moment to get off his chest a grievance which had been boiling there for a long time.

As he prayed for the workers, the farm and the future, Lavigerie asked God also to bless the colonials—official and civilian—and urged that they show through their deeds the unity of the land, that "from the freedoms of France might come a freer Algiers." Bowed heads popped erect.

"By that," Lavigerie continued solemnly, "I mean civil, religious, agricultural, and commercial liberties which we still lack. These benefits I would expect to come from the reason and justice of a truly Mother Country."

Before the prayer was finished, reporters rushed off to cable their stories to Paris. One paper described the reaction as "sensational," and another said that Arabs had burst into applause right in the middle of the prayer. From Algiers to Paris there were major explosions throughout official circles. Lavigerie was accused of stirring further revolt. Particular agitation broke out in the Arab Bureau, which was supposed to set policy for relations with the natives of Algeria. Strong voices charged Lavigerie with "unwarranted criticism by a newcomer." But, surprisingly, there were others in the Bureau who felt that Lavigerie was right, that only through religion would there be any unity in the country, and for a while these men urged that Arab and European children be sent to the same schools as the first step in overcoming the antagonism which existed between the two peoples, but the idea was crushed officially before it could be tested. Whatever harmony had grown in the country during famine and epidemic apparently faded as soon as the threat had passed.

Governor MacMahon was furious. Searching for revenge, he struck at Lavigerie's most sensitive spot: MacMahon accused him of proselytizing the Arab orphans and, using similar charges against Bishop Pavy in 1851 as a precedent, he ordered the orphanages closed. In reply, Lavigerie stated his position plainly:

If the orphans are not taken from us, and if we continue to receive funds from charitable Christians for their support, we shall soon have a flourishing nursery of good citizens who, we may openly say, will be Christian Arabs. These children know no more about religion than they do about anything else; therefore they are practically unprejudiced against us, and in time they will probably ask to be baptized. That will be a beginning of the regeneration of this people, and of a unity between them and ourselves, which has long been aimed at but can never be reached while the doctrines of the Koran are taught. To believers in the Koran we are "Christian dogs," and will remain so for a thousand years, and it will always be a praiseworthy deed to overthrow our influence and cast us into the sea.

To solidify his position, Lavigerie organized an association of prayer among the laity for the conversion of the Arabs and the revival of Christianity in North Africa. Dedicated to St. Augustine, who had been born in Eastern Algeria and was once a bishop there, the association required its members to say one Hail Mary a day for a year.

MacMahon took these to be prayers aimed against him. He wrote heated reports to Paris, begging to have Lavigerie moved out of the country. Lavigerie warned him: "Help the Arabs or they will one day rise up against you." But MacMahon considered this a threat Lavigerie intended to urge upon the Arabs, and this opinion too he sent on to Paris. In response, Lavigerie, well versed in history, wrote a lengthy evaluation of French mismanagement in Algeria since 1830, pinpointing every mistake the government had made, and concluding with vivid clarity that continuing along the same road of domination and disinterest would inevitably result in the destruction of the French Empire in Africa. The report was prophetic, as the French discovered some seventy-five years later, and like most prophecies it was ignored by the people who would benefit from it.

Napoleon III was confused and annoyed. He wrote Lavigerie:

"Limit your zeal. Work with your own people. Leave the natives to the government."

Now it was Lavigerie's turn to be furious. He went immediately to Paris to see the Emperor, but before he could arrive, MacMahon took off after him, passed him en route, and reached Versailles first. His story alarmed Napoleon III, who, to avoid Lavigerie, left quickly for Biarritz. Discovering this, Lavigerie went there after him. Attempts were made to keep him from the Emperor, but Lavigerie refused to be denied and practically beat on the door until he was admitted. He received a very cold welcome.

"Sire," Lavigerie said, "why have you ordered me to stop the very work you so heartily approved the last time we were together?"

"Because I hadn't expected you to start a revolution," Napoleon returned.

"Believe me," assured Lavigerie, "I am pursuing the only path that can prevent one."

"Not according to reports I receive."

"Reports can be distorted," said Lavigerie. "Come to Algiers yourself and see what I am doing."

"You know very well I can't go to Algiers now," Napoleon said impatiently. "I'm having troubles enough right here in Europe."

"You will have no trouble in Algiers if you keep your promise to the people."

"What promise?"

"In your message to Algiers just a few years ago, you said: 'Providence has called us to shower on this country the benefits of civilization. We shall not fail to do so.'" Lavigerie waited a moment, then added: "That is what you said. Well, Sire, how can I do anything else but that?"

Napoleon looked away, evasive. "Must you do it with such fury?"

"It is not I who causes the fury."

"Your latest remarks apparently stirred some excitement," the Emperor said pointedly.

"Such remarks," replied Lavigerie, "have caused excitement for centuries among certain people who refuse to grant others their freedoms."

"What do you mean by freedom?" asked Napoleon. "Are you forgetting that Algeria is French, part of the French Empire?"

"It will not be for long, unless the government there corrects its mistakes."

"Like what?"

"For one thing," said Lavigerie, "Governor MacMahon has threatened to close my orphanges, throw the children into the desert to starve, to die. Those who are fortunate enough to survive will grow up in bitterness and hatred for France, and for you, Sire. Do you expect them, as adults, to be any more peaceful than their parents have been?"

"MacMahon says you are trying to convert the children," Napoleon announced flatly.

"I admit to it," Lavigerie replied in the same tone.

"He says this is a mistake, that it will only ruin the people."

Lavigerie almost laughed. "Sire," he asked, "have you ever known Christianity to ruin a people?"

38

"But the people don't want Christianity," the Emperor said. "Your priests haven't converted a single adult Arab."

"I admit to that, too, and I tell you it will take a hundred years—"

"Then doesn't that prove—" Napoleon broke in.

"—a hundred years," Lavigerie emphasized, "of acts of charity on our part to pierce the hearts of the Arabs and convince them that ours is the better way of life. These days, we are not even trying to convert the adult. It is wiser for the time being to trust their un-baptized souls to the mercy of God rather than make Christians of them now only to watch them fall away later when they discover the difficulties of being Christian Arabs among their antagonistic Moslem relatives. Our hope is in the children, perhaps not even these children, but their children, or their children's children."

"Well," said the Emperor, "if you have so much patience with souls, why are you so disturbed about liberties? For that matter, what have liberties to do with religion?"

"A man's rights," Lavigerie stated, "are as much a part of Christianity as a man's prayers, and they should both be the concern of a good government. No matter how hard I work to save a man's soul, he will never listen to me until he learns first, from the liberties you can give him, that he is a dignified human being, a creation of God, with a soul that is worth being saved."

The Emperor studied Lavigerie silently for several moments, then asked quietly: "What do you want me to do?"

Lavigerie held up his hands and shrugged; the familiar French gesture of helplessness. "Sire, you know what I want you to do."

The next day, Lavigerie received word that the Emperor had written to Governor MacMahon, ordering him to leave the orphan-ages alone and return them to Lavigerie's supervision, adding that in the future Lavigerie should be left free to pursue any measures he felt would be contributive to the welfare of the country. Also, he urged all the Europeans in Algiers to perform whenever they could effective acts of charity which, he said, were inseparable from Chris-tian civilization. MacMahon replied speedily that he had not in-tended to close the orphanages permanently, but had closed them, he said, because he felt it was the best thing to do at such a moment of unrest. He promised the Emperor to co-operate with Lavigerie in the future, assuring him that he had always done so in the past, and he approved the Emperor's definition of Christian civilization. All this news Lavigerie sent to his priests at the cathedral in Algiers, and when he arrived at the city a week later, three of them were awaiting him on the quay. Their joys over what they considered Lavigerie's triumphs with the Emperor sparkled in their eyes. They kissed Lavigerie's ring and said happily, "Now we have peace, eh, Your Grace?"

Lavigerie looked at the destitute Arabs milling on the quay; he glanced ahead at the city and saw the Casbah: human hells on a mountainside; he thought of the plains beyond the mountains and the desert beyond that, full of Arabs sick and starving of soul and body, and he wondered if there would ever be enough time for France as well as himself to reach all of them.

He turned to his priests and said soberly: "Not peace, just a pause."

V

It was a pause in which Lavigerie hoped to push ahead with his plan to expand the Church far beyond the city limits of Algiers, and to achieve that he needed priests. His diocese stretched hundreds of miles to the south, embracing an area larger than France, but he had only a fraction of the staff he had had in Nancy. Bishop Pavy had managed to attract a few priests from various religious orders, like the Holy Ghost Fathers, the Lazarists, the Jesuits, the Premonstratentions, but far from enough. Men of the secular clery in France had also come to Algiers, and there was a small seminary in the suburbs, but it would be many years before the diocese could stand on its own. Government restrictions had limited the work of even the small staff that Lavigerie had. Besides, these priests were not trained for the job Lavigerie had in mind. His eye was on the Arab, and to make any headway with the Arab required a special kind of priest. The men he had certainly were able enough and they were necessary for the work among the French. However, they were not in any way prepared for the task with the Arabs. None of them spoke Arabic, except possibly a few words they had picked up; none of them had more than a fragmentary knowledge of the Arabs, their history, their culture, their religion. It was Lavigerie's opinion that his appoint-

41

ment to Algiers made him a missionary to the Arabs as well as bishop to the French, and he felt that he was only partially armed for the double responsibility. His shortcoming was always clearest to him when he went to the seminary at Kouba to rest and pray. Seeing the young men at their studies, he often thought how well he could use them among the Arabs—if only they had the specific training. Frequently he discussed the predicament with Father Girard, the Lazarist priest who headed the small faculty.

"The boys ought to be studying Arabic," Lavigerie often said, "and the Koran. They leave here completely unprepared to do any work among the Moslems, and it shouldn't be that way."

"You are right," Father Girard agreed, "but they already have so much to study as it is. Besides, even if they learned Arabic and the Koran, they wouldn't have much opportunity to use it under the circumstances."

"True," said Lavigerie, "but circumstances will change someday, and then what happens? We will have to start from the very beginning and it will take years to get ready."

"Years to learn Arabic?" Girard was a little surprised. "The students are intelligent, Your Grace. It shouldn't—"

"Knowing the language isn't enough," Lavigerie asserted. "Even knowing the Koran isn't enough. A successful priest among the Arabs must *think* like an Arab, dress like him, react like him, live like him, be as much like him as a priest can. It is the only way to get into the Arab heart, and you can't achieve that overnight. You can't even achieve it in the three or four years the students are here. No," Lavigerie said slowly, and he got up and went to a window, "what we need is a group of men especially trained for Africa, who will love Africa as much as their homelands—more; who will become Africans, no matter what they were born, who want to live for Africa, the whole of Africa, and die here, and who are willing to go through their entire priesthood with only the slim hope that maybe someday they'll convert just one single Arab, most likely not even that; men who love Africa and the Church so much that they are willing to serve both completely without expecting rewards of any kind from either as long as they remain in this world."

"You make it sound so lonely," said Father Girard.

"It wouldn't be lonely for a man who had enough love in him,"

Lavigerie replied, turning. "A man is lonely when he thinks he isn't being loved, but certainly a priest knows that God loves him. And if he has enough love for God, then what else is necessary but doing God's work? What more could God want a priest to do than lift this dark continent to Him? And I am sure there would be enough work to keep any number of priests too busy to have any time to be lonely."

The two men often discussed the idea, until it became for them almost a fantasy they enjoyed sharing but never really thought would materialize. When it did, they were both greatly surprised.

As superior of the seminary, Father Girard gave the daily spiritual talk to the students. It took place at seven in the evening and lasted twenty minutes, and it was followed by ten minutes of meditation during which the students thought about what they had been told and applied it to themselves. Then in silence the seminarians went to their dinner, during which they remained in silence while they were read to. Afterwards came forty-five minutes of recreation before night prayers and bed.

One December night, 1867, Father Girard spoke to the students about the kind of priests Lavigerie wanted for Africa. Among those listening to him were three particularly attentive young men: Charles Finateu, who was just a year away from ordination, Eugène Barbier, and Louis Pux, who were a year behind him. Finateu's family lived in Algeria; the other two had come from France.

Having lived and studied together for so many years, the seminarians knew one another well. At the beginning, when they were younger and impressionable, their spirits had soared between zeniths of outrageous piety and incredible devilment. But they were boys then, and most of what they did was mere defense against their doubts and loneliness. Whatever their home backgrounds, they were all somewhat startled by the austerity of seminary life when they first began it, wherever the beginning took place. The long dim halls, the drab classrooms, the stark dormitories, the dreary menus, the chapel heavy with the smells of burning candles and incense, elsewhere in the house the pungent odors of strong soap and floor wax, the long silences, the endless studies and the frequent periods of prescribed prayers all tended to arouse in the young students an air of sobriety that sometimes frightened them and would have alarmed their mothers. The priests who were their professors had been

43

through it all themselves and knew all the ropes and understood that the soberness would wear off as soon as the strangeness did. To prolong the peace, the priests were often too firm, too strict, constantly reminding the students of the severity of what they were trying to achieve. Nothing shocked the seminarians quite as much as the sudden departure of one of the students, whether by his own decision or by faculty command. And nothing unsettled them more than being called in by the dean of studies and told with disinterested clarity that one's marks were not quite up to standard. Had the peace lasted too long, however, the faculty would have worried about the normalcy of the student body. Its length, therefore, depended on the timidity of the individual student, and the boy who finished his first school year without being caught breaking rules at least three times was looked upon by the faculty as being too saintly or too shrewd, either a terrifying influence to have in a seminary.

Infractions of the rules were usually harmless in themselves, but the exaggerated discipline imposed by the faculty made the slightest waywardness look like a capital offense. A boy might talk during a silence period, he might wander into an off-limits zone of the campus, he might sneak a smoke or secret food from home into the dormitory at night for an after-lights party, he might perform his chores halfheartedly or not at all, he might scribble a letter when he should have been at his books, he might be tardy for a class or unprepared, he might get into a fight or act uncharitably, he might kneel through Mass or rosary, his mind wandering, without saying a prayer, or he might be the influence which made others do any such things. Surely none of these acts could be considered contributive to delinquency, but their urgency was emphasized for the seminarians in order to impress upon them the importance of obedience in the religious life and to prepare them for strict adherence to the sacred vows of the priesthood which they would take at ordination. Certainly the rules were broken, but most often impulsively; but when the violation was willful, springing from pride or resentment or sheer boredom, it was only a matter of time before the student went on his way, of his own will or his superior's. Factors of the devilment were recognizable to the faculty: the weather, the burden of long semesters, the pressures of examinations and the rush of freedom afterwards, the weight of demanding spiritual exercises, approaching vacations, the normal loneliness of a boy away from his

44

family. There were personal factors, too: trouble at home, doubt of one's vocation, dislike for a student or priest or perhaps too strong an affection, preoccupying concern with a hobby or sport, a girl back home suddenly remembered, the puzzling inability to be able to study or even to pray.

All these traits the priest-faculty watched for, and seeing them did not wait for the student to come forward for guidance but went to him. The task at times involved a certain cruelty: the spiritual pattern of the priesthood had remained unchanged since the apostles, and whatever other qualities an aspirant might have, if he had not this pattern, he was in the wrong place; a priest could recognize it in a seminarian as a parent could see himself in his son. It was therefore the frequent and unpleasant task of the priests at the Kouba seminary—and in every seminary, for that matter—to take a student aside, sometimes even a model student, and tell him bluntly that he did not have a vocation; doing this was occasionally a mistake, but not doing so could often be a greater one. The devilish student usually needed only a firm admonition. But as the years passed the problem became more complex, more awkward to evaluate, for just as it could be difficult for some men to hide their spirituality, so it was difficult for others to reveal theirs, and thus the responsibility of the faculty became greater. It also became greater for the students themselves. The last months of the seminarians' life were therefore as sober as the first, but for different reasons. The end was near; the time was soon when, man by man, they would kneel to take vows they must keep throughout their life, a difficult life in which their only strength would be their spirituality, their union with God, their complete submission to Him, which they had spent a dozen years nurturing. Gone was the superficial piety they had affected as boys; now their prayers meant more: they meant everything. With their absorption years closing, whatever they thought, read, heard, saw was gravely important to them. To the last moment, there would be some who would be shocked to be told it was best for them to leave, and there would be others, privately shaking their heads, who would wonder how in the world they had made it. Among those who survived there was a bond that made them closer than brothers and yet as separate as hermits. They had given themselves to God, and in that was their unity; in their individual strug-

45

gles for sanctity they needed no one but God, and in that was their separateness.

The night Father Girard spoke to the seminarians about Lavigerie's idea of a special apostolate among the Arabs, Charles Finateu, Eugène Barbier, and Louis Pux moved deeper into their separateness than they had ever before. During the brief meditation following the talk, the three young men thought of the definition of the apostolate Girard had given:

"It would be a difficult work, perhaps killing, with no immediate rewards, and certainly none of the spiritual rewards a priest finds in giving the sacraments to his people. It would be a job for men of great piety, who would be able to sustain themselves on nothing but their own deep love of God. Yet who knows but in this room tonight there might be one or two or possibly three who would desire to devote themselves to this kind of missionary work?"

The three were there. Of them, only Finateu had previously thought of working among Arabs. Raised in the country, he knew Arabs better than did the others, had had boyhood Arab friends, and understood the good that could be in them as individuals yet the terror they effused as groups. He had hoped as a priest to be able to do something about it. Knowing all the difficulties involved, he concluded that such a priest would have to be a man of intense prayer: a Trappist in the marketplace. How that could be arranged was something he had never figured out. Now he had heard Father Girard, and he wondered if this was what he was seeking.

Barbier and Pux reacted differently. The apostolate Father Girard described had never occurred to them before, but the idea of it stirred a restlessness in them, a curiosity, which haunted their meditation, their silent meal afterwards, and was foremost in their minds during the chapel visit before recreation.

The rule at Kouba, to encourage intermingling among the students and preclude special friendships, required that recreation always be taken in at least groups of three, any three who happened to reach the door at the same time. That night when Finateu reached the door he turned and saw Pux coming down the stairs; at the same moment Barbier stepped from the cloakroom. The three of them went outdoors together, as they had every night for years, together or with others. But there was something special about this night.

46

They walked in silence down the garden path, and at last Finateu asked: "What did you think of the spiritual talk tonight?"

"I found it interesting," Pux said.

"So did I," said Barbier. "How about yourself?"

Finateu bit his lip before admitting: "I've never been so struck in my life."

"How do you mean?" asked Barbier after a moment's silence.

"It's just the kind of thing I've had in mind for years."

"Really?"

"Yes. I think I'm one of those two or three in the room Father Girard mentioned."

Almost reluctantly, Pux said: "I haven't been able to think of anything else for an hour."

The others looked at him and Finateu asked: "Does it appeal to you that much?"

"I don't know if it's an actual appeal or just a crazy idea that's excited my fancy," Pux said. "I just know that I'd love to try it."

"So would I," said Barbier.

They stopped in their tracks, looked at one another quickly, then burst out laughing. Disapproving heads of other strollers turned toward them, and they controlled themselves. Then Pux asked: "Is it coincidence or Providence that we three met at the door tonight?"

"Three," Barbier said. "Father Girard said three. Let's go and tell him what a prophet he is."

Excited, they took a step, but Finateu paused. "Just a minute," he said. "Let's not get carried away. If I remember rightly, Pux, you got just as excited last year when that missionary came here and tried to talk us all into going to China."

"That was different," Pux said defensively.

"It was," Finateu granted, "but so might this prove to be. If we go rushing to Father Girard right now, do you think he'll have much confidence in what we say? There's a certain amount of adventure in this idea, and that's exactly what Father'll accuse us of."

"That's the disturbing element," Barbier conceded. "I'm not sure but it's the adventure in it that's got me worked up."

"That won't take long to find out," said Pux. "After all, Father said it wouldn't be an easy life."

"Is a priest's life ever easy?" Barbier returned.

47

"You're ahead of yourself, Pux," Finateu said. "A lot will have to be done before we reach that stage."

"What should we do now?"

"The best thing is to think it over," Finateu said. "Let's make a novena, the three of us, and if we still feel the same way, we can go to Father then."

Pux and Barbier agreed and Barbier said: "I wonder how much of this Archbishop Lavigerie has figured out in his own mind. Let's pray for him, too."

"Good idea," Pux said. "And since we're being so sensible, I'd like to suggest something else. I don't know about you two, but the more I discuss a new idea the more excited about it I become and I find myself leaping before I look. I suggest we don't talk about this to anybody during the novena."

"Not even among ourselves," Finateu specified.

For nine days they prayed, asking for guidance in the decision they were about to make. They also prayed that the idea would not gnaw at them as persistently as it was doing and they tried to occupy their minds with other things, but every time their eyes met, they grinned. On the afternoon of the ninth day they met, quite by accident, in the corridor outside Father Girard's office.

"Well?" asked Finateu.

"Let's go," said Pux.

The priest was surprised to see the three young men enter together. He looked up at them expectantly.

"Father," Barbier said, "over a week ago you gave a spiritual lecture on the new missionary society the Archbishop is thinking of organizing."

Girard said: "Yes?"

"We'd like to join it."

Girard looked from one to the other. He tried to conceal his astonishment; he hadn't thought he'd made much of an impression with that talk. "What makes you think so?" he asked.

"What makes a man go into a seminary?" exclaimed Finateu. "The desire, the urge, the conviction."

"God has something to do with it," the priest pointed out.

"We feel He may have something to do with this conviction, too," Barbier said.

"Perhaps. I think the best thing for the three of you to do is make a novena."

"We just finished one," said Pux.

"Then," said Girard, looking at him evenly, "make another one, Come see me again when you've finished."

Abashed, the three students nodded obediently and left the room; they had expected a heartier reaction. They went to the chapel and began their prayers. Alone, Father Girard sank back in his chair, unable to believe what had happened. Had he been too crisp with the three students? How terrible to have discouraged them by what he considered prudence. Still, young men, particularly those on their threshold of ordination, were inclined to short-lived zeal; he had witnessed it any number of times. Nevertheless—Girard smiled—the news had been so unexpected that he had come close to throwing his arms around the three of them. Wouldn't the Archbishop be delighted! Girard fought an impulse to write Lavigerie immediately, forcing upon himself the prudence he had imposed on the seminarians. He got up from his desk, walked to the chapel, and knelt in the back alone. In a front pew were the three young men. All the priest could pray was: "Thy will be done."

The nine days dragged by, both for Girard and the three students, and on the last day Father Girard waited impatiently for the students to come to him. It was late afternoon before they appeared. They were filing into the room when Girard said: "Ah, the missionaries."

"That's right, Father," Pux said, and he smiled.

"You've finished the novena?"

"Yes, Father," Barbier said. "Just a few minutes ago."

"And?"

"We still feel the same way," said Finateu.

"Good. I'm glad."

"What do we do now?" Finateu asked.

"The next step, I suspect, is for me to write to the Archbishop," said Girard. "He'll want to meet you, and if he is ready to go ahead with his plans, he will tell you what to do after that."

"What do we do meanwhile?" Barbier asked.

"Well," said the priest, "since you have taken this great task upon yourselves, I think it would be well to fortify yourselves with

49

more prayers, don't you?" He glanced at each of them and saw their mild surprise. "And now," he said, "I'd better get that letter off to His Grace." He picked up his quill and reached for a piece of paper. The young men turned and went to the door. "By the way," he called after them, "you might as well wait until tomorrow to start the next novena; I imagine you have a lot you want to talk about tonight."

The three students looked back at the priest, smiled happily, thanked him, then hurried away, content like the young, the pure and poor with small pleasures.

When the door was closed, Father Girard put down his quill and opened a desk drawer. He took out an envelope addressed to Lavigerie: the letter was already written. He went down the hall and outside to an Arab boy who was waiting with the mail pouch, waiting as the priest had hopefully instructed him.

"Before you go to the post office in the city," Girard told him, "take this envelope to the Archbishop's palace at St. Eugène. Wait for an answer."

Back in the house, he went to the office of the priest who was bursar of the seminary and told him all that had happened. "I think it would be fitting," Girard said, "to serve wine at dinner tonight, and I will make the announcement."

"But certainly," the bursar said. "It is a wonderful occasion. I think those three boys will make fine missionaries."

Father Girard shrugged. "That is for God to determine," he said. "I have seen too many students come and go in this house to predict anything like that. Remember, these youngsters are not even ordained yet. But tonight they have done one important thing: for a long time the Archbishop has talked to me about the missionary society he wanted to establish, but he never got around to it; now he has three volunteers, and his society is therefore launched, Africa will always be indebted to these young men for that."

VI

THE orphans were still pouring in from all corners of Algeria. They needed food, clothes, medical care, a place to sleep. And there were adults, too, with the same needs. When they discovered they could get these things, however limited the supply, from the priests at chapels throughout the country, they flocked there, waiting with endless patience on the doorsteps until they were cared for. The responsibility of raising the money to meet the incredibly vast needs fell almost entirely on Lavigerie. Frenchmen in Algiers gave what help they could; the government, still smarting from the diplomatic defeat with Napoleon III, did nothing at all. Lavigerie appealed directly to his friends in France, and he kept three secretaries busy ten hours a day. He was up at five every morning, finished his prayers and Mass by seven, and was at his desk for two hours before his staff arrived. All day he dictated letters, then wrote more himself while his secretaries copied those he had given them. He managed somehow to see the endless parade of callers who came to his house at St. Eugène in the hills west of Algiers and several times a day he darted from the house for firsthand observations of the welfare work being done in the city and in the nearby country. He remained at his desk long after midnight, finishing the day's work and preparing

51

tomorrow's. He cared nothing for food or his own health, and he was impatient with people who tried to pamper him. He slept badly, and when he could not sleep at all, he would get up and return to his desk, piling up work for his staff, often doing their jobs for them.

All this did little to soothe Lavigerie's sensitive temper. He was constantly at the boiling point. His secretaries quit with shameless rapidity, usually in hysterics. Male assistants probably would have assaulted him, had he not been an archbishop. One man paused long enough to flood Lavigerie with violent invectives before stalking out of the office. Lavigerie watched him go and asked mildly: "What's the matter with him?" When told that he had been quite rough on the man, Lavigerie went immediately to his house and apologized, adding: "We have a lot of important work to do. I would like you to come back, but not if you expect me to apologize to you every five minutes." The man came back.

Priests who worked for Lavigerie could not expect the same apologies, and rarely got any. In obedience to their bishop, they had to take whatever treatment he gave them. With his lay staff, Lavigerie would occasionally tolerate a little loafing, but he expected his priests to be as dedicated as he was. Time and again many a young priest, red-faced with fury, lifted his eyes to a crucifix on the wall and prayed for the virtues of patience and charity—for Lavigerie as well as himself. There were moments, however, when Lavigerie displayed a histrionic repentance that embarrassed his priests. He would come from his private office, tears in his eyes, approach a startled young priest, and say: "I have just made a brief examination of my conscience and I realize I have been brutal to you. Please forgive me. I am a savage." Then would come a gruff but paternal embrace, with Lavigerie's great beard scratching the young man's cheek. Back Lavigerie would go to his office, ignoring everyone else in the crowded room, leaving the priest to his blushes. A moment later he would storm out again, waving a sheaf of accounting papers, rush upon the recent object of his affections, and bellow: "Are you the idiot around here who thinks he knows arithmetic?" Then it would start all over again.

Lavigerie's temper was widely known. On a trip to France he was waiting one day for a train at a countryside station when a local priest strolled up to him. "I noticed your beard," said the priest. "Are you a missionary?"

"Yes, I am," Lavigerie said.

"Where?"

"Algeria."

"Oh, then you must know Lavigerie. He used to be the Bishop of Nancy."

"I'll say I know him," said Lavigerie.

"Is he still the same?" the priest asked.

"The same?"

"Hard to get along with. He used to be a regular monster."

"Oh, he's worse," Lavigerie said, "now that the African sun has hit him. Absolutely unbearable."

"I'm not surprised," the priest said. "I saw that in him from the beginning. I size up people fast."

"Yes, apparently you do."

"Yes," the priest agreed. "He tried to get me to be his vicar general when he went down to Algiers, but I refused. I'd rather die first. You couldn't get me to work for a man like that."

"Heavens, no," said Lavigerie. "You'd be a fool."

The train pulled in. Lavigerie opened his overcoat and exposed the large cross which, as a bishop, he wore on his chest. The priest stared at it, then at Lavigerie, and asked: "You say you were from Algeria?"

"I told you the truth," Lavigerie said with exaggerated sweetness, "and everything you told me was the truth, except one thing. I never asked you to be my vicar general, and I wouldn't, even if you and I were the only two priests on earth. Now, if you don't want to hear any more of my opinions, perhaps you'd better get into a different car." Which the man did.

Despite his thunderous temperament, Lavigerie was able to arouse the deepest and most effusive love in men who managed to survive their first few weeks with him. He was impatient and exacting, but he was so pleased when things were done right that he could not conceal his delight which at such moments was enough to inspire every man to perfections. He drove his workers to exhaustion, but the instant he learned a man's lassitude came from some personal problem, spiritual or material, he immediately took

53

him aside and stayed with him, no matter how long, until the problem was resolved. He loved the pomp of the Church, everywhere, and the part of his house the public saw was elegantly furnished, yet his own quarters were austerely simple; there was not even a comfortable chair in his room. He received medals from kings and presidents and popes, but he never wore them, and when he died, they were found in a shoe box at the back of his closet. With the budgets of his archdiocese he was almost unreasonably parsimonious, but his own money he threw around recklessly, unable to resist anyone who even looked as if he needed funds, and so he never had a balance in his own bank account for more than a couple of days. Though he could terrify men, with children he was as submissive as a new father. Children adored him, probably because he did not treat them as children. Many times he was overheard telling them his greatest problems, then listening to their advice as if they were patriarchs. He was, beyond all else, a deeply spiritual man. He let nothing interfere with the regular periods of prayer and meditation he had prescribed for himself from the first days of his priesthood. At times when his staff would fall exhausted on their beds, he could be found in his chapel, surrendered in intense adoration. From such moments, he often said, he drew all his strength. And he had the strength of armies.

On the night Father Girard's letter arrived from the seminary, Lavigerie had a particularly wearisome day, and by the time his staff left, every bone in his body ached. Lavigerie had been seriously ill twice in his life: on one of his trips to Rome he suffered such severe attacks that people thought he was going to die and he was given the last sacraments of the Church. Though fatigue rarely bothered him, a series of disappointments could depress him almost to the point of lethargy. These days, he was having more than his share of disappointments. So many of his plans were failing because he had neither the money nor the personnel to do all that had to be done. He began to wonder if he was really following God's plans.

Such were his thoughts when, alone late that night, he finally found time to reach for the envelope the messenger had brought from the seminary. At first he could not believe what he read, and he read the letter again. His vigor suddenly restored, he immediately wrote Father Girard: "Never before have I more needed evidence of God's concern for Africa and my part in its future. Bring the young men to me as soon as you can."

On January 29, 1868, Father Girard and the three seminarians arose at dawn and went to the Our Lady of Africa basilica at Algiers, where Girard said his Mass and the students received Communion from him. Without pausing for breakfast, they walked the mile through the suburban hills to Lavigerie's house at St. Eugène. He was at his desk, and when they entered the room, he rose to greet them. The four of them knelt, kissed Lavigerie's ring, and asked for his blessing. Then he helped them to their feet and told them to sit down.

"I cannot tell you how happy you have made me," he said, "but now I'm going to do everything I can to dissuade you from your decision."

The seminarians were puzzled. Finateu said: "Dissuade us? Your Grace, we thought you wanted volunteers?"

"I do," Lavigerie said, "but when a man agrees to die for you, I think you should give him every opportunity to change his mind."

He began to question them then, about themselves and their lives, about their knowledge of Arabs and Africa. Repeatedly, he cited the hardships ahead. "I have no money to give you," he warned. "You will be poorer than desert spiders."

"We're ready for that," Pux said.

"I will put you through a novitiate that will break you," continued Lavigerie.

"We do not break easily," replied Barbier.

"I want men who are tough," Lavigerie said. "Tough enough to live like Arabs without succumbing to the Arab life, and I mean to test every muscle you have, in your body, your mind, your heart and soul, before I will call you my sons."

"We're ready for that, too," said Pux.

"Ready to start now," Finateu added.

So they began.

Because of the training he planned for them, Lavigerie wanted to remove the young men from the seminary where they lived and put them in a house of their own, but Girard opposed him. The priest felt that the seminary influence was too important at this stage of their spiritual development to isolate them, and he suspected, too, that it would be unwise to single them out from the others at what might be a premature hour. Lavigerie went along with him.

Alone or with the others, Finateu, Pux, and Barbier were nevertheless different from their fellow seminarians. They were going to be missionaries now; they had an identity; they were set apart. Eagerly they began studying Arabic and they struggled with the Koran. They were, therefore, permitted to spend more time among themselves, and on their Thursdays off they left the other students and went out among the Arabs. They pooled whatever money they had, either giving it to the Arabs or buying things for them; they played with Arab children. Sunday afternoons they spent with the orphans Lavigerie had taken in. Certainly they were sincere, and they were very happy. Their unity created a great friendship, and they made plans as if they were going to be together for the rest of their lives. Yet in making somewhat a game of what they were doing, they forgot some of the things Lavigerie had in store for them, and thus they were not prepared for these things when they appeared.

The novitiate, like basic military training, was to be a toughening place. In joining a religious society, a man admits his intention of accepting the society's rules, philosophy, and aims, all of which he usually knows before he starts. He also knows the restrictions of the priestly vows, and he is ready for them. But there is one more thing. He must acquire the ability to put out of his mind whatever plans he might have for himself and replace them with the plans of his superiors, and this he must do without discussion, resentment, bitterness, or hesitation; he must even like it. Of all the priesthood, this is the most difficult part to learn. Teaching it is the task of the novice master, and to succeed at it he has the authority to resort to any measures he deems necessary to destroy in a man the much underrated vice of pride. Pride is blatantly evident in stubborn children; in adults preferring a path of harmony it is mostly a secret sin. The novice master's job is to dig it out, and he stops at nothing. The importance of his success is reasonable: the priest who, if only in his mind, violates his vow of obedience is more likely to run the risk of violating his other vows; whereas the priest who is truly submissive to the will of his superiors also develops a more receptive submissiveness to the will of God, and with this double reliance always keenly in his mind his personal conflicts are lessened, and he is a better priest, and a happier one. Acquiring the proper attitude is not an easy adventure; it is, rather, a devastating one. Many novices fall out, others require a breather before they can resume their regular studies, and some are never quite the same.

To establish his missionary society, Lavigerie needed Vatican approval. He wrote for it, and when it seemed too long in coming, he went to Rome to see if he could push things along. The delay was understandable; papal offices had to study Lavigerie's plans and his rules for his priests to be certain they were in keeping with the Church's attitude and its own plans. Lavigerie had just arrived in Rome when the Vatican announced that the Missionary Prefecture of the Sahara and the French Sudan had been established and that Lavigerie was to be director of it. This was the first expansion of Lavigerie's prelate jurisdiction in Africa. Back in Algiers, Lavigerie wanted to put the three seminarians into the novitiate immediately, but Father Girard suggested it would be a better idea to let the students spend the summer with their parents before beginning the strenuous routine. Lavigerie agreed.

The novitiate began on October 19, 1868. By now, Charles Finateu had been ordained; Barbier and Pux were just a few months away from it. Two men who were already priests in Algeria learned about the society and wanted to join it. Both of them entered the novitiate, and one of them brought two young men from his parish. The building itself was in the hills of El-Biar at the southern limits of the city, just a short way from the orphanage Lavigerie had opened at Ben-Aknoun. It was an old building, unused for years, and it looked like it.

Because of the importance of novitiate training, Lavigerie was careful in his selection of a novice master. The best such training available at the time was that of the Jesuits, and from the Jesuits in Algiers Lavigerie chose Father François Vincent to be trainer of the new missionaries. Lavigerie's instructions to Father Vincent were brief: turn the young men to saintly, obedient apostles. It was the kind of challenge a Jesuit loved.

There were others at the novitiate. Victor Cordier, who wanted to become a lay brother in the new society, though plans for the duties of the brotherhood were still not clear even to Lavigerie; a young Negro named Luigi who had been educated in Italy by the Verona Fathers and who now taught Arabic to the novices and catechism to the orphans nearby, François Boulac, then twenty-three, who had been orphaned at six and raised by Arabs but who ran away when they tried to marry him to a Moslem girl. Boulac did odd jobs until Lavigerie took him on to work with the orphans; at the novitiate he was assistant bursar and instructed the novices in customs of Arab life. There was also Father Gillet, a Sulpician priest whose failing health forced him to give up parish work; he taught philosophy. And Doctor Maurin, who gave instructions in emergency medical treatment.

Novitiates being what they are, there was outbound traffic from the very beginning. One of the two priests who had joined felt that, since he was already ordained, there was no reason why he should undergo further spiritual training, and he left in two weeks, taking along the two young men he had brought with him.

The life was rough. The novices slept on the floor, they ate the food of the poorest Arabs, and they were to speak Arabic as much as possible. Besides their studies and spiritual exercises, they had to repair their house and grounds and grow as much of their food as they could. Father Vincent watched them closely for any violations against obedience and humility, correcting them sternly. The novices were obliged to bring to one another's attention whatever such violations they observed in their confreres, and each novice daily made what amounted to a public examination of conscience. This did not go down well with several of them, particularly Barbier and Pux. Grumblings began; they reached Lavigerie. As badly as he needed missionaries, he decided the beginnings of his society were too vital to its future to tolerate leniency. On December 12, he went to the novitiate and sent for Barbier and Pux. Finateu, who was bursar, was away, and when he returned he learned that Lavigerie was with his two friends. From sounds emanating from the room, he gathered that they were apparently not having a casual conversation—Lavigerie was roaring. Finateu waited in the garden, and soon Barbier and Pux came running to him, all tears and sobs. They threw themselves into his arms and said: "We've been expelled!"

Finateu rushed to Lavigerie and asked: "Your Grace, my two friends are leaving! What am I to do?"

Lavigerie looked at him evenly, foreseeing further trouble. Paraphrasing Christ he said in Latin: "You are the rock on which I shall build my mission," and Finateu tried to take heart from that. Barbier and Pux left that day and the second of the two Algerian priests went with them. Both Barbier and Pux went on to the priesthood; Barbier became chaplain to the Sisters of the Poor at Bone, and Pux went to work among Moslems in Turkey, where he died shortly afterwards.

The society continued through its growing pains. Victor Cordier, who wanted to be a lay brother—a man who, while giving himself to the religious life, does the manual work thus freeing priests to take care of the spiritual needs of the people—turned out to be a thief who made a career of entering monasteries, remaining a few weeks while he cased them, robbing them, and then disappearing. He robbed the novitiate but was caught later and imprisoned for a long line of offenses. Also, the society, looking about for saints to whom to dedicate itself, came upon Geronimo, who, according to legend, had been a Christian hermit in the desert who was beheaded when he refused to become a Moslem. He seemed to be the perfect man, until careful studies at the Vatican uncovered that he had never existed.

The traffic continued at the novitiate. Men either loved or loathed the lives they had to endure, and the ardent novices were in the minority by far. Like any new religious society, the group had to develop its own personality. Had Lavigerie nothing more to do than nurture that personality, the process might have been simpler, but he had an important archdiocese to manage, he was trying to establish a society of missionary nuns, he was burdened by the political unrest of the country. Further, the bishop of Constantine, in eastern Algeria, was ill, and Rome instructed Lavigerie to take over his duties. And also it was at this time that the infallibility of the Pope was about to become dogma. Lavigerie strongly supported this step, but there were many bishops opposed to it, and thus Lavigerie was engaged in lengthy doctrinal correspondence with dozens of bishops, defending the logic and philosophy of the idea. And brewing in Europe was the War of 1870 between France and Germany.

The novitiate managed to move forward, stumbling though the

progress was. Lavigerie decided his society, which he then called the Society of Missionaries to Africa, should have a distinctive clerical habit. Since they were destined to work among Arabs, he wanted them to dress like Arabs. He therefore ordered that they were to wear a *gondoura*—a full-length, loose-fitting white robe; a burnoose —a white cape with hood which Arabs also used as a blanket, and a *chechia*—a red fez. To identify them as Christians, they would wear around their necks a large rosary of black and white beads. Other priests in Algiers were wearing the customary black, and when the orphans saw the novices in their new habit, they were delighted and one of them said: "The others are black Fathers; you are white Fathers." As simply as that the name was born by which the society eventually became officially known.

Of the ten who began the first novitiate of the White Fathers, only four finished, Finateu among them. They were surprised, in the last days of their training, to be told that, in keeping with the Jesuit idea, they would now be sent on a long pilgrimage on which they would have to beg for everything they needed. Their goal was a shrine in Oran, almost three hundred miles away. They were to walk most of the way, but there was a train they could pick up near Oran if the trip took too long. En route they were to perform acts of charity for Arabs, and they were given medical kits for that purpose. There was a certain appeal in getting away from the novitiate for a few weeks and an attraction in at last making contact with Arabs, but the idea of begging was uncomfortable: the Arabs had never been known for their generosity. Just before they left, they received a message from Lavigerie: "Let me be your first benefactor. Here is a hundred francs for each of you."

They were back in a month, weary but triumphant. Their relations with Arabs had proved far more successful than they anticipated. The first aid they were able to give stirred a warmth which they had not expected. The trip had been rugged, but they got used to it. They learned a great deal about the Arabs, and their reports proved helpful when the White Fathers later began their caravans into the Sahara. The Bishop of Oran was startled to see the four white-robed, flea-laden young men drag into his house some four weeks after they had left Algiers, but he was so pleased by what he observed of them in the next few days that he wrote Lavigerie glowing opinions of their piety and personality. They took the train back to Algiers, and when they arrived, they were heroes for a brief moment until they became novices once again.

The War of 1870 broke out. Priests in Algeria were called into service. French troops in the country were shipped to the European front. The Arabs took advantage of their departure and began attacks on French farms and villages. Father Vincent felt that, under the circumstances, his place was with the people he had served before becoming novice master, and he asked Lavigerie to relieve him of the job. Vincent went to Fort Napoleon in Kabylia and was there when the Arabs besieged the fort the next year. He worked day and night attending the wounded, the dying, the sick, the hungry; he literally worked himself to death in a few months.

Everywhere was disorder and anarchy, springing not only from the injustices of the Algerian government but also from the traditional Arabic hatred of Christians. Lavigerie was convinced that had he been able to proselytize even moderately much of the chaos would have been avoided. He pointed this out in a letter to the authorities at Paris, claiming that where chapels had been erected throughout the country there had been little disturbance. He concluded:

For years, our priests have been forbidden to preach the Gospel, our sisters even to exercise charity. Well, here is the fruit of that: the fanaticism protected and encouraged by the government now breaks out in the open in the burning of villages and the massacre of the population. Will this sight at last open everybody's eyes?

But it did not.

With France at war, Lavigerie was unable to get any money to support his vast archdiocese. The time came when he did not have a penny. Because of fighting in the country, all farming had stopped. The orphans went months with only potatoes to eat. The novices were eating a stew made of weeds and dog meat. At remote chapels, the menu was mice. Though the Arabs were suffering as much, they ignored Lavigerie's pleas for an armistice so that farmers could return to work and produce food the country so desperately needed. On the contrary, they accused Lavigerie of starving the orphans into submission to Christianity and threatened to attack the institutions and take the children away.

At the novitiate, Lavigerie had chosen Father Creusat, another Jesuit, to be the new novice master. Creusat was a far different man from Vincent. He had been in the country almost twenty-five years, and though he, as a Jesuit, heartily approved the Jesuit-type novitiate, he felt that since the novices were destined to work among Arabs their training should be more missionary-slanted than it was. With Lavigerie's permission and without diminishing the spiritual aspect of the training, he ended much of the severe discipline of the novitiate and put an emphasis on the study of Arab life and religion. He was a very gentle man and the students found it easy to confide in him; fewer of them left than before, and he himself went out looking for new ones. His gentleness affected the students: despite the miseries of the times, there was no complaining among the novices. Everybody worked hard, and though they were far from happy they were not discontent.

Father Charles Finateu, having finished his studies, was appointed superior of the first White Fathers' house, at Maison Carrée. Three others were with him. They had hundreds of orphans to take care of, plus the huge farm which, because the uprisings had taken away all the Arabs, they had to work themselves. Few of the orphans were old enough to be of much use at the work. The priests were able to grow very little, which meant that they had to scrounge through the community for food for the children. Their days were crammed with chores, and at night they had scarcely enough strength to drag themselves to bed. The house rule required that the priests get up at three-thirty in the morning for their prayers and meditations before Mass in order to have more daylight hours for the farm work. As the months of torment stretched on, they found it more and more difficult to fulfill this duty. Father Finateu began letting the others sleep in the morning, getting up himself as often as he could manage it.

News of this reached Lavigerie. He was greatly disturbed and he sent for Finateu. "You must remember," he said, "that you are priests, and you must not neglect the spiritual side of your vocation simply because of the physical burdens you now have."

"Your Grace," Finateu said, "I cannot bring myself to order these men out of bed in the middle of the night. They are working very hard; they need their sleep."

"There have been others who did not refuse to be crucified for Christ," said Lavigerie. "Is it too much to ask a man to give up some sleep for Him?"

"But—"

"I know," Lavigerie broke in, "that you try to fulfill your morning spiritual duties, and I think that is fine. You should. And I can sympathize with your concern for your brothers. That is fine, too, but you shouldn't. A priest must spend a portion of his day exclusively in adoring Christ by prayers and meditation. Your concern for the others only permits them to neglect this duty."

"But isn't the work prayer, too?"

"It most certainly is," said Lavigerie, "but for a priest it is not enough."

Finateu sank back in his chair and sighed heavily. "Oh, what's the use?" he muttered.

Lavigerie was a little surprised. "What did you say?"

"I said what's the use," the priest repeated. "Can't you see, Your Grace, that the whole thing is doomed? We can't go on any longer."

"What is doomed?" Lavigerie asked carefully.

"The White Fathers. We have no men, we have no money, we're nowhere near the work we're supposed to be doing. Nothing is going the way it should. We might as well try to sweep away the Sahara."

"I'm sorry you feel that way," said Lavigerie. "None of us expected this would be easy, but we felt it was just a matter of time."

"I'm afraid I can't wait any longer."

"What do you mean by that?"

"I mean, Your Grace, that I'm asking you for permission to withdraw from the society."

Lavigerie studied the young man. "Why? Because I have reprimanded you?"

"Oh, no," Finateu said, tired. "It's been on my mind for some time. I just don't think I'm the man for the job; I can't go on at this pace any longer. If I could believe it might all come to something, perhaps it would be different, but I doubt that."

"I could appoint a new superior at Maison Carrée and let you go somewhere else," Lavigerie offered.

Finateu shook his head. "That wouldn't make any difference."

"What will you do?"

"I'd like to stay in Algiers, if you will permit me. Perhaps you could appoint me to a parish—that's if you want me around. Otherwise I will have to look for another bishop to accept me, I guess."

Lavigerie struggled to keep tears from his eyes. He had grown to love this young man very much, and to hear his words was a great pain. "I think that can be arranged," he said, "but I wish you'd think it over."

"All right, Your Grace," Finateu said, "but I'm sure I'll feel the same way."

Alone, Lavigerie was too crushed by the experience to move, and he sat in the growing darkness, thinking. What Finateu had said was partly right: things were going very badly. In some three years, twenty-four priests had joined the White Fathers; all had left but eight. Why? Was he too rough on them? He could be rough on himself, but perhaps he should not expect the same from them. How he loved them all, and how it hurt to lose them! Yet if he tempered his treatment of them, if the novitiate was eased too much, would he be getting the kind of men the job demanded, men resilient of body, of mind, of soul? The worst years certainly were ahead. As soon as possible the men would have to go deep into the Sahara, into Central Africa, and quite surely the trials that awaited them there would be considerably worse than what they were suffering now. Was it possible that these men were leaving because God knew that, good priests though they were, they were not fully capable of the task ahead? Or was it possible that God, instead, was merely trying to show that he was not the man for the task at hand? It was late and the night was black when Lavigerie finally left his office and went quietly through the house to his chapel.

Finateu did not change his mind. Lavigerie appointed him parish priest at Duperré. Father Charmetant, a young priest who had made the pilgrimage to Oran, replaced him as superior at Maison Carrée.

The situation in Algeria grew worse. France lost the war and was occupied by Germany. Napoleon III was dethroned. The birth of the Republic of France was declared by those who rushed in to take over the government. The Arabs interpreted this to mean the end of the Empire, and taking advantage of the weakened French forces in Algeria, they tried to destroy the influence of France in the country, once and for all. There were great assaults, terrific battles, many people were killed. Freed from fighting in Europe, French troops were sent to North Africa. Strength was gradually built up, which indicated a huge fight, certain to be costly to both sides. Vice Admiral de Guedon, in command, went to Lavigerie and asked for his prayers.

"This is going to be a terrible battle," the Admiral said. "I wish there were some way to avoid it."

"I don't know how you can avoid this one," Lavigerie said, "but I know how you can avoid future battles."

"How?"

"Instead of constantly fighting the Arabs, the French might make an effort to grant them a few of their rights."

"And what is it that they want?" asked the Admiral.

"I'm sure they have a long list of grievances, most of them just," said Lavigerie.

The Admiral shrugged. "But it is too late for talk, I'm afraid."

Lavigerie did not think so. Mokrani, the leader of the insurrectionists, was a friend of the White Fathers. Some time before, he had brought his infant daughter, covered with ulcers, to Father Charmetant, and the priest had succeeded in curing her. After that, Mokrani had helped the White Fathers when they needed food or clothes for the orphans. Since the fighting had begun again, Mokrani stayed in the Kabylia hills, but Lavigerie was convinced that if he could be reached he would, out of trust in the White Fathers, be willing to talk to de Guedon. Lavigerie therefore instructed Father Charmetant to make the attempt.

"I don't want you to take any chances," Lavigerie warned him. "Don't go beyond the front lines unescorted. For that matter, don't even accept an escort into the Arab area unless you already know the men in it. If you cannot reach Mokrani yourself, then do what you can to get your message to him. Just remember, however, that I order you in Holy Obedience not to risk your life."

Charmetant set off for the mountains. When he reached the

Boudouaou River, he found that the French of the adjacent town of Alma had put an impassable road block across the bridge. He went into the town and found the mayor and said he wanted to cross the bridge.

"What for?" the mayor asked.

"I want to reach Mokrani."

"You will be killed in the attempt."

"That is my risk."

"What do you want of me?"

"I need some help at the road block."

"I cannot move it," said the mayor. "You will have to leave your horse here and proceed the rest of the way on foot. I assure you that you will not have to go far to meet an Arab."

Father Charmetant climbed over the road block, and he had not gone a hundred yards on the other side when a Kabyle stepped from behind a rock and aimed a rifle at him.

"Put down that rifle!" Charmetant called to the man. "I am a friend. Take me to Mokrani."

The man paused. Instantly a dozen other Arabs appeared and surrounded the priest. The first man indicated that Charmetant should follow him, and the entire group moved upward into the hills, into the thicket bush. They came upon a tent, and Charmetant was told to go inside and wait. In about ten minutes, a man entered, a chief, gorgeously dressed. "I am Mokrani," he said.

"You are not," Charmetant told him. "I know my friend Mokrani too well."

Surprised, the man almost smiled. "I am one of Mokrani's lieutenants," he said. "Mokrani is at Dra-el-Mizen. What is it you want of him?"

"I have a message from the Great Marabout at Algiers."

"Lavigerie?"

"Yes."

"What is the message?"

"I am to tell Mokrani that the Great Marabout has sent me to take stock of the grievances of the Kabyles and to assure Mokrani that the Great Marabout will do all in his power to see that the Kabyles get their just rights, provided they will not fight now."

"Not fight?"

66

"If Mokrani will talk with the commander of the French, it may not be necessary to fight."

The lieutenant raised his brows in doubt. "Mokrani is our leader," he said, "but I do not think he has enough influence over the Kabyles to make them put down their arms."

"Isn't that for Mokrani to decide?" Charmetant asked.

"And you want to go to him?"

"Yes."

The man was silent a moment. Then he said: "I will talk to my men. I will arrange an escort for you."

Charmetant had seen the men, and he remembered Lavigerie's orders about an escort. Also, one attempt had been made to deceive him; he was wary of another. He said: "I have instructions to go no farther than this. We thought Mokrani was here. Can you take my message to him? Give him my name, and he will know that I have spoken the truth to you."

"If that is the way you want it," said the lieutenant.

It was late at night when Charmetant returned to St. Eugène. Lavigerie was relieved to see him. They told de Guedon all that had happened, and everyone realized there was nothing they could do but await Mokrani's reaction to the message. Apparently he never received it, or he did not believe it, or he realized his limited power over his people. The battle broke out; it was vicious. Thousands were killed, including Mokrani himself.

The French won the battle and there was peace, but a peace that was not to last. Lavigerie was fully aware of that, particularly when after the fighting the grievances of the Arabs were ignored. The country was completely devastated. Lavigerie evaluated his own position and came to the conclusion that he could not possibly continue all the work he was doing. Also, his conversation with Charles Finateu was always in the front of his mind. Perhaps the priest had been right; perhaps the society was doomed. In any event, it would be too cruel to expect the priests in the society to go on in such poverty and misery. He sent for Charmetant and said:

"I appoint you, as the superior at Maison Carrée, to inform all the White Fathers that I am disbanding the society."

Charmetant bellowed: "What!"

"Yes," said Lavigerie calmly. "They are free to go. I cannot possibly hold them to their vows any longer. They have suffered enough."

"But I don't want to go," said Charmetant. "Your Grace, you don't know what you're saying."

"I know too well. I am happy you would want to stay, but I have no work for you. It is all over."

"What about the orphans?"

"I will keep the young ones," said Lavigerie. "The sisters can take care of them. The older ones will have to go. I can put some of the priests in parishes, and I will help the rest find other bishops. If any of you want to continue living in the community, I will ask some other society to take you."

"Your Grace," the young priest said strongly, "I don't want a parish, I don't want another bishop, and I don't want another society. I've been very happy the way things are, and I want them to stay that way."

"Happy? How could you be happy?"

"The only way a priest can measure happiness: the good that's been done and can be done."

Lavigerie looked at the priest sadly. "You haven't had a decent meal or a good night's sleep in two years."

"Oh, I'll be the first to agree that it hasn't been easy," Charmetant said. "In fact, it couldn't have been rougher. But also it couldn't have been more efficacious. I'm sure those of us who survived are better priests because of it."

"You can speak only for yourself," Lavigerie said.

"Let the others speak for themselves and they will tell you the same thing."

"I don't intend to listen to them," Lavigerie said. "They are free to go. The society is finished."

By morning the other White Fathers either wrote Lavigerie or went to his house, begging him not to go through with his decision. One of them said: "If I were anywhere else, in any other work, I would not be doing what God wants of me." The appeals continued all day. Lavigerie was overwhelmed, but still uncertain. At last he announced: "All right, but just for six months. If nothing happens in that time, my original decision will be carried out."

He decided to make one more attempt to get men, and he sent

68

letters to the bishops and seminaries of France. He hid nothing, revealing details of all that had happened, the failures, the miseries, the sufferings, and he added:

"It is to this life of poverty, danger, trials of all sorts and martyrdom that we dare to write our brothers in France to whom God has made known in the bottom of their hearts the call of His grace."

The response was immediate. Thirty-three men, most of them priests, wrote that they were on the way to the novitiate. Eleven men asked permission to join the society as lay brothers. A bishop wrote: "These days the young men of France speak only of the White Fathers. I cannot imagine what stirs this attraction you hold, unless it is the rich approval of God."

Among the first arrivals was a young priest. Following regulations for traveling priests or those assigned to a new area, he went to the Bishop—to Lavigerie—for the necessary permission to say Mass in the archdiocese. Lavigerie signed his application form with: *Visum pro martyrio*—approved for martyrdom. The priest glanced at the words then looked directly at Lavigerie.

Lavigerie asked: "Are you prepared for that?"

The priest said: "It is what I have come for."

It was the end of the beginning.

VII

To LIFT up the Arab, as Lavigerie wanted to lift him from his stagnant Moslem world, required more than providing the means to make his life easier. The Arab could be instructed to farm intelligently, he could be given medical care, he could be taught to read and write so that he might discover for himself what was going on in the world beyond his own small sphere. Yet these things would not change him sufficiently to turn him into the kind of man Lavigerie wanted him to be. What was needed was a change in basic attitudes, changes that would make him tolerant not only toward Christians but toward his own people. Islam as practiced in Algeria was a man's religion. Women mattered little, either in the mosque or in the home. Lavigerie believed that the best gauge of civilization was the way a nation treated its women, that if the Arabs were to derive any benefit at all from the new Christian influence around them, the first place for it should be in the liberation of Arab women from the ranks of slaves. At that time, Arab women could be bought and sold, and their price depended on how much work they could do in the house and in the field and on how many children they could produce. Arab princes had their harems, to be sure, but chances of getting into one were so slim that mothers dreamed of it for their daughters.

Prostitution though it was, it was better than the bleak life of suffering that otherwise faced any Arab girl born outside a palace. Most Arab women died young from disease or exhaustion. They were constantly pregnant, and the majority of their children were either stillborn or lived only a short time. A woman who for any reason was unable to do her share of the work was simply turned out of the house, and if she had no family to return to—and her family did not want her back—she could only hope that some man might take her in. Making the Arab woman more helpless in her plight was the fact that actually there was very little about her to make a man feel any different toward her. She had no education, she could not cook, sew, or take care of her children properly, she did not know how to run her house. Indeed, she could not even call the place where she lived her house because most often she shared it with two or three other wives of the same husband.

Reports on the miserable state of Arab womanhood piled up on Lavigerie's desk from White Fathers as more and more of them became available and moved out to set up missions in the ramshackle chapels that had been established beyond Algiers years before. There was very little the priests could do about the problem. Being men, they would have been shot by an Arab who saw them getting too close to one of his wives—not because he treasured the woman in any way. A stranger would have been shot had he tried only to get close to a dying cow. The priests were also helpless because they themselves knew nothing about the skills that should be taught to Arab women if they were ever to earn the respect of their men. The teaching was a job for other women—for nuns, nuns who, like the White Fathers, were especially trained for the job in Africa. The answer, Lavigerie realized, would be in establishing the White Sisters.

There were already several congregations of sisters at work in Algeria when Lavigerie first arrived, but they were too few and too busy. They were nurses, mostly, or teachers in schools for Europeans, and they had only the briefest contact with Arab women. When Lavigerie began taking in orphans, he sent for the Sisters of St. Charles of Nancy. He gave them a house at Kouba, two hundred acres of land and three hundred orphan girls. The nuns were excellent; they worked with astonishing zeal, and the girls found them incredible: they did not seem to eat or drink or sleep. Despite their excellence, however, they were not the type Lavigerie wanted to work with the Arab women. They were highly educated, owing greatly to Lavigerie's influence when he was bishop of Nancy; they were well bred; they were genteel. They had neither the temperament nor the ability to get out into the fields and reach the Arab woman at the only level she was available.

"What I need," Lavigerie said, "are simple and strong hard-working farm girls. Certainly there must be girls like that in France who would want to come here and fulfill this important mission."

For a long time, it did not seem so. Lavigerie's appeals to French newspapers and magazines brought no results whatsoever. On his trips to France, he talked up the idea, but the two or three girls he convinced to go to Algiers stayed only a short time. The sad truth was that the Sisters of St. Charles of Nancy, whatever virtues they had, did not know how to conduct the type of novitiate Lavigerie asked them to establish for his new nuns. Part of the trouble, Lavigerie felt, was that there were only one or two aspirants in the novitiate at a time, and this made the experience all the more lonely and difficult. In August of 1869, he sent a priest to France on another hunt for prospects.

"Go to Brittany," Lavigerie instructed him, "and talk to every unmarried farm girl you can find. Stay there until you get at least four."

In a month, the priest was back with eight. They ranged in age from seventeen to twenty-eight. They were big and muscular and healthy. All of them had worked on their fathers' farms; a couple of them had been to school. This was the first trip away from home. It was also the first time they had been on a train or a boat. Traveling through France, they had received considerable publicity, also a new experience for them which they greatly enjoyed, and this resulted in an additional twenty-two girls, who were suddenly eager to go to Algiers. They were all hearty girls, loud and cheery, they had huge appetites and they liked their wine and beer. This was more than the mild Sisters of St. Charles of Nancy could abide.

There was trouble of all kinds. Lavigerie's plan was to have the girls do farm work, for it was in the fields that they would be able to meet Arab women and thus begin their influence. Though the aspirants still faced their novitiate, Lavigerie was anxious to discover what they knew about farming, and as soon as he could he hurried out to Kouba and led all the girls out to the orphanage farm. Cow-pulled plows were waiting. Lavigerie told each of the girls to have a try at it.

The result was catastrophic. None of the girls had ever seen such a plow before. They dug rows that curved all over the field. "Here," Lavigerie said impatiently, "let me show you." Getting behind a plow, he spent the rest of the morning working his way up and back across the fields, the girls trailing at his side, occasionally trying their luck, only to have Lavigerie grab the plow from their hands in disgust. To add to his annoyance, he soon learned that none of the girls could sew well and none of them knew much about infant care. It was all very disheartening.

The Sisters of St. Charles of Nancy were no happier. They seemed completely unable to instill in the girls any of the daintiness typical of nuns, and they were not sure that all the prayers the girls were obliged to say were actually getting through to them. The girls themselves were not too pleased. They had arrived with the impression that the White Sisters were already established and they did not enjoy taking orders from nuns who they felt were not truly their superiors, yet a little too superior for women who did not even know how to chop wood. So there was discontent in the house, pouting and stubbornness, factions, and occasional outbursts. Certainly the girls were willing to work, but even in this they found small satisfaction. The Sisters of St. Charles of Nancy were finicky, and no efforts at housework were quite good enough for them. In the fields, the girls found the ground too hard, full of rocks, too dry, and what grew was scrubby, withered and tasteless—completely unlike home. On top of that, several of the girls acquired severe dysentery, which made them most unhappy. Of the thirty girls who had arrived in September, only six were left at Christmas. And a desolate Christmas it was, for everyone concerned.

As months passed, Lavigerie realized clearly that the major obstacle was the inability of the Sisters of St. Charles of Nancy to provide the specialized novitiate the White Sisters needed. He knew that sooner or later there would have to be a change. The War of 1870 precluded any such change. In fact, during it Lavigerie, eager to protect the nuns from the bands of wild men who roamed the countryside, ordered the White Sisters to go back to France, but they refused. The eight who by then had taken the habit were too engrossed in their work with the orphans and they were just beginning to make their first contacts with backward Arab women. To go now, they said, would erase whatever good they had achieved and would make starting anew more difficult than starting originally. He let them stay. The war ended. He notified the Sisters of St. Charles of Nancy that they would be relieved of the training of the White Sisters and, in France, he made arrangements for them to be replaced by the Assumption Sisters. At the same time, he temporized his demands on the White Sisters, visited them more often, lessened their farm labors and encouraged them to spend more time preparing for the social work that would one day be required of them. He knew that from among those he now had would come the future leaders of the society; he studied the girls for likely candidates, but he also realized that he would have to start appealing for vocations among the higher-type young women of France. Much of Lavigerie's new sensitivity toward those who worked for him had been aroused by the departure of Charles Finateu: not only was he afraid that he might lose the people he had, but he felt that he had not displayed the love and fatherly concern for them that he should have, and he tried to make it up. Unlike the founders of most societies who usually had only the task of getting a new organization on its feet, Lavigerie had besides his societies many Church responsibilities both in Africa and in France. Nevertheless he gave the White Fathers and White Sisters far more of his time than he could spare. Upon them, he felt, rested much of the future of Africa, and nothing meant more to him than that. Though he was at times violently impatient with the shortcomings of those who had followed him into this work, he was also deeply moved by the miseries they were willing to suffer for his sake, the Church's sake, Africa's sake. He tried to show this. Learning that vineyards at the White Fathers' farm were heavy with grapes which the priests would have to pick themselves because they had no Arab helpers, Lavigerie went out to the farm, put on work clothes, and went into the fields with the priests. For a while, he thought seriously of resigning his archbishopric and becoming a White Father himself, even though one of the young priests he

74

had trained himself might be his superior. He had a set of White Fathers' clothes made and enjoyed wearing them. Still hanging at Maison Carrée is a painting of him in the White Fathers' Arablike habit. So imbued did he grow with the idea that he actually wrote the Vatican and asked for permission to carry it out. The Vatican refused, hinting that it had bigger plans for him.

Lavigerie's plans for the White Sisters were still not out of the rough. The arrival of the Assumption Sisters increased their morale considerably, if only because the novices were happy to wave goodby to the Sisters of St. Charles of Nancy. Too, the Assumption Sisters had experience at training novices, and the difference was noticeable almost immediately. One White Sister—Sister Gonzaga—was soon capable of becoming superior of the mission at Attaf at the surprisingly young age of twenty-two. It was at Attaf that Lavigerie had built a settlement for orphans who were becoming too old to remain at the regular institutions. The country offered no employment for the teen-age boys; to help them earn a living, Lavigerie created the settlement and gave each boy a small farm. Many of them had become Christians, while others who hadn't nevertheless had developed the tolerance toward Christianity which Lavigerie hoped to cultivate throughout North Africa.

Also, Lavigerie thought it was high time the young men married. Under Moslem circumstances this would have been out of the question because of the dowry customs. Attaf provided an opportunity to get rid of that. Lavigerie gave the youngsters a talk on marriage, then suggested that they visit the house where the girls lived with the White Sisters and see if there was anyone there they'd care to marry. The young men were amenable. They went to the house, and when they saw what they liked, they pointed it out to Sister Gonzaga. The nun introduced the couple and, in her presence, they were permitted to get better acquainted over a period of a few weeks. If by that time the girl decided she liked her suitor, they were allowed to marry.

Lavigerie warned Sister Gonzaga: "No matter how well or how little newlyweds know each other, they all face certain obstacles in the process of settling down. Sooner or later, these girls are going to come running to you with tears and complaints. Stay out of it. The time may come when you will think you are living in the middle of a battlefield. I command you to keep out of the combat."

The combat started almost immediately, and Sister Gonzaga found it impossible to remain neutral. She began writing Lavigerie for advice, and the newlyweds wrote him, too, that they were discovering their mates were not quite so sweet as they had pretended. Lavigerie wrote Sister Gonzaga: "Don't you have enough to do? If I hear once again that you have time to listen to the woes of these young people, I will order you to return full time to your farming which, as I recall, you did not enjoy." To the newlyweds he said: "You are discovering what married people have been discovering since the beginning of time. Time, too, is the only solution. Practice patience and charity, and gradually you will discover much in each other to love."

Peace slowly came to Attaf, but there was not much of it at the White Sisters' training center. Excellent though they were, the Assumption Sisters could not forget that theirs was an older order, well established, with a colorful history and an outstanding record, and they did not let the White Sisters forget it either. This was a source of much contention at the training house, and all of it eventually reached Lavigerie. He threw up his hands. "'I'm going to call this whole thing off," he told the White Fathers one day. "If those women can't get along, they shouldn't be in the religious life."

The White Fathers urged against it. They pointed out that the White Sisters were certainly necessary, that they had already done wonderful work with the orphans, and if they were being looked upon as an inferior group, hadn't Lavigerie purposely chosen women who were more brawn than brain? Educate them, they suggested, and meanwhile find some way to erase the difference between the two societies of nuns. Lavigerie came to the conclusion that the priests were right. He picked out a few of the brighter White Sisters and sent them to school. To remove the difference between the two groups, he announced that no longer would they be two separate congregations, but one. And he appointed Sister Mary of the Sacred Heart, who had been an Assumptionist, to be Superior of the new society.

On the surface, this looked like the answer, but it was not. The friction between the two societies was too deeply rooted to be

vercome merely by changing labels. It wasn't long before Sister
Mary of the Sacred Heart decided it would be a good idea to
classify the nuns according to their potentials—the leaders, the
possible leaders, and the drones. She made the classification on her
own. Oddly enough, all former Assumption Sisters were in First
Class; one White Sister made Second Class; the rest were all in
Third. This did not help matters at all. Lavigerie learned what had
happened and threw out the entire classification. He replaced
Sister Mary of the Sacred Heart and appointed as the new superior's
assistant the White Sister who had managed to make Second Class.
When the smoke cleared, he went out to the training house one
morning and called all the nuns into the chapel.

"Obviously," he told them, "there is a reason for all the discontent
here, and I believe that those who are responsible for it should leave.
But it is not for me to say which that should be. You know better
than I who are the troublemakers. I have brought with me this
morning some black marbles and some white ones. Now, we are
all going to pray for fifteen minutes. Then I am going to go through
your roster, and one by one you are to come up here and vote who
is to go and who is to stay. The responsibility is yours. And if I have
any more trouble with you after this, you are all going to get out."

The sisters were terrified. The responsibility was indeed a great
one: each sister realized that not only was the burden of deciding
another's fate a serious one, but she also raced a tally through her
own mind to determine how many friends she had around her.

Lavigerie began the roll call. With each name, the nuns approached one by one to vote. When Lavigerie noticed that one nun
invariably reached for a black marble, he decided she must be one
of the busiest malcontents, and when the time came to vote on her,
he didn't bother to count the marbles but simply announced: "Black-
balled."

By morning's end, there were twelve nuns at the chapel doors,
sobbing their hearts out, hurt, insulted, furious. Lavigerie sent the
ousted Assumptionists back to their society; for White Sisters who
still wanted the religious life he arranged entrance into other congregations; the others who were voted out he put on a boat to
France. The situation certainly had been an unpleasant one. To
some it would seem extremely distasteful and unnecessary. But

the nature of the religious life in the Catholic Church required th
complete self-abnegation of those who entered it. The intellectu
and moral error of self-centeredness could not only threaten th
individual's personal pursuit of sanctity but it might detour th
society itself from its common goal—the glory of God. Rather tha
destroy personalities, the self-surrender tended to crystallize then
Rather than weaken talents for leadership, it afforded a great
understanding of authority and the ability to accept it or exercise i
whatever the situation might be—and the situation often turne
completely about by periodic elections. The obedience and humilit
nurtured in the religious life provided both the single-mindednes
which was necessary for any kind of success and the fervent unit
which had been a major cohesive factor of the Catholic Churc
Newcomers to established religious societies had the benefit c
steadfast foundations already laid from years of trial and effort, an
it was thus easier for them to become assimilated into the societ
while preparing to make their personal contributions to its aim
In a new society with almost everyone fresh from the world c
prides, ambitions, jealousies, envies, and competitions, the pre
requisite group unity of mind and soul was slower to achieve an
harder to come by. But it had to be achieved, or the common goal—
the glory of God—was unattainable.

Following Lavigerie's housecleaning among the White Sisters
there was a period of quiet. During it, he was able to observe th
specific needs of the society. There still was no one who knew how
to keep books properly, who knew how to run a house efficientl
and economically, who could provide the young nuns with the knowl
edge they would need for the highly specialized work in the Africa
missions. What was needed was a woman of daring and vision an
fortitude, and these were gifts acquired in the cradle: one had then
or did not, and Lavigerie's chore was to find a woman who ha
them. Actually, the woman found him.

One day Lavigerie received a letter from Marie Louise Grande
de l'Eproevier, whose family he already knew. It was an importan
family of France; the girl's father was a general in the French Army
At nineteen, Marie was bright, brilliant, proud, and beautiful. Sh
wrote Lavigerie that she had long been interested in Africa and
had read a great deal about it. She was now convinced that she

hould become a nun and work in the African missions. Lavigerie vas most anxious to get her into the White Sisters, but he was fraid that the haughtiness typical of girls with her social background vould make her somewhat uncontrollable. He wrote her a carefully vorded letter, stating how pleased he was by her vocation and that he certainly hoped something would come of it, and he urged her o consult her confessor before going too far with her plans. He varned: "It is a difficult life in Africa, even for women who knew he difficult life in France. Do not come here unless you know what you are in for. For that matter, it may be best for you to wait until you are of age before making up your mind."

Soon afterward, he saw her in Paris. Because her family had many friends among the hierarchy, she was not overwhelmed to be in the presence of the Archbishop of Algiers. Lavigerie enjoyed her ease with him, but he wondered how this would work out once he was her direct superior in Africa. Now that she had declared her intention of becoming a nun, he expected her to imitate the demeanor of nuns, and he thought it would be a good idea for her to practice this gentleness for a year or so as a laywoman before actually attempting the religious life. He urged her to follow his suggestion that she wait until she was twenty-one before going to Africa.

"I don't know if I have the patience," she said, "but I'll try."

She was just a few months short of her goal when she arrived in Algiers. By now, Lavigerie had reorganized the White Sisters further. More girls had entered the society, and it was beginning to acquire its own personality. Lavigerie decided that only girls who had begun their religious life with the desire to become White Sisters should be in the society, and the Assumptionists who had been held over needed little encouragement to return to their own congregation. When young Marie entered the novitiate, the Superior General of the White Sisters was Mother Salome, a firm, solid woman, of moderate intelligence, unlimited perseverance, a certain heavy-handedness in performing her duties, and a remarkable piety which Lavigerie considered her greatest asset.

He told her: "I want you to be careful how you handle Marie Louise. She comes from a rich and noble family and is used to the best of everything. She has a great deal of pride, self-assurance, and a natural tendency to assume authority. Knock it all out of her. Give her no preferential treatment; give her the lowest and dirtiest and most humiliating jobs you can find. If she seems to resent them, think up something worse for her. She is beautiful and she knows it, so if she shows the slightest concern for her appearance, put her to work in the manure pile. I leave it to you to mold this young lady into a perfect nun, and I will support you to any extent you care to go."

Then he took Marie Louise aside and said: "You will find life here far different from what you have known, my child. Even the people will be very different; after all, none of them have had your advantages. I'm sure you will find the easiest way to get along is to do whatever you are told. Be particularly obedient to Mother Salome. She is a simple woman, from the humblest background, and at times she may ask you to do things which strike you as useless, almost idiotic. But always remember that, here at least, she is your superior. Furthermore, she has more sanctity in her little finger than you have in your whole body and until you become more like her you won't be of much value to anyone, will you, my dear?"

Thus he started a little game of his own. In private conferences with Mother Salome, he learned that Marie Louise had been busy washing pigs, emptying rat traps, and painting latrines, and he thought this was very funny. With Marie Louise, he was sweetly solicitous.

"How are things going?" he asked her one morning. "Feel free to tell me anything on your mind. Speak to me as you would to your father."

"Oh, all right," she said evasively.

"You have no complaints?"

"No."

"None at all?" Lavigerie persisted. "The truth, now."

She bit her lip. "Well," she said at last, "it does seem odd that I always get the unpleasant jobs around here, but maybe it's because I'm new."

"Perhaps," said Lavigerie, "but there are others here as new as you."

"I know. That's what puzzles me. There seems to be a concerted drive going on to make my novitiate one long series of revolting

80

chores that no self-respecting woman of France would even think of doing."

"You are no longer a woman of France," Lavigerie said. "You are a woman of God who has given her life to Africa."

"That's just what I want to be," Marie said quickly, "and I know that's what I'm supposed to learn in the novitiate, but I don't see how I'm to learn this from some of the work I'm told to do. Do you know what I had to do the other day?"

"What, my dear?"

"I had to scrub the *outside* of the chapel—all by myself," she said indignantly, "while everybody else was working inside. Now, wasn't I good enough to be inside with the others, or was I picked for the outside work just to humiliate me further?"

"Well, now," Lavigerie said kindly, "I would say the outside of a building has to be cleaned occasionally."

"With the rainy season just a week away?" the girl said pointedly.

"That may have slipped Mother Superior's mind."

"I don't think much slips Mother Superior's mind."

"That," Lavigerie said, "could have been an uncharitable remark. Remember, you must love Mother Superior."

"I do," Marie Louise insisted, "but I can't understand her. At first I thought she was being attentive because she knew this life would be difficult for me, but now I think she's determined to wear me down until I get discouraged and go home."

"Are you thinking of going home?"

"No."

"Because you don't want to admit to your friends that you failed?"

"I don't care what my friends think."

"Or because you won't concede to Mother Superior that you might not have a vocation after all?"

"I know I have a vocation."

"Oh, well," Lavigerie said with a sigh, "I'm not surprised that you're having a rough time. After all, you were raised on the luxuries of life."

"Yes, I have enjoyed the luxuries of life," she said, "but I guess I can enjoy the miseries, too."

"Which do you prefer?"

"It makes no difference to me," the girl said.

81

Lavigerie stayed for lunch that day, and during it he threw one of his familiar darts at Marie Louise. The community was eating in silence; Lavigerie was chatting softly with Mother Salome. Suddenly he looked up and, addressing her by the name she had taken on entering the novitiate, called across the room to Marie Louise: "Sister Mary Claver, what was that idiotic remark you made to me this morning?"

She stood and faced him and said simply: "Which of my idiotic remarks are you referring to, Your Grace?"

For a moment he was caught off balance, then: "You said something about enjoying miseries."

"Yes, Your Grace?"

"It just occurred to me," he said, "is that quite a sane thing to say?"

"Perhaps not, Your Grace."

"I didn't think so, either," he said. "After all, one can offer up his miseries to God as prayers, can't one, but to enjoy miseries for themselves is rather perverse, isn't it?"

"If Your Grace says so."

"Well, really," said Lavigerie, sounding a little shocked, "a child learns that in his earliest catechism, doesn't he?"

"Yes, Your Grace. "

"Didn't you learn it, or did you just forget it?"

"I forgot it, Your Grace."

"Then you admit it was an idiotic remark?"

"Yes, Your Grace."

"Thank you, my dear. I just wanted your confirmation." He sent her a seraphic smile of innocent joy and returned to his meal. He had embarrassed her in front of the entire community, he knew it, and he wanted it. He did it frequently. But he also knew that it was possible for him to go one step too far, not that she would have been unable to take it, nor that she would have lost patience with him and rushed away, but that it might have roused in her a deep doubt about herself which could have sent her packing. Of course, he could have defended himself in that situation by concluding that she had not had a vocation in the first place. Like other superiors in similar positions, he might have been right, but he might as easily have been wrong; a mistake in either direction would be most serious. He therefore occasionally sent her a book, or a postcard

82

while he was traveling, and from these she derived a certain comfort during the long stretches of soul-searching uncertainties which every novice, man or woman, undergoes.

She made it. When the time came for her to receive the simple habit of the White Sisters, Lavigerie himself presented it to her. For the next year, she worked at various posts near Algiers, always performing her tasks, whatever they were, with brilliant efficiency. Lavigerie felt he need no longer worry about the White Sisters. After her first year, he recalled her to become novice mistress, clear evidence of his satisfaction with her: she had learned how to rectify in herself the traits which had endangered her vows of obedience and humility, and he believed she could now spot these same traits in others and teach them to make the same corrections.

The change by no means made her meek and obsequious; merely, she had learned to substitute the "we" of the society for the "I" of herself, in both her heart and mind, and she looked upon her promotion not as a personal honor of any sort but rather as an opportunity to serve the society better. Lavigerie was anxious for her to have even greater opportunities. Shortly after her appointment, the White Sisters held a Chapter—a conference at which current projects would be evaluated, new ones planned, and leaders elected or re-elected. Lavigerie was present during the elections, and he was disappointed when Sister Mary Claver was not put into a position of high authority. He openly said so.

"But, Your Grace," said Mother Salome, "she has only been in the society a year."

"That has nothing to do with it," he said. "As your founder, I hereby appoint her your First Assistant Superior General."

"But the vote—"

"I don't care how the vote went. That's an order."

It was also a wise appointment. Sister Mary Claver held the office for seventeen years. Admitted years later was the fact that she actually ran the society, yet never with top honors, never full authority. That, too, was in Lavigerie's plan. Yet he was wrong if he expected he would have in her an efficient personal delegate who would blindly carry out his orders. She frequently and openly opposed him whenever she felt he was in error, and repeatedly subsequent events proved her to be right. Lavigerie liked her straightforwardness with him, and at the same time he loathed it. One day he sent her a list of appointments he wanted made which she did not entirely approve. She learned he was about to leave on a long journey and she knew the problem would have to be settled immediately. Hurrying to him, she found him in the sacristy of the cathedral where he had just finished a solemn ceremony and was in the process of removing his vestments.

"These appointments, Your Grace," she began.

"Yes, Sister, what about them?" Lavigerie asked, almost off-handedly.

"There are a few of them I should like to change."

"No need for that. I have given the matter considerable thought," said Lavigerie, "and I'm quite sure it's the best solution to the problems you're facing." He continued taking off his vestments.

"I'm sure," she said, "but at the moment we need two of these sisters at the Motherhouse, and the one you want sent to Attaf should really be—"

"Sister," Lavigerie said, tired, "I have a great deal to do before I leave Algiers this morning and I haven't time for all this. Carry out my my orders and I'm sure everything will work out fine."

She said simply: "I'm afraid I can't carry out your orders."

He spun on her. "Are you talking back to me?" he demanded.

"No, Your Grace," she said, "I'm only trying to explain why I cannot obey you this time."

He was furious. He bellowed: "You dare stand here in the house of God and tell your superior to his face that you can't obey him!"

She said: "Please let's step outside, Your Grace."

"By what reason," he went on, "can you possibly have—"

"I thought you would ask for reasons," she said, "and I have prepared a list." She took a paper out of her pocket.

He grabbed the paper from her and tore it to bits. "All right," he shouted. "Do it your way!" Then, suddenly deflated, he turned to others standing nearby and declared helplessly: "This woman is the devil."

She worked like one. When she was not at the mountains of paper work on her desk, she was out touring the White Sisters' posts, guiding and encouraging the nuns, reprimanding them when she felt she must. Scarcely a day passed but what she found time to spend a

84

few moments with novices, in a firm mood or gentle, whatever the situation required, and she knew the situations so well. Somehow she managed to maintain a voluminous correspondence with friends in France, getting money and aspirants for the society. Soon after White Sisters made the arduous journey into Central Africa, she went there after them for a firsthand study, to find what was needed, what must be done, what the nuns were learning that could be taught in the training of future White Sisters to prepare them better for the mission life. It was there, in Tanganyika, that she died with shocking suddenness at the age of thirty-nine. Her heart stopped without warning as she rushed about on her heavy schedule. No one could believe she was gone, and in a way she wasn't. The imprint she had made on the society was so deep that the others, even without discussion, found themselves pursuing both her ideas and ideals. Nuns who knew her intimately were infected with her zeal and would not content themselves with anything less than her energetic devotion to Africa. Novices who had trained under her virtually became reincarnations of her, passing on, in turn, to others what she had taught them, thus perpetuating all that she was. Just as the White Fathers soon outgrew their French origin and began receiving members from all over Europe and North America, so did the White Sisters. And as the priests were to lose their lives in the course of the campaign they had launched, so were the nuns. It was a price they paid without hesitation on their first treks into Central Africa seventy years ago, and a price they paid in recent months.

In September, 1956, two White Sisters were kidnapped from the mission at Ighil-ali, deep in Algeria. Rebels notified the mission that they had taken Sister Pierre Fourier, who was French, and Sister François Solano, a Canadian, because they desperately needed nurses. "We will not harm them," the rebels said, "and we will respect them. They will be released when we are ready to leave this area, but we need them now to take care of our wounded."

They were prisoners almost a month. On the night of Tuesday, October 16, the rebels were ready to move on and they made plans to escort the nuns back to their mission. A dozen men walked with the nuns out of the hidden camp, across the fields and to the road. They had gone perhaps a mile on the road when they were spotted by French troops. A skirmish broke out. The rebels tried to shove the nuns out of the way, but the French guns were fast—and they were careless. Sister François Solano managed to duck behind rocks in time, but Sister Pierre Fourier was hit several times and died almost immediately. The rebels retreated. Somehow the facts were garbled, and when the news of the incident reached the world it appeared that the rebels themselves had killed the nun, and there was no mention of the skirmish. It looked like ruthless murder, but it was not. Later, Sister François Solano assured that the nuns had been respected during their weeks of imprisonment, that they had considerably more freedom than they expected, and that they were given time to themselves for their usual spiritual exercises. They would have returned safely had they not been caught in the reckless crossfire of the ambush. She was asked if she hadn't been in constant terror during the imprisonment.

"Just at first," she said. "But we knew we were going to be all right when we were allowed to pray."

The death of Sister Pierre Fourier did not dim the efficacy of the prayers; she had died as she had expected: in the service of Arabs. Lavigerie had trained the White Sisters to want exactly that.

VIII

The kind of respect displayed by the rebels for the two nuns had been among Lavigerie's earliest hopes. The ambush was a tragic climax to what otherwise was shining evidence supporting Lavigerie's conviction that, given enough time, the Arab would recognize that missionaries were his friends, respect them, and admire them. The next steps were obvious: the complete acceptance of the missionaries and their religion and the tolerance to let others become Christians if they wanted to. Out of that progress, Lavigerie was convinced, would come Arab priests, Arab bishops, the Catholic Church restored in North Africa, and a church that could exist harmoniously side by side with Moslems who wanted to remain what they were. The Christian influence would be re-established among the people—in the people, and that was what was important. That possibility, even to Lavigerie's closest friends, seemed fantastically remote when he mentioned it. Arabs in Algiers itself were used to seeing priests on the streets but ignored them. The priests were restricted by government regulations from contact with the Arabs, and so there was little they could do; the Arabs, in turn, merely looked upon the priests as the marabouts of the French. From the start, Lavigerie was determined to change that attitude. The

White Fathers—and later the White Sisters—therefore became the first missionaries in North Africa expressly for the Arab. Their work with the orphans and their tireless labors during the famines and epidemics mellowed Moslem antagonism in the city and for some miles into Kabylia. But there were thousands of miles and millions of Moslems beyond the mountains who would remain untouched and unchanged as long as the missionaries were kept from them. Lavigerie had visions of a string of missions throughout Africa: oases of civilization, spreading their influence in all directions in an irresistible network of good. To be effective, the network had to grow fast and wide. The French were content to leave the Arabs as they were, so long as they submitted to Paris rule. That attitude conflicted entirely with the most elemental precepts of Christianity, precepts which had once already lifted France itself out of its swamps and were able to do so again whenever she returned to them. Lavigerie was anxious to let Algeria be a new proving ground for these precepts, and though he knew the task would be long and slow, he was eager to get started with it. He faced obstacles other than the colonial government. He faced, specifically, the entrenched hatred of Moslems who as yet had no idea what the missionaries could do for them and, in general, the understandable Arab distrust of all white men. And he faced the obstacle of Africa itself.

To the south was the Sahara: a continent of emptiness. Yet living along its fringes were some fifty million people who had become Moslems. Few of them had been reached by the Christianity which thrived in North Africa during the first centuries of the religion. Only Berbers still had traces of Christianity in their culture, hundreds of years after Islam swept across the Mediterranean shores. With the advent of Islam in the west, a door seemed to close on Africa, shutting out the world. None of the progress which was then lifting civilizations in Europe and North America, even remote Asia and India, penetrated beyond the African coasts. Explorers tried to fight their way into the wilderness, but most of them were never heard from again. The few who returned brought tales of millions of people living in extremely primitive societies, and they reported, too, that they had found cities, large cities, which seemed to pop right up out of the jungles and out of the sands. The cities were so inaccessible that even the name of one of them—Timbuktu—came to signify the far ends of the world. But Islam had reached there. For a thousand years, Islam had crept across Africa, and what it could not conquer in battle it overcame by osmosis. By the time the first European explorers reached Timbuktu in 1487, it was already an emporium of Arab slave traders and a thriving forest of mosques. The extreme remoteness of the city kept it isolated for another four hundred years. Locked in the Moslem grip, the city in all these years had not taken one step forward.

The papal creation of the Missionary Prefecture of the Sahara and the Sudan made Lavigerie the Bishop of Timbuktu. He looked forward to the day when he could send his first missionaries there. The most feasible route appeared to be from Algiers southward to Laghouat, then across the desert. It would mean a journey of almost two thousand miles, mostly over sand wastelands. Getting ready for it required many years. Until the White Fathers had enough men, Lavigerie used diocesan priests to staff the string of chapels which stretched south from Algiers and he sent the Jesuits onward to Laghouat, some three hundred miles further. All of them had orders to attend only to the spiritual needs of Europeans.

Lavigerie had no illusions about the Moslem attitude towards Christianity. Since the days of Mohammed himself, *Jihad*—the Holy War against Christians—and the promise of Paradise to those who died in it had been inspiration enough to send Moslem armies rampaging across Africa, to make two unsuccessful attempts to conquer Europe, and to plant an advance guard throughout the Far East in the guise of missionaries. To rush a holy-water font to such people was an invitation to disaster. At this point, Lavigerie was not interested in baptisms; he made them as difficult as he could to receive. He established the rule that anybody who wanted to become Christian must undergo a four-year catechumenate of preparatory studies, and this applied even to children. Exceptions were permitted only in the case of serious illness and imminent death. The wisdom of the rule proved itself repeatedly in subsequent years. Lavigerie also ordered that, even after the training, children could be baptized only with the written permission of both parents or legal guardians, and this was practically impossible to obtain. Orphans completely alone in the world were baptized, with the understanding that they would live among Christians; orphans adopted by Christians were bap-

89

tized. On occasion, adults were secretly baptized, but only if they could go to the mission regularly without provoking the suspicions of their Moslem relatives and friends: the visits enabled them to perform their religious duties while carrying out whatever ordinary business took them there. Also, adults able to prove that they were going to live in a Christian community elsewhere could be baptized before departure. These rules of Lavigerie's were later issued as a papal dictum applicable to missionaries working anywhere in the Moslem world. The caution was justified not only out of the physical dangers a converted Moslem risked from his relatives, but even more because of the possibility that environmental pressures might discourage a convert into denouncing the indelible responsibilities of baptism which he had freely accepted, reverting to his former errors, and thus threatening his eternal welfare far more seriously than had he never been baptized at all.

As more White Fathers became available, Lavigerie sent them to replace other priests at the outpost stations, and he gave them a four-point plan of action: education, charity, example, and prayer. He told them, too, that they must respect the Arab and his religion. The Arabs had no schools and did not even realize their need for hospitals; both must be supplied for the good of the people. However, Lavigerie ordered, at no time was Christianity to be forced upon them, for this was the pressure they were expecting, and it would have been a mistake. Christianity was not even to be discussed, Lavigerie instructed, except possibly in an historic sense or in answer to direct questions. This did not mean that the priests were to hide their religion: the Arabs prayed openly; the priests were to pray openly, too. Though Islam had brought nothing good to North Africa, only approbation of what was bad, it had nevertheless given the Arab and awareness of the duty of prayer, and this in itself was a very good thing. It was the basis on which the priests could approach the Arab, it was the link between them, it was a source of mutual respect. If that respect were to grow, the priests would have to demonstrate that, at this point, it was all they wanted. Certainly the Arabs realized what the priests had in the back of their minds, and it was this that made them apprehensive of the Christians who came among them. The Arabs were uneducated, but they were not ignorant. They knew Islam itself had proselytized, but with the help of the sword, and they expected something of this sort from the Christians. France had taken over the country by force; the Arabs looked for the same tactics in missionaries. They were therefore distrustful of the priests, aloof, belligerent. Progress, therefore, could only be made by carefully trained men, a training which other priests then in the country did not have. The Jesuits at Laghouat, despite orders from Lavigerie to restrict their pastoral work to Europeans, attempted to spread out among Arabs. They met only opposition and coldness. When Lavigerie sent a group of White Sisters to Laghouat, the mayor decided the Christians had gone too far and refused to let the nuns stay. Suddenly the mayor was stricken with a serious illness. Without waiting to be asked, the sisters went to his house, treated him, and in a week cured him. A few days later, he sent for them.

"Well, now," he said, "I suppose you think I owe you something."

"No," Sister Superior said.

"You would like me to let you stay, though, wouldn't you?"

"Of course," the nun said. "But if you want us to go, we will."

"Why did you come here?" the mayor asked.

"To open a school."

"And teach what?"

"Sewing, cooking, taking care of babies, things like that."

"And religion?"

"No, no religion."

The mayor was doubtful. "No religion? You are nuns; teaching religion is part of your job, isn't it?"

"So is living our religion," said Sister. "That is the opportunity we want here."

"And you'd do that by teaching our girls all these things?"

"Yes."

"But you'd like us to become Christians, wouldn't you?"

"Naturally," the nun said. "Wouldn't you like us to be Moslem?"

The mayor was amused by the answer. "Very well," he said. "You can stay—for a while, anyway. Rest assured I'll keep an eye on you. One attempt to convert—"

"There won't be any attempt."

"Good." The mayor hesitated. "Would you accept my daughter in your school?"

"Happily."

"She will be there in the morning," he said. "But just remember I'm not doing this because I think I owe you anything for taking care of me when I was sick."

"If that was the motive you have," said Sister Superior, "it would destroy the motive we have."

"What is your motive?" the mayor asked.

"We want to help."

With that motive, the White Sisters and White Fathers gradually began to reach out across Northern Algeria.

When the Jesuits were relieved at Laghouat, they were glad to go. They reported to Lavigerie that it was impossible to do any good there: the government was hostile, the people were stubborn. Lavigerie was well aware of the excellence of the Jesuits, but he was also aware that they did not have the specific training he felt essential to missionary work among the Algerian Arabs.

The White Fathers did. They went to their station well acquainted with the Arab, his religion, his life. They were, in effect, Arabs themselves. Further, they were armed with Lavigerie's excellent advice.

He had prescribed that they must always live in groups of at least three, and he put strong emphasis on the rule. "Give up a mission station before you give up this rule," he ordered. "Abandon your entire society rather than abandon this rule." There was greater wisdom in it than at first met the eye. Its first advantage seemed to be that it allowed for one man always to remain at the mission for emergencies while the other two went out among the people, but there was more to it than that. As new missionaries, the men would be full of fervor and their days would be crammed with work. But a man was a new missionary just so long, and then he became an old hand at it. He eventually found himself leading what amounted to a routine life. For any man, routine in itself could be a danger to the mind; to a priest alone among Moslems it was deadly. Two priests together would not make the task much lighter. Their duties would frequently separate them, their long periods together would pale their friendship, and nothing could create more disharmony than for one to harp on the fading spirituality of the other. Yet if the spiritually faded, the man himself became a very weak instrument of God, if he managed to remain one at all. The safeguard, then, was in the three, with the superior not only responsible for the success of the mission, but also the interior lives of his two assistants. Lavigerie felt so strongly on this point that he forbade a missionary to be alone for more than fourteen days, even when on treks to outposts remote from the main mission station. When he received a letter from Central Africa, from a White Fathers' caravan, proposing that the men split into smaller units so that one or two men could be sent out to cover more of the vast area, he replied in quiet indignation that he was surprised the men would consider such a thing in view of the rule he had given them. It would seem, at a glance, that Lavigerie did not trust his men on their own, but that attitude misses the point completely. He simply knew the difference between men and angels, and he also knew that the only man who had successfully resisted temptation was Christ, but Christ had the advantage of being God as well. Lavigerie had said, in his first searchings for White Fathers, that he wanted saints. Sanctity grew not only from the good things a man did for others, but more so from his personal relationship with God, a relationship built on adoration, prayer, obedience, meditation, mortification, a deep love. Whatever a man might do for others, his deeds would be little more than philanthropy unless his acts were balanced by a true interior life. From this life, too, came the strength necessary to endure against the burdens and privations of Africa—or anywhere else, for that matter. If, because of a heavy schedule or even sheer monotony, the interior life dimmed, then so did the man, and not only did he become worthless as a missionary but he endangered the welfare of his soul. That, to Lavigerie, was more important than anything else.

With remarkable foresight, Lavigerie gave his men advice on their dealings with Africans, whether the Moslem of the north or the pagan at the Equator. He said the first acts should be medical treatment, and he suggested that initial contact with Africans should be to seek out the sick and care for them. If further medicine was needed, a relative of the sick person was to go to the mission for it, thus acquiring the habit of looking to the mission as a source of help. Next, he said, priests should go into the fields and look for ways to make immediate contributions to agriculture, no matter how simple at first. All Africans were notoriously bad farmers and needed this help. As soon as possible, the priests were to start their own farms, teaching modern methods to the people by hiring them. Eventually workers would return to their own farms, would take with them all they had learned, and the entire community would profit. Then schools should be started; when nuns were nearby, girls should be urged to go to them for training. From such frequent contacts, Lavigerie foresaw, a curiosity would arise about the missionaries, and then the questions would come. As long as the priests lived up to the answers they gave, the people would respect them, trust them, and, sooner or later, imitate them.

"Do not Europeanize the people," Lavigerie instructed. "Rather, make yourselves what they are, as far as your priesthood permits. Speak their language, adopt their customs, live among them as the brother to them that you are. Even should they become Christians, encourage them to retain all of their culture which does not outrightly conflict with their new faith. If you can give Christian interpretations to their customs, their songs and dances, do so, but change nothing that you cannot replace with something of value."

Knowing that the political structure of Africa put authority into the hands of Moslem sheiks or pagan chiefs, Lavigerie told his men always to respect the established leaders and to win their friendship. A ruler who opposed them for any but a religious reason certainly would not let the priests associate with the people; the religious differences would not present a serious problem as long as the priests did much more for the people than merely campaign for converts. Actually, it would be the leaders and intellectuals of tribes who would want to discuss religion, he said, and only then should the subject be gone into. Lavigerie likewise warned his men about their contacts with women and children. He knew that throughout Africa a male's interest in sex began the day he learned to walk and could thereafter run down whatever appealed to him. Among Moslems, the gender of the object of pursuit made no difference whatsoever. It would not take long, Lavigerie warned, for people to discover that the priests had a vow of chastity, and they would find it difficult to believe. The moment, therefore, anyone saw a priest pay particular attention to a woman or a girl or a boy, doubts about adherence to the vow would race throughout the community and the priest would lose his effectiveness completely. Lavigerie felt so strongly on this point that he commanded his priests not only to avoid such public displays of interest—however innocent—but also never to be alone with a woman or child behind closed doors, even to treat their illnesses or—when the time arrived—to hear their confessions. The years proved Lavigerie right on this point, time and again.

"Be men of prayer," he told the priests. "Do not hesitate to kneel at your prayers in public. The people will admire you for it. Besides, you will need all the prayers that you can say. There is a great deal of work ahead for everyone. Among Moslems, you have centuries of hatred to overcome; among pagans, centuries of fear. A single imprudence on the part of one of you can ruin everything. Therefore, do not rush, don't be in a hurry for success. A hundred years will pass before the world sees the fruits of your efforts. I warn you that you are destined for failures and frustrations; sometimes you will feel so desolate you will want to quit. But remember you are there for God. Him you must never fail. For His sake, the less you succeed, the more you must endure."

IX

THERE was no limit to what the young priests were willing to endure. Imbued by their training with astonishing zeal, they thrived on hardships, flourished on deprivations. They were as poor as Arabs but far happier: they had a purpose. Settling in a new mission held for them all the excitements of world discoveries, and they could not find enough time for all that they wanted to do. They knew they were not wanted when they arrived, and they overcome this by making themselves needed. Adhering to Lavigerie's instructions to provide medical care, they stalked the streets in search of anyone who looked as if he had so much as a headache. Arabs who came to the mission, with problems or merely with curiosity, received royal welcome. That they should be allowed just to remain in a new village or a new valley was encouragement enough for the priests. Often they were hungry, many times they were sick, but they were never depressed.

They were, on the other hand, restless to do more. They agreed with Lavigerie that they would be most effective if they advanced with the surprise speed of shock troops, fanning in all directions as fast as possible. There would be time enough to take root; it was important now to cover the surface so that wherever an Arab went he would see priests, would get used to seeing priests, and would eventually want to see priests. Each southward mile therefore became somewhat of a triumph in itself, and each mile took them nearer the goal they had picked: Timbuktu, the western Mecca. To explorers and to generals, the conquest of Timbuktu assured the victory over Arab hold-outs of the Sahara, but to the White Fathers it meant penetration into the stronghold of Islam and the chance to soften the fierce rays of anti-Christian hatred that emanated from Timbuktu into every grain of sand in the desert. Not until the priests could extinguish the hate at its source would the good they achieved elsewhere be firm and lasting. Thus Timbuktu was important, and for a long time it seemed unattainable.

For many months after the War of 1870, nests of insurrectionists had held out in the mountains south of Algiers. French troops, freed from the fighting in Europe, went up into the hills after them, but the soldiers soon found that they had more than rebels to fight. Roaming through the country were small bands of gangsters taking advantage of the unrest. Mostly they attacked small villages, isolated shops and remote farms, but at times several gangs united for big assaults on sizable towns, even cities. The gangsters, for the most part, came from Sahara tribes, like the Chamba and the Tuareg, and they had rarely been seen in the north. All that was known about them was that they were a cruel and treacherous people. To Lavigerie, they had a special importance. They knew the desert; they could, if Lavigerie was able to persuade them, lead missionaries across the Sahara to Timbuktu. Lavigerie, therefore, was most anxious to make contact with them.

By January, 1872, French troops had pursued insurrectionists and outlaws to Ouargla, some five hundred miles south of Algiers, and at the end of the year they reached El Golea, another two hundred miles ahead. That November, Lavigerie sent an inspection team, headed by Father Louis Richard, to evaluate possibilities of sending the first missionary caravan into the Sahara. Richard was able to go as far as Ouargla, where he met a French explorer, Soleillet by name, who had traveled all the way to In Salah, a thousand miles south of Algiers. Lavigerie had contributed to Soleillet's journey, with the hope that he might bring back helpful information about the distant regions. His information was helpful, but not very hopeful. The southern area, he reported, was full of political refugees and dissidents from Algiers, and mingling openly among them were thieves and killers who preyed upon anyone who looked like an easy victim. The district was tense with great dangers, he said; it was no place and certainly no time for defenseless priests. Lavigerie decided to postpone his plans until a safer day, but the young White Fathers were restless and impetuous. They pleaded with Lavigerie for permission to go as far south as was possible so that, when the time came, they could push out across the Sahara quickly, effectively.

This Lavigerie was willing to permit. After all, French troops were stationed along the route, providing both protection and a reason for the priests to start spreading out. In the next few months, mission posts were established at Laghouat, Biskra, Géryville, Metlili, and Ouargla. Father Alfred Paulmier took a group all the way to El Golea. The steppingstones to Timbuktu were falling into place.

The first missions got off to far better starts than anyone expected, and the priests were anxious to move further south. Held back until replacements could arrive, they squirmed with envy as French troops, with whom they could have traveled, moved on without them into the Sahara. Occasionally they received jolts to remind them of the shifting sands on which they were building. In April, 1874, Dourneau Dupéré, an explorer, left Algiers in a southeasterly direction, with the idea that by advancing through Ghadames and Ghat he could pick up the routes to Timbuktu used by Arab traders. He was on the road just ten days when his expedition was attacked and he and two other Frenchmen were murdered. No matter, then, how well things might be going in the towns, out in the open desert there was still danger.

The Berber gang which had killed Dupéré was well known. For ten years, it had rampaged throughout Southern Algeria, robbing, killing, destroying. Its leader was Salem ben Seghair, a member of the Chamba tribe, and he used Ouargla as his headquarters. The gang was small but fierce and shrewd, and though the police had enough evidence to hang every member of it, they seemed always able to elude capture. There were some people, however, who had taken just about as much as they could stand from the gang, and among these was the Arab mayor of Metlili. The mayor learned in midsummer of 1875 that the gang had left the In Salah area on a raiding tour of the Metlili district. When they arrived on July 1, the mayor was ready. A brief but violent battle took place in the fields outside the city. Salem ben Saghair was seriously wounded and was put out of action, a man was killed and two escaped. Ten prisoners—three Chamba, five Tuareg, and two Saharans—were taken to the Metlili jail.

It was there that the White Fathers encountered them. The priests were especially anxious to meet the Tuareg. Their tribe was probably the most powerful of the Sahara. By reputation, they were traders, and they knew the desert thoroughly, but they were also raiders, attacking not only Europeans but weaker tribes of the Sahara, and when their opposition grew too strong, they hurried southward to the safety of Timbuktu. No one had ever been friendly with Tuareg. They were like bands of hermits who discouraged all attempts of intimacy. They were known for their cruelty, their black-heartedness, their deception. Nevertheless, they were important to anyone wanting to cross the Sahara, and Father Jean Baptiste Charbonnier hastened to the prison as soon as he learned the five Tuareg were there. He was given a cold and savage reception. The Tuareg would have nothing to do with him. They expected to be shot for what they had done and they were not interested in this young man who had come to them with a thousand questions about the Sahara. The Metlili jail was far from a pleasant place to be, even for desert men. They were fed irregularly, if at all, there was little fresh water and no fresh air. Determined to make the men talk to him, Father Charbonnier broke down their stubbornness with gifts of food and water, and he arranged for them to have a few minutes a day out of their cells. Slowly, they began to pay a little attention to him. Before a month had passed, they spoke to him freely, almost friendly, telling him much he wanted to know about the desert. Passage across it was not so difficult as people supposed, they said, especially if one had good guides. There were oases in the most unlikely places, they told the priest, and if you knew them, you would have no trouble at all. True, the people along the way were not hospitable by any means, but that was because they were afraid of the French. But priests—particularly priests who spoke Arabic— should get through easily enough, more so if they brought along

99

money and cloth, even weapons, to give to the sheiks in return for permission to pass through safely.

Charbonnier was fascinated by what he learned, and he wrote long letters to Lavigerie with all the news. He knew that he was dealing with Tuareg, but he felt that under the circumstances he could believe what they were telling him. There seemed no reason for them to lie. They were convinced they were going to die, and at such moments most men are more honest than ever in their lives. Lavigerie replied with countless questions; he ached with the desire to interview the Tuareg himself.

Late in August, the ten prisoners were transferred to Laghouat for trial. Oddly enough, the cases against the three Chambas were dismissed on the grounds that there was not sufficient evidence to prosecute them. The five Tuareg and the two Saharans found themselves on the way to Algiers. This was most unusual, and only someone with the influence of Lavigerie could have brought it off.

The prisoners were welcomed into Algiers as if they were visiting nobility. The entire city fought for a glimpse of them. They had been washed and given new and colorful robes; they wore their traditional veils. Tall, slender, sullenly proud, they strolled freely about Algiers as if the city was theirs, and it virtually was. The government interviewed them, the Army interviewed them, and both occasions amounted to parties. Hostesses competed to fete them: they were celebrities. No one had ever seen anything like them before. In the contest for a close look, everybody forgot that they were killers and thieves, and the Tuareg themselves never gave it a thought.

Lavigerie saw them several times, each time questioning them in great detail. The prisoners quickly perceived his plan for a missionary caravan to Timbuktu and they assured him glowingly that it was an excellent idea that should be pursued immediately. Convinced that he was getting priceless information, Lavigerie reciprocated by interceding with the government on the prisoners' behalf, and the charges against them were dropped. Then Lavigerie offered to give them the money to get back to the Sahara.

One of them, by name Idda ag Guemmun, said: "That is most generous of you. We do not wish to impose on you more than we already have, but under the circumstances we must accept the money. But we want to do something for you. We know you want

100

to reach Timbuktu. Why don't you return to the desert with us and let us take you there?"

Lavigerie smiled sadly. "Nothing would give me greater happiness," he said, "but I am not free to go."

"Well, then," the Targui said, "give us some of your sons who can go with us. If we have to carry them on our backs, we will get them there."

Now Lavigerie was full alert. "This may be just what I've been waiting for," he said. "But would the priests be safe?"

"Even if they had their *chechias* full of gold pieces, there would be no danger," Idda ag Guemmun assured.

The opportunity was too tempting to resist. "Let me think about it," Lavigerie said, but before the prisoners were out of the house, he was already completing his plans. He wrote Father Alfred Paulmier at Metlili and appointed him superior of the first caravan, naming to it Father Pierre Bouchand, who was also at Metlili, and Father Philippe Menoret, who was working with the orphans at Attaf. They were eager and strong young men, all in their mid-twenties, certainly capable of enduring the hardships of the trip. When they received news of their appointments, they were ecstatic with joy. Other White Fathers wrote them with open envy, asked God to protect the young priests, and promised them prayers. It was a great moment for the society; at last it was fulfilling its aims.

At the end of December, 1875, the three priests met at Laghouat to await the prisoners coming down from Algiers. Lavigerie sent them careful instructions for their behavior among the Moslems at Timbuktu and he commanded them to write him regularly. "Write me every day," he said, "even though you may not be able to send the letters on for weeks. Report everything you see, hear, do, think, for it is from what happens to you on this journey that others will learn how to prepare for the future."

United with the prisoners, the priests spent a few days in consultation with them, then moved on to Metlili. By now, news of the trip had gotten out. French officials were strongly against letting the priests travel beyond the zone of military protection. The Arab mayor of Metlili told them:

"I know I cannot stop you from going, but I insist that you sign documents showing that you leave here against my advice. I don't want to be responsible for you."

On January 14, 1876, the priests signed the document and left the city. White Fathers from surrounding missions had come to see them off. There was a great deal of merriment, teasing, and joking. At the last minute, all the priests knelt in a final prayer, then they kissed good-by and the caravan departed. In it were the three priests, the five Tuareg and two Saharans, four camel drivers, and a teen-age Arab boy named El-hadj'-ben-Boubeker who had become attached to the priests and insisted upon going with them despite his family's strong objection.

At a White Fathers' conference in Algiers a week later, Lavigerie announced: "Three of our missionaries are at this moment among the Tuareg on their way to Timbuktu to set up a mission in the Sudan and, if necessary, to give up their lives for the love of truth."

It was a prophecy. January ended, and February passed away with no word from the caravan. At the end of March, rumors seeped back from the Sahara that the priests were dead. White Fathers at mission outposts ran down the rumors but were unable to verify them. On April 11, the French commander at Laghouat telegraphed Algiers that according to the Arab Mayor of El Golea the rumors had been confirmed. Two days later, on Holy Thursday, Lavigerie was strolling the country road toward his house at St. Eugène when a messenger caught up with him and handed him the telegram, forwarded from the Governor's office. He read it, then passed it to the priest who was walking with them. Without a word, they turned and began retracing their steps the mile back to Our Lady of Africa basilica. They had taken just a few steps when Lavigerie intoned the *Te Deum,* and for the rest of the walk they continued singing the hymn. At the basilica, they went to the priests who had been elected assistant superiors of the society and told them what had happened.

"I don't want the others to know just yet," Lavigerie said. "Tomorrow is Good Friday, a day of great mourning for the Church, and though we have lost sons that we love, we do not have reasons to mourn further."

On Easter Sunday, he called all the White Fathers together and announced the massacre. Everyone was shocked. Lifelong friends of the dead priests openly broke down. Lavigerie said: "As the Church does not wish that we recite the *De Profundis* for martyrs, we will sing together the hymn of thanksgiving." And again he intoned the *Te Deum*.

He wrote the priests' families and told them that though they had certainly suffered a great loss, they should rejoice in knowing that their sons had earned the crowns of martyrs and might one day win the thrones of canonization. The Paris newspapers did not look at it that way. They accused Lavigerie of consciously sending the young men to their deaths and they demanded he be recalled from Algiers. They pointed to the other young priests he had under his influence, and they warned that the same thing would happen to them. They urged a complete investigation, with every effort to recover the bodies in order to determine exactly what had happened. Lavigerie, too, wanted the bodies recovered, not only to learn the circumstances of the deaths but also to give the priests a proper burial. Also, if it could be established that they were true martyrs, their bodies would become the sacred relics of saints.

Finding the bodies seemed impossible. No one was sure where the killings had taken place. Even the four camel drivers, who had returned to Metlili, knew nothing. The first two said that the caravan had met some Tuareg a few days south of Metlili. Feeling that the newcomers knew the desert better than the camel drivers, the priests had dismissed two of them. The other two said that a few nights later they heard the Tuareg planning to murder the priests; frightened, they had run off.

They were asked: "If you knew the priests were in danger, why didn't you warn them?"

One of them replied: "If a man does not know when he is in danger, it is not my business to tell him."

Such was the callous indifference the White Fathers encountered wherever they turned. If there were any witnesses to the murders, no one would talk out of fear of complicity. Several Arabs claimed to have helpful information, but they would talk only if they were paid. They were paid, but their stories made no sense at all. The months rolled away with no success. The Arab mayor of El Golea offered a reward of a thousand francs for the bodies, but this only encouraged a parade of dishonest informers. Some of them even

103

brought bones to the White Fathers, which turned out to be the bones of animals. A year passed and nothing happened, and then another year. Pressure from French officials grew. White Fathers were ordered not to make any more long trips, assured that if any should try troops would be sent after them and they would be imprisoned for breaking the law. For a time, several of the missions were closed, by order of the French, and Lavigerie had to exert all his influence to have them opened again.

Late in 1878, Father Louis Richard, then superior at Ouargla, heard that a band of Arabs was touring the area with a package they claimed held effects of the massacred missionaries. They were offering the package to the highest bidder, reluctant out of fear to take it themselves to the police or the White Fathers. Through Arab channels, Richard got word to the tribe, assuring them his protection against the police if they would bring him the parcel. They agreed—for fifteen hundred francs. Richard raised the money among friends in Ouargla, and the Arabs came to his mission. The package contained some bones and some books and papers Richard recognized as effects of the priests.

"Where did you get this?" he asked the tribe leader.

"I will take you there for five hundred francs more," the man said.

Richard got the money. He was then taken to a place known as Hassi-Targue, in the valley of El Meksa, north of the Oued River. There, half buried in sand some distance off the road, he found two skulls that had been burned, more bones, pieces of an altar stone, books and manuscripts. There was no third skull, and no sign of the Arab boy who had gone with the priests. Richard felt he had enough evidence to conclude that these were the remains of the missionaries. He was certain, at least, that they were the bones of Christians: there was an unwritten law among Moslems against the decapitation of other Moslems because the head was supposed to contain the soul; the victim of such a death would be unable to take the rest of his body into heaven and would therefore haunt the man who had killed him until the end of the world. This law was not applicable to Christians, who, according to Moslems, were damned anyway.

Richard sent all he could find to Algiers, and his own conclusions were supported by authorities there. That seemed the end of it.

Several months later, however, an Arab came to Father Richard and said he knew the details of the murder. For a fee he was ready to tell.

"How can I believe you?" Richard asked. "Others have come here and told only lies."

"El-Oufini, El-Meneir, Idda ag Guemmun," the man said, naming three of the Tuareg prisoners. "I have seen them in the desert and they told me everything."

Father Richard got the money the man asked, then listened to his story.

From the beginning, the Tuareg had planned to kill the priests. Their plan developed further when, on the road, they met other Tuareg, and they urged the priests to dismiss the camel drivers. Only two were replaced; the Tuareg decided to wait. Then, one morning, they found that the other drivers had run off in the night. Now it was only a question of when to fulfill the plan. They waited a few days until the carvan stopped to spend the night in an isolated place. It was El-Oufini who started it. He took out his saber and went to Father Paulmier, suggesting that the priest learn how to use the sword in case of attack. Demonstrating, he made several thrusts with the saber, then turned quickly and hit the priest on the head, scalping him. Father Bouchand ran forward to help Paulmier. El-Meneir shot him in the head. Father Menoret turned to flee, but Idda ag Guemmun jumped on him and stabbed him several times in the neck and chest with a small dagger. Dying, the three priests crawled to each other and fell in a heap, whispering absolutions as they grew weaker and weaker. The Tuareg cut off their heads and burned them, then went through the supplies and took whatever looked valuable.

"What about the Arab boy?" Father Richard asked.

"The Tuareg saw his affection for the priests," the man said, "and thought he must have become a Christian. They therefore felt justified in using their sabers to cut him to pieces."

X

On the second of January, 1878, Lavigerie sent to Rome a secret memorandum which subsequently became one of the most widely discussed documents among organizations involved in the Christian missions in Africa. Most of the discussion has been utter conjecture because, until now, details of the memo have never been released. Secrecy meant the risk of misunderstanding, but the risk was necessary in this case. Had the memo's contents become known when it was written, the Church, confronted by anticlericism on all sides, would have suffered more than she did. Wary non-Catholics immediately assumed that the memo contained some dark plot intended to turn Africa over to the Pope, lock, stock, and ballot box, and the resulting antagonism has persisted widely even to this day. It was an antagonism which, quite normally, grew from ignorance, plus—in Africa—a distorted alarm over a report that was amazingly shrewd regarding conditions at that time and impressively clairvoyant in terms of much that has happened since. The secrecy enshrouding the memo was, clearly, a diplomatic necessity in order to safeguard Catholic life elsewhere in the world. In many ways, this was unfortunate. Certainly there were few political leaders in Europe in 1878 who could have been seriously influenced by what Lavigerie had to say; had this been otherwise Africa today would most likely be a far more peaceful continent. But the European rulers were not interested in peace.

In 1876, the Belgian King, Leopold II, summoned to Brussels delegates from several European countries and large industries which had displayed expansion interests in Africa. The meeting was a forerunner of the subsequent Berlin conference at which Africa was chopped up into political zones of influence. Leopold's intention was to correlate the efforts and expenses of the commercial and political explorations then going on in Africa. Until that time, such explorations rarely penetrated into the interior. A few professional explorers did manage to advance well beyond the coasts before they were forced back, and the missionary efforts of both Catholics and Protestants were commencing. Outstanding among Protestants was Dr. David Livingstone, whose expeditions were in part supported by a geographical society. A bulletin describes him as a "missionary of the gospel of science." This was in keeping with what Leopold had in mind.

Religion as such was relegated to the background. The official report of the Brussels conference claimed: "The establishments which we are going to create [in Central Africa] will be of a purely secular nature. Commerce will civilize the interior of Africa. To raise up, at once and considerably, the level of the moral and social conditions of the native people, it will be sufficient to organize among these people the arts and trades of Europe."

The proposed establishments were to be way stations where expeditions could rest and stock up for further travel. Some of them would have doctors to treat expedition members. Between expeditions, the staffs at the stations were to occupy themselves with scientific research. At the beginning of the conference, the subject of antislavery measures was on the agenda, but it somehow slipped from view and was not mentioned in the final report. Funds for the extensive network of stations were to be provided by member nations of the committee, with headquarters in Brussels and Leopold as permanent chairman.

The absence of Catholic influence at the conference was too noticeable to be a coincidence. No invitation to send a delegate had been offered to the Pope, a surprising affront in view of the fact that most of Europe recognized him as a bona-fide sovereign with a justified interest in the development of Africa. The only priest present was a bishop who, to everybody's astonishment, had been brought along as a part of the Austrian delegation. The two strongest countries represented were England and Germany, both Protestant. Delegations from other nations were composed almost entirely of Protestants and "free thinkers"—a now obsolete term once applicable to atheists and Freemasons. The conference appeared stacked.

Lavigerie felt that the Catholic missionary interest in the future of Africa could not be completely ignored by the conference and was even anticipated—the missionaries were to be kept out, or at least controlled. The conference agreed that no expeditions of any kind would be allowed into Central Africa without the commission's approval, and there could be any number of reasons for a refusal. Further, the commission's praise for Livingstone, the missionary of science, indicated the kind of apostles the commission preferred. Also, the declaration by some of the French that they planned to permit in Southern Algeria the sales of slaves to Arab traders was additional assurance that countries at the Brussels session wanted no interference from quarters which had a higher regard for human life.

Lavigerie's secret memo dealt with all these points, deducing from them that several of the European rulers were as anxious to keep the Catholic Church out of Central Africa as they were to destroy the last embers of its moral influence in Europe itself. The moral obligations inherent in Catholicism had been a yoke around the necks of exploiting rulers for years; to escape it, they had twisted the efforts of Martin Luther to their own ends and they had backed Henry VIII's severance from Rome when the Church denounced his depravity. Lavigerie saw in this new crusade of commerce the same type of exploitation which had kept Europe on the battlefield for centuries, which had caused the American Indian practically to be wiped out, and which had produced in South America a new race of slave labor. Successive popes had descried such exploitation, reminding rulers of their duties to the people they ruled, but to no avail. And now it looked like Africa's turn.

Lavigerie advised Pope Pius IX—and on his death, the new Pope, Leo XIII—that the Chuch should move fast to get into Central

Africa before the door was shut. If missionaries could not enter the area before the Brussels' expeditions, they should at least get there at the same time. Let the others import science and commerce, he said, but let the Church import humanity and justice.

The great threat Lavigerie saw in the Brussels idea was the danger of transforming Africans into Europeans. Africa is for Africans, he said, and they must be permitted to develop it along its natural lines. To teach European arts and trades to an African, to force him to dress, eat, live, and talk like a European would make him as foreign to his own country as snow. "The advantage achieved by such methods is purely negative," Lavigerie wrote Rome. "It removes an obstacle but it does not give a solution." The solution, he felt, was to adjust the knowledge of Europe to the African way of life, not the other way around. The solution was in helping the African, not using him.

There were three realms in which Lavigerie felt the African needed help: education, agriculture, and medicine. As important as these were, they were not so vital as the religious life that would lead the African to God. Unless all four factors progressed together, there would be no progress at all. And true progress would come only when the Africans themselves, having learned all they could, turned around and taught other Africans. The duty of Christian civilization, as Lavigerie saw it, was to help people to help themselves. That moment would not be achieved without hard work, Lavigerie declared. There would first be failures and frustrations, headaches and heartaches. Though Islam had not the same grip on Central Africa that it had in the north, the Moslems were most certainly in the area and at work. There were also centuries of paganism to combat, years and years of tribal rule by fear and suspicion. This would have to be overcome before there could be one step forward, and Lavigerie assured that the step would be slow. The greatest mistake, he warned, would be sudden and violent change, the kind of change indicated at the Brussels conference and based on the attitude that what was best for Europeans was also best for Africans. This attitude in missionaries would be a grievous error. "We must close our eyes to such false pity and false self-love," Lavigerie advised Rome, "and resign ourselves to seeing at our sides for a long time young Africans continuing the customs of their

109

country, living in straw huts instead of houses, sleeping on the ground instead of beds, eating sorghum and manioc instead of bread, wearing leaves instead of pants. The African does not suffer in these conditions; it is the imagination of the missionary that suffers." The time would come, he said, when the African would be ready to borrow from European civilization whatever he considered of value to his life in Africa, but to force that moment or to pressure any foreign part of it would result only in chaos. Important at the beginning was to win the trust and love of the African by trusting and loving him.

Lavigerie's secret memo outlined a simple plan: first, get priests into Central Africa; there were none there now. Oblate, Holy Ghost, Jesuit, and Verona Fathers were working along the coasts, but they were few in number and could not be spared. Therefore, send in other priests, and a lot of them. Lavigerie offered the White Fathers, now growing in membership and eager for just such an assignment. On arriving in the African interior, the priests had as their first duty to treat the sick, and they were to limit themselves to this as long as necessary while winning the confidence of the people and the chiefs. At the same time, they were to make contact with the caravans of slave traders and buy back all the people they could, especially children. When possible, the children should be returned to their tribes; otherwise they were to be housed in orphanages. Education of these children was to be started immediately, and with the children of nearby tribes as soon as permission of the chiefs was granted. Medical assistants would be trained at the first opportunity, Lavigerie urged, and every effort ought to be made to improve farming methods.

All this would take a long time, of course, and while it was going on, the missionaries would also be laying the foundation for their proselytizing. The aim was obvious: the establishment of the Catholic Church in Central Africa with the day always in mind when the Africans could take it over. This meant ordaining African priests, consecrating African bishops, establishing congregations of African nuns and brothers. Through such people, Lavigerie said, the ideals of the Church would be crystallized in Africa, ideals reflecting the dignity of the individual, the family, society itself: the Catholic Church of Africa governed by Africans for Africans. How far off that day might seem! But, Lavigerie assured, it was actually as close as the hearts of the men who were willing to start the work: the White Fathers.

Such hearts were quite different from those that beat at Brussels. Forty battle-torn years in Algeria occupation had taught the French nothing, and they were now about to invade Tunisia with the same strong-arm tactics. Portugal had occupied chunks of the African coasts, then sapped the strength out of them. Germany, Italy, Spain, and England were about to divide what remained of the continent. Leopold II had already claimed the entire Belgian Congo as his personal property and ruled it for years with shocking cruelty.

Predictions of the many years of chaos which grew out of the Brussels conference were made by Lavigerie in his secret memo. The inevitable chaos would have been obvious to anyone whose ambitions were other than for power and wealth. Had the memo been made public at the time, Lavigerie and the Church would have been accused of rabble-rousing, disloyalty, and bigotry, and the repercussions from it would have been felt in every humble chapel in Europe. There would have also been accusations that the Church was merely trying to regain its lost temporal influence; in fact, when the existence of the memo became known and its secrecy was noted, those very accusations sprouted in misguided non-Catholic circles and have never completely faded. Because of its shattering evaluation of the Brussels conference and its amazingly accurate forecasts which reflected against member nations at the meeting, and also because it advocated sending Catholic missionaries to Central Africa regardless of the European machinations, the secrecy imposed on the memo was quite wisely a prudent decision.

Two days after the memo arrived in Rome, it was approved by Cardinal Franchi, director of the Propagation of the Faith, and submitted to Leo XIII. The Pope quickly approved it.

The papal approval was dated February 24. It was the first official act of the new Pope. Two weeks later, the first White Fathers' caravan to Equatorial Africa was on its way. At almost the same hour, the influences of commerce and of Christ entered the heart of Africa. It was up to the Africans themselves to determine which would succeed.

XI

THE murder of the three young priests in the Sahara brought Lavigerie's work in North Africa to a standstill. Only through his own influence in Paris was he able to keep open the missions he had already established in the earlier days of the White Fathers. Even so, there was a retreat of some measure. Men were pulled back from the desert fringe and assigned to safer missions; newcomers anxious to get to work among Arabs found themselves teaching catechism to children at the Algiers orphanages. Notoriety resulting from the murders brought an onrush of applications from seminarians and priests throughout Europe who discovered in the White Fathers the kind of challenge that would give their vocations deeper meaning, and soon the novitiate at Maison Carrée was packed. In a few months there was a backlog of White Fathers, looking for something to do. With the Sahara closed to the society, it appeared that all that could be done was to wait until the French colonial authorities calmed down and permitted the White Fathers to resume their southward expansion, slowly this time, cautiously. Lavigerie was in the awkward position of knowing that some day he would need a lot of priests yet being unable to use those he already had. Then the papal permission to go into Central Africa arrived.

Once again there was great excitement at Maison Carrée. Men watched the bulletin board with the tense hope that they would be assigned to the first caravan, and there was a scramble in the library for books and maps—anything pertaining to the interior of the continent. A new vocabulary appeared in the house, words full of vowels that rolled deliciously on the tongue—Uganda, Tanganyika, Nyasa, Bagamoyo.

Bagamoyo, on the Tanganyika coast of Africa opposite the island of Zanzibar, is in British territory today, but when the White Fathers arrived to begin their first trek into the interior, it was under the jurisdiction of the Sultan of Zanzibar. The Sultan was a tremendously rich man, deriving his wealth from percentage claims on the sales of slaves, gold, and ivory brought by Arab traders from the inlands. His permission was necessary to enter the mainland, a permission attainable by payment of a fee. Also for a fee, he was able to supply porters and soldiers, but they had to be paid as well. Safe passage through the bush could only be assured—and not absolutely assured —by payment to chiefs along the route, payment in cloth, arms, jewelry, animals, food, all of which had to be purchased at Zanzibar. With the increase of traffic into Africa, Zanzibar became a highly prosperous city.

Lavigerie appointed ten men to his first caravan, nine priests and one lay brother. They were to proceed together as far as Tabora in Central Tanganyika, then split up, one group going northward to Lake Victoria, the other west to Lake Tanganyika. Father Léon Livinhac was named superior of the first group; Father Joaquim Pascal superior of the second. Lavigerie's plan was to set up vicariates as quickly as possible, and it was obvious from the beginning that these two men, as soon as enough priests had arrived, were destined to become bishops.

They were going into territory that was practically untouched by the missionary influence. Only Dr. David Livingstone had made any notable penetrations in Central Africa, and though he covered a vast area, his influence upon the people was necessarily slim because he was alone. Most important, Livingstone proved that white men could survive the hardships of journeys into the deep interior, and his personal efforts established that the hidden tribes were receptive to Christianity. Moreover, his reports on the vicious Arab slave trade

113

made clergymen everywhere realize that they must rush to the African's defense if the race was to be saved from extinction. Previously, severe government controls, the great hardships of travel, and hostile tribes made missionary attempts into the inlands either impossible or imprudent. For centuries, Christianity was therefore limited to the fringes of the continent, and the ministers who settled there were more chaplains to the Europeans than missionaries to the natives. The few who tried to enter the interior either did not come back or returned convinced that the inlands, at least for the time being, were impenetrable. Sadly enough, the people who actually opened Africa were those who were causing its greatest disasters: the time came when Arab caravans traversed the interior with alarming frequency, easing their travel by enslaving Africans as highly expendable beasts of burden. With the new concentration of European interest in Africa, more and more explorers began piercing the interior darkness, but their intentions did not include any specific aid to the people. Livingstone was the first man of science to be also a man of God. After him, Protestants erected several small missions on the routes he had opened, establishing tiny oases of Christianity in the incredibly vast wilderness. The Catholic Church, too, wanted to reach the people while the opportunity existed, particularly in view of the apparently anti-Catholic plans formulating at Brussels. Priests already on the African coasts could not be spared, and existing missionary societies were committed elsewhere. The White Fathers, however, their work in North Africa restricted by the many conflicts there, were available and eager for the challenge of the interior, and thus they became the Catholic pioneers in a world that was filled with dangers and death.

On March 12, Lavigerie gave his men personal instructions for all phases of conduct on the trip, ordering them to keep the instructions with them at all times. Two days later, the official farewell was celebrated at Palm Sunday ceremonies at Maison Carrée, and the following Wednesday, the caravan left by boat for Marseilles. Father Charmetant and Father Toussaint Deniaud, who was one of the caravan members, left France immediately for Zanzibar to make arrangements for equipment necessary for the journey; the others followed them in a week. When the men were all en route, Lavigerie went to Belgium to see King Leopold II to tell him that the caravan was on its way. Leopold was considerably surprised, but since the caravan had already left and because it had been organized by an archbishop who had the clever audacity to walk into his palace and tell him about it, there was nothing he could do under the circumstances but wish the men good luck. Lavigerie then returned to France to get financing for the future caravans he planned to send off in rapid succession. Money for the first expedition had been granted by the Pope from a special Vatican fund intended for welfare work among children.

The missionaries themselves felt like children. They were, of course, imbued first of all with the missionary nature of their trip, but Central Africa itself had become a goal they were now about to achieve. From their first student days they had read all they could about Africa, memorizing it, talking about it with such intimacy that they sounded as if they had lived there all their lives. They liked saying the names of the countries, the towns, the tribes, pronouncing them with exaggerated correctness, carefully in a way that revealed both their love for the continent and their newness to it. They had read Livingstone and admired him for what he had tried to do. After Livingstone's death, his effects had been taken to Zanzibar and sold at auction. Most of it was soon scattered all over the world, but Father Charmetant managed to find in a side-street shop a pair of puttees Livingstone had worn and the mattress he used. The young priest bought them both, and he was very proud of them.

On the sixteenth of June, the missionaries left Bagamoyo and crossed the Kingani River to the fields where the porters were waiting. Five hundred men, porters and escort soldiers, had been hired. They were at camp, waiting to start off, and the sight of them deeply impressed the missionaries who were meeting black Africans for the first time. They were handsome men, magnificently built, strong and sleek. They moved with the grace of panthers. Many of them were nude, while others wore a neatly folded loin cloth which they used as a blanket at night. The field was full of them, some resting on pack boxes, some finishing their breakfast of manioc root and sorghum seeds, others clustered around fires, smoking their water pipes. Most of them had been on safaris before; this one was just another job. They were easy and casual among themselves; their deep laughter burst forth: small, happy thunder. They glanced at the missionaries walking among them, knew they were being evaluated, and evaluated the priests in return. On previous safaris, they had gone in search of gold, ivory, animals, even Africans, but this time, they were told, they were simply to escort the white men to the interior where the missionaries planned to stay. This the Africans did not understand; not understanding, they were not interested.

It was decided to break the caravan into three groups. Father Théophile Dromaux and Brother Amans would head the forward group; Father Deniaud and Father Henri Delaunay the second, and the others bring up the rear. There was never to be more than a day's journey between them. Runners would maintain contact between the sections. For as long as possible, the missionaries would ride on mules, the only animals able to resist the bite of the tsetse fly. The priests wore their usual white robes, hip boots because of the swamps ahead, and large, cork hats. They carried rifles and canteen belts. They looked very different from the men who had left Maison Carrée, and there was a great deal of joking among them because of it.

The first section, comprised of two hundred men, moved out. Accompanying it were twelve soldiers leading nine mules loaded with provisions. Further provisions were carried by the porters: small boxes were tied to the ends of firm branches which men carried over their shoulders. Heavier boxes were attached by the middle of a branch and carried by two.

Next morning, the second section was prepared to start, when the *Kirangozis,* who were somewhat like foremen, announced that they had not as yet received their *djoho,* and were not moving a step until they did. *Djoho* was the piece of colorful cloth which had been agreed upon as the daily salary. The men could wear it as a cloak or a turban, and it was negotiable. The missionaries had decided among themselves to distribute the *djoho* periodically, rather than waste time on it every day, and so the bulk of the supply was still in Bagamoyo waiting to be brought over and transported with the third section. The *kirangozis* were adamant. There was nothing to do but send for the cloth, and it was two in the afternoon before it arrived, too late in the day for the second section to make

116

much progress. Father Livinhac said it would be better for both sections to leave together the next morning. The porters asked for permission to spend this last night with their families, which struck the priests as a reasonable request, but one of the *kirangozis* warned: "If you let them go, they'll come back late, drunk, or not at all."

"Well," said Father Livinhac, "evidently they want to go, and I doubt if we could stop them if we tried. It's better to let them go with permission than tempt them to be disobedient. There'll undoubtedly be discipline enough once we get moving."

The priests prepared their evening meal. They dug a hole, inserted chips of wood, and started the fire. On it they put a pot of water for rice. They placed a chicken on a stick over the escaping flames, and in the cinders they buried manioc roots. This was the way they would eat for months to come with none of the bread and wine Frenchmen love. But they didn't think of themselves as Frenchmen any longer. They would work and die in Africa; they were Africans. After the meal they sat around for a long time talking, confidently and confidentially. Missionaries for a week, they liked thinking they were old hands at it. Already they could recognize sounds in the night. They wanted to sleep under the open sky, as the Africans did, but they were told they were too new in the country, and until they got used to the sudden changes of night climate it would be wiser for them to sleep in their pup tens. Chagrined, they obeyed.

They were up at three in the morning and eager to go, but, as the *kirangozis* had warned, the porters were slow in returning. It was six before they could break camp, and nine before they were ready to leave. Last-minute mail arrived; the priests checked it quickly to see if any of it needed an immediate answer, decided none did, and the caravan began its long trek westward.

Three miles ahead, they encountered the first swamp. The rainy season just ended had covered it with a shallow lake of water, and it was impossible to tell where it suddenly plunged deep. Porters moved to the front and used long sticks to test the depth. Progress was slow. Often the caravan had to reverse to a new path. The laden mules had especially tough going. With each step they sank deep into the muck. The swamp was about two miles wide, and the caravan lost four hours crossing it. Out of it at last, they moved faster, and their spirits raised a bit. The countryside was beautiful.

High manioc grew along the road, and there were rice fields as far as they could see. In the distance lone mountains popped out of the ground so unexpectedly that they almost looked surprised. The sky was magnificently blue clear, except for the small puffs of bright white clouds that clustered low over hidden lakes. The afternoon was warm, but there was the typically African breeze: soft and constant against the face but too gentle even to move the leaves. People came from villages and roadside huts to see the caravan, making quick jokes that brought raucous laughs from the porters, staring in shy-eyed curiosity at the priests.

Suddenly the caravan stopped. Father Deniaud came from his post at the head of it. "There's a river," he said.

"A bad one?" Father Livinhac asked.

"Just a creek."

"Then what's holding us up?"

"The banks are steep," Deniaud said. "We're having trouble with our mules. You'd better bring yours up now so we can get them all across at the same time."

The creek was only three yards wide and three feet deep, but sheer banks of five feet dropped from the ground level to the water. The mules refused to make the jump. Stretched across the creek nearby were felled trees, put there seven years before by Henry Morton Stanley on his search for Dr. Livingstone, but they were too narrow for the mules. There was only one way to get them across. Their packs and saddles were removed, and ropes were tied around their necks; then men got behind and pushed them over the side. Men on the logs above led them across the water by the rope, then pulled them up the opposite bank. It was a rugged and noisy procedure. Tempers of man and beast flared. Coarse curses and brayed screams crashed through the quiet air, bringing people from their nearby homes, to watch and to wonder. The porters soon lost all patience and threw the mules into the river as if they were rubbish. One mule landed awkwardly and caught its head in the underwater growth. Seeing it, Father Simeon Lourdel jumped into the creek and freed the mule. They both reached the opposite shore muddy and smelly. Seconds later, Lourdel again plunged into the water on a similar rescue. He was coated with a putrid muck, and when the caravan was at last ready to move on, the other priests suggested that Lourdel bring up the rear.

That night, everyone was too weary for much talk. The missionaries went to their tents immediately after their meal. In the morning, Father Charmetant said good-by and returned to Bagamoyo to prepare for other White Fathers who were on their way from Algiers. The caravan proceeded, leaving the plains and dipping towards the jungle lowlands. The road was good, but the day was crushingly hot and no one felt like talking. They paused occasionally at small villages and they saw other caravans heading back to the coast. Some of these were slave caravans, with Africans chained to each other at the ankles and wrists, bound in pairs at the neck by forked yokes. Many children were among them, and young women. The priests' hearts ached from what they saw. They knew that, at this moment, they could not buy any of the slaves and give them freedom; Father Charmetant would be able to do that at the coast. But they went among the slaves and gave them water and food and tried to console them. Never had the priests seen such misery, and at night sitting around their fire they could think of nothing else.

"Will we ever have enough money to buy freedom for all of them?" Delauney wondered aloud.

Joseph Augier said. "I'm sure not. There are millions. But is buying them the way to do away with slavery? They would only be enslaved again, somehow, and the cycle would go on and on."

"Money could never do it," Livinhac said.

"How?" asked Ludovic Girault. "Bullets?"

"Not bullets either," Livinhac said. "Christianity. Africans aren't Christians—yet, and neither are the Arab slave traders. We are here to make as many of them Christians as we can, and maybe from that they will learn that they must not buy and sell each other."

Father Deniaud said: "It might be a good idea if we do some praying for the Europeans who are taking over this continent so that they remember that they're already supposed to be Christians."

All of them nodded, knowingly.

Early the next morning they were again on their way across the low, rolling plains. Crowds of birds filled the dark mango trees. At one point, a herd of great monkeys peered out at them through the heavy foliage, silent, sober, and unmoved. In the midafternoon, the caravan arrived at the Kingueni River and found piled up on the shore the advance section that had gone on ahead. The river was wide and swift.

"We'll need boats to get across," Brother Amans said. "The porters are making them now." Downstream the men were hewing dugouts from huge logs.

Lourdel glance at them. "How long will that take?" he asked.

"The rest of the day, at least. Maybe more."

"I'll have our men help," said Father Pascal. "We can spend tomorrow ferrying everything across, and after that I think we ought to stay closer together. We'll be running into a lot of these problems from now on and we'll need all the man power we can collect."

Night brought a sudden chill, and Father Pascal found himself shivering. Father Augier asked: "Are you all right?"

"Just the cold, I think," Pascal said.

Augier left him and went to hunt out the medical kit; it might be the cold, but here in Africa it could be anything else.

In the morning, Father Pascal still felt ill. He seemed unable to hold up his head, and his eyes would not focus, and he was a bit sick to his stomach. By midafternoon, Father Lourdel was complaining of the same discomforts. That was the start of it. For the next weeks, no day passed but one or two of the priests were debilitated, sometimes so weak that they could not hold themselves on their mules. For two days, Brother Amans had to be carried in a stretcher. Another time, Father Barbot was completely unable to travel; Father Livinhac stayed behind with him until he regained his strength. They called their disease "the fever," but they had no idea what it was or how they caught it. They observed that the porters did not get fever as much; the Africans smoked their water pipes a great deal, and the priests wondered it there might be something in the smoke that protected them. There was: the smoke drove off the mosquitoes. But no one knew mosquitoes were to blame. Water was often to blame, too, even when they just walked through it. Tiny bugs bit them and underwater growths tore at their legs and infections developed. Everyone suffered violent headaches, intense cold, delirium, and morbid visions at night. Their only treatment was a strong laxative and a heavy dose of quinine. This had a certain over-all effect, but at the same time it left them weaker than before. None of them wanted to be a problem to the others, and so they sometimes went two or three days before admitting how desperately ill they were, by now so ill that none of the medicines helped them. They needed rest, but no one could be convinced to take it.

The farther west they traveled, the more troublesome the porters became. There were desertions every day, fights among the men, and stealing. At Msuwa, the priests bought corn from a village to pay the porters, but the men refused it. They wanted their piece of cloth so that they could buy their own food, and they insisted on more than the half cubit of cloth of their original agreement. They wanted a full cubit. There was nothing the priests could do but pay them.

Each day brought new people who also had to be paid. Chiefs and village rulers demanded a fee for safe passage through the area. Most of the fees were outrageously exhorbitant, but again the priests had to pay without compromise. Within a month they gave away a large portion of the supplies they had brought along, and they were certain they wouldn't have enough left to reach their destination.

Often at night the caravan was attacked by robbers. The *askaris* hired from the Sultan of Zanzibar proved to be weak protection indeed. Instead of the soldiers they were supposed to be, they were little more than proud porters who refused to carry anything more than a rifle, demanding a double salary for it. They were poor shots, clumsy with their weapons. One *askari* blew off three of his fingers, while cleaning his rifle, and required medical treatment which the priests were not equipped to give. Robbers terrified the soldiers. A cry of warning anywhere along the caravan sent the *askaris* scurrying into the bush, far from where they were needed.

The priests realized their own helplessness. Traveling with them was an army they did not know how to control. So great was the waste of time, equipment, and men that only sheer momentum kept the caravan moving. Father Livinhac wrote Lavigerie that it would be wise for future caravans to bring along laymen who were trained in leadership, and since certain spiritual qualities would be required of such men, he suggested that Lavigerie try to get the services of formal Papal Zouaves, the corps of European noblemen who had volunteered to protect the Pope during attacks on the Vatican.

Correcting the disorders of the caravan was certainly the task for a general. Exhausted from disease among themselves and weary from constant bickering with porters and chiefs, the priests soon reached a point of lethargy when they cared about nothing except moving ahead. There were days when they scarcely moved at all. Thick jungles rose in front of them like solid walls, and hours were lost as porters tried to hack a pathway. Deep ravines full of acacia trees forced them to detour through mucky swamps or into mountains where huge granite and quartz boulders blocked every step. Most trying of all were the *tirikeza*—the forced marches across wide arid stretches where they would see no water for two or three days and each wasted step meant that someone else in the caravan would be a moment nearer death from thirst. The days were brutally hot, dry, and dusty; many nights were robbed of sleep by lions and leopards that prowled savagely just beyond the firelights and would not let men rest.

A month after leaving Bagamoyo, the missionaries reached Mpwapwa, where there was a large Protestant mission. It was a magnificent station, rich and well equipped; a million francs had gone into it—more than Lavigerie had to support all his missions for a year. The Protestants said they had heard from the people that a caravan was coming through, but they thought it was another Arab group heading west for more slaves. Seeing how sick and weary the priests were, the Protestants insisted that the caravan pause for a few days to give everyone time to rest. They warned that ahead was much trouble, from hostile tribes that had never seen a white man, from herds of wild animals, from the rugged terrain.

The White Fathers needed little persuasion to accept the invitation. Father Pascal was still very ill, and the others had reached the end of their resistance. Gratefully, they fell into clean beds for the first time in weeks. The warm soup brought to them seemed finer than anything they had ever tasted; the fresh bread was a feast in itself. In three days, they were like new men; even Father Pascal appeared wonderfully revived. This was the first contact between Catholics and Protestants in Central Africa, and its indications of future harmony greatly pleased both groups. Certainly, neither would send prospective converts rushing into the arms of the other, but that was to be expected from ministers of opposing convictions. History and national traits might put them at further odds, but they found they could respect each other as individuals and they discovered that their interdependence as white men facing the tribulations of Africa created a special sphere of co-operation. Everyone was satisfied with the visit.

Ready to move on, the White Fathers organized their caravan with their old zeal. Even news that many porters refused to go any farther could not dim their spirits. They started off. In a month, they had covered just two hundred miles; ahead to Tabora was more than twice that distance but they felt, despite the warnings at Mpwapwa that the worst was over. They had hardened and were ready for anything.

But Africa would not let herself be conquered quite that easily. A week on the road found the White Fathers confronting even greater problems than before. An epidemic of *bilharzia* broke out, derived from lake waters infected by poisonous snails and causing blindness. Afflicted porters were left in villages, with money to pay their way home when they could make the trip. One porter died from fever, and others began to say that the caravan had been cursed by devils. The *honga* passage fees demanded by chiefs at Debwe and Mbala almost entirely depleted the caravan's stocks, and it became necessary for everyone to eat whatever wild things grew along the way. Unused to the foods, the priests suffered extreme cramps and nausea. Fever again struck Father Pascal, and then he developed black water. He grew so weak that he could not ride his mule. He was put back on a stretcher and carried by Deniaud and Augier to assure smoother handling than from the impatient porters.

By mid-August, a month from Mpwapwa, the caravan had not even gone half the distance to Tabora. It was evident to everyone that Father Pascal could not last much longer. To ease his pains, the caravan moved slowly, on some days not at all. They were in the country of the Ugogo tribe, cruel savages who were frequently hired by Arabs to attack the villages of other tribes and capture slaves. Many of the Ugogo had become Moslems through the slave traders' influence, and though few of them had ever seen a white

123

man, they had learned from the Arabs that white men were hated enemies of Islam. Pagan urges still flourished beneath their Islamic veneer, and the Ugogo were as anxious for a human sacrifice as they seemed to be for the huge *honga* they demanded of the priests.

"We cannot pay all that," Livinhac told the tribe's chief. "We have very little left and we have still a long way to go."

"You will pay it," the chief threatened, "either in cloths or in lives." He took out his knife and stepped to Livinhac.

Pascal heard it all. Unnoticed by the others, he struggled to his feet and stumbled forward. Sweat poured down his discolored face, his bloodshot eyes were almost sightless, his body twitched in painful spasms. He forced himself through the circle where the others were talking and stepped between Livinhac and the chief.

"If you must kill," he muttered, "kill me."

Stunned, the chief stared at him. Pascal reached out, took the man's knife away, and let it fall to the ground. The chief turned and walked quickly into the bush. Pascal collapsed in Livinhac's arms.

"Put up a tent," Livinhac ordered crisply, and when it was ready, he carried Pascal into it. He remained alone with Pascal a long time, preparing him for death, then he sent for the others. "We will stay here until it is over," he said.

That night, sixty men of the Ugogo tribe attacked the caravan and carried off all they could carry. Two porters were killed in a brief gun battle, but there was no more fight left in anyone and the tribe was free to ransack as it pleased. At three-thirty the next afternoon, Father Pascal died.

"We must not let the porters know about this," Livinhac told the priests. "We have trouble enough. They already think we're cursed."

"What are we to do with the body?" asked Father Lourdel.

"Tonight," Livinhac said, "when the porters are sleep, three of you will take the body on ahead and bury it in the bush. Then return to the road and wait for the rest of us. We will get an early start so that you don't have to wait long."

"What about the tribe? Do you think they will let us out of here?" wondered Brother Amans.

"We will have to take that risk."

In the morning, the porters noticed immediately that Father Pascal was not there, and when they asked about him, they were told that he and the others had gone on ahead. But when they reached those who had left the camp the previous night and still did not see him, they began to suspect what had happened. They thought, however, that the body was still with the caravan. They wondered who was carrying it, and they became afraid. In twos and threes they put down their boxes and disappeared into the bush.

Suddenly out of the undergrowth stepped the Ugogo chief with some of his men. He called to Livinhac: "Where is the man who is sick?"

"He is not with us," Livinhac replied.

"Is he dead?"

"He is gone," Livinhac said evasively. "He is not with us any more."

"The porters say he is dead and you are carrying him with you," said the chief. "It is an evil thing to move the body of a dead man, and if you are doing this, you must be punished."

"I tell you he is not here," said Livinhac. "Look for yourself."

With a gesture, the chief ordered his men to inspect the caravan. They moved quickly through it, almost relieved that they did not find a body. The chief asked: "What have you done with him?"

"Nothing."

"Where is he, then?"

"Back there." Livinhac pointed down the road. "If you go that way, you will come upon him."

"Why have you left him? Is this a trick to get out of my country without paying the *honga*?"

"You should not expect a *honga* after what you have already stolen from us."

"I stole nothing," the chief said. He moved closer. "Now, if you want to pass, you will pay me two hundred cubits of the smooth cloth."

"I don't have that much," said Livinhac.

"Then give me what you have."

"If I do that, I will have nothing for the chiefs of the countries in the north."

"I don't care about other chiefs," the man said.

Dromaux stepped to Livinhac. "Father, don't argue with him.

125

Give him what he wants so we can get out of here. There aren't enough porters to carry what we have left, as it is."

"I know that," Livinhac said, "but if I give in to him too easily, he will be all the more difficult with the caravans that come after us."

"Well," said Dromaux, "let's pray that they too don't have a body to hide."

Their eyes met. Livinhac said: "All right."

He gave the chief what satin he had, perhaps a hundred and fifty cubits, and the caravan moved on. They had about a hundred porters with them. A week later there were sixty left, and a few days later there were twenty. Then one morning the missionaries stepped from their tents and discovered that they were completely alone.

XII

THEY were not sure where they were. They were on a road, but Africa even then was a network of paths traveled by slave merchants, traders, explorers and expeditions. The race for the continent was on; men with all kinds of incentives rushed to Africa. Expeditions organized as a result of the Brussels conference reached Equatorial Africa two months after the White Fathers, and of the eighteen men who came to set up the political-scientific stations only five were alive three months later. The three stations they established soon withered when the European countries involved cooled to the idea of unified efforts and began their individual pursuits. England and Germany were the busiest, entering the territory from various points along the East Coast. England, with a state religion of her own, realized the social influences of missions and backed those of the Church of England to a considerable extent, often putting up her religious and political-scientific emmissaries on the same plot of ground. Deducing wrongly that so-called Catholic countries intended to follow the same procedures, a representative of the Church of England went to Lavigerie soon after the departure of the first White Fathers' caravan and suggested the establishment of separate zones of influence so as to avoid religious competition. The sug-

127

gestion completely disregarded both the basic theological differences between the two denominations and the fact that reputedly Catholic European countries were not co-operating with the Church because of their lack of control over it. Lavigerie rejected the suggestion, an attitude which Protestant leaders could not understand. On the other hand, he had already instructed his priests not to set up their own missions close to Protestants in order to preclude complaints of competition, but he also told them to feel free to spread Catholic doctrine wherever they could. "If," he said, "you have anything worthwhile to offer the people, they will come to you wherever you are." He told them, too, to be friendly toward the Protestants, to assist them in any material way possible, and to respect them for their efforts. The Catholic Church would find its roots in Central Africa in the hearts of the people, he said, not in making conversions some sort of competitive sport.

At the moment, the White Fathers were having trouble enough just trying to stay alive. On the morning they discovered themselves abandoned in the middle of Tanganyika, only three of them were well enough to walk. They had two mules left out of the dozen they had started with, the rest having died or been stolen by the deserting porters, and they had perhaps fifty boxes of supplies. They were completely out of medicine, and there was no way to treat those who were ill. All they knew about their location was that Tabora, their destination, was somewhere to the north. How far, they had no idea.

"We cannot just stay here, yet we cannot all move on," said Father Livinhac. "I think those of us who are well enough should try to reach Tabora. The governor there is the brother of the Sultan of Zanzibar; maybe we can get some help from him."

Under the circumstances, there was nothing else to do. Deniaud and Barbot were able to travel with Livinhac. They packed what they needed on the two mules and started off. Those who remained behind moved the supplies off the road, set up a camp, and waited. For ten days, the three travelers worked their way northward, praying against further encounters with troublesome tribes, like those of Ugogo. With the inexplicable speed typical of Africa, news of them raced ahead. Their arrivals at villages along the route seemed less and less a surprise; the *honga* gradually diminished. Certainly

128

they met no overwhelmingly friendly tribes, but neither did they find any of the hostility that had plagued them for over three months. As they drew nearer Tabora, they became increasingly aware of the Moslem influence spread by Mohammedan merchants and the government in the city. In every village was a mosque made of clay, surrounded by walls of clay, even with clay minarets pointing ten, fifteen feet into the air. They saw veiled women, men in robes and turbans, nude boys who were circumcised. Often they came upon dozens of men at a mosque, squatting in neat lines at their prayers, bowing toward Mecca to the east. This much they could admire about Moslems: they prayed. Other factors the priests considered to be implicit in religion—health, education, the welfare of the people, and the dignity of womanhood—were missing. These things, plus the recognition of Christ as God and savior, the priests hoped to provide.

On September 12, six months after leaving Algiers, the first White Fathers entered Tabora. They were expected. Governor Abdullah ben Massib told them other caravans had brought word of them, messages had come through the people themselves, and his brother, the ruler of Zanzibar, had advised him by letter that credit arrangements had been made. He fed the three priests and gave them a house in which to stay. He sent some of his men southward to pick up the White Fathers who had remained behind, and by the end of the month the missionaries were together again.

It did not take them long, however, to learn that ben Massib's hospitality sprang from purely commercial interests. He knew that the White Fathers would have to restock their caravan completely and he expected to sell them what they needed. Somewhere in the area was Philippe Brayon, a Swiss traveling merchant who maintained warehouses in Tanganyika. The priests had hoped to do business with him. They became more hopeful of this when they discovered that the Governor was ready to charge them seventy francs for a cubit of satin for *honga* purposes which Brayon was selling for eight. There was a rumor that Brayon was with the powerful chief Mirambo, a hundred miles to the northwest, and the priests decided to look for him.

The Governor said: "I would warn against that. Mirambo is a savage. The farther away from him you stay, the better off you will be. I know why you want to go there, and just to prove my concern for you I have decided to lower my price to fifty-two francs per cubit of satin."

The concern was still unattractive. Livinhac named Lourdel and Deniaud to search for Brayon in the Urambo country, but they were back in two weeks with the sad news that Brayon was not in the area and that Mirambo was off at war. Thus the only source of men and supplies was the Governor. Reluctantly, the priests made arrangements to equip the caravan. They were ready to leave by early November, but the rains began and held them up for a month and so they spent the waiting time refreshing in their minds the instructions Lavigerie had given them.

Among the Equatorial Africans they would not face the same problems that had confronted the White Fathers in the north. The local religion was mostly paganism; Islam was entrenched along the principal roadways, and Protestants who had followed Livingstone had set up a few scattered missions. The caution required in North Africa was not necessary here. The same widespread, deep hatred did not exist. Of course, one must be prudent. Religious and political control were in the hands of witch doctors and sorcerers who were shrewd enough always to act favorably toward chiefs. These men were not fools; they would struggle to defend positions they knew they would lose should a tribe become Christian. The missionaries should therefore, Lavigerie said, first win the admiration of the chiefs by acts of charity and hope to derive from this the privilege of teaching religion to the people. Most advisable, naturally, was the conversion of the chief, and even if this could not be done for a while the chief should nevertheless be consulted on all matters pertaining to plans for mission expansion.

From the outset, the priests were to buy what slaves they could from the Arab traders. Most such slaves, particularly children, would probably come from tribes in other regions, and if after being purchased they were set off on their own they would only be enslaved again soon afterwards. Lavigerie advised orphanages for the children and huts on the mission grounds for older purchased slaves. He suggested, too, that early postulants for baptism should live on mission property in order to benefit from mutual moral support and to get accustomed to living in a Christian community. Such postulants, he instructed, were to undergo a four-year preparation for baptism, during which they were to be taught to read and write as well as receive religious training. "Do not let the neophytes' falls discourage you," Lavigerie told the missionaries. "They will fall often. You have read St. Paul's reproachments against drinking, incest, and perversion, and remember that he was talking to people who were already Christians. Your people will have a great struggle to overcome the vices in which they have lived for generations. Therefore, do not be astonished by the immoralities you see even among those who announce their desires to become Christians. In time they will learn to live as they should."

Polygamy would be the greatest problem; polygamists could not be baptised. Nevertheless, Lavigerie said, polygamists should not be refused religious instructions. There were, after all, four years of training to go through, and during that time marital difficulties could be straightened out.

There could be another problem, but whether or not it arose depended on the priests themselves. In sensitizing the consciences of the new Christians, there was the risk of putting such emphasis on the eternal punishments of evil that the people could become overly scrupulous and then a form of Jansenism might sprout. Certainly the awesomeness of God's judgments should be clearly defined, Lavigerie said, but so should God's mercies. He said: "Go over again and again the themes of confession, penance, and absolution until the people realize they are to receive Communion not only when they consider themselves worthy but also to make themselves even more receptive to the graces of the sacrament. The remission of sins is one of the great strengths of the Church, and if by being too severe with your people who go astray you thereby frighten them away from the sacraments, you will be committing a grave error that will threaten everything you are trying to achieve."

As soon as possible, the priests were to start schools and everything should be done to encourage children to attend, especially boys. Then, by prayer, example and gentle guidance, the apparently more spiritual boys should be led to consider the priesthood as a vocation. Those who responded were to receive the full seminary training which aspirants for the priesthood anywhere in the world underwent. In Africa, at first, it would take longer, perhaps twenty years in all, but that made no difference. True, the majority would fall out, but, for that matter, the vast majority of seminarians anywhere did not reach their goal, for any number of reasons. Inevitably, however, some of the Africans would succeed, and others would follow them. In time, there would be enough to choose a bishop from among them, and then everything the White Fathers had meanwhile accomplished—schools, churches, hospitals, orphanages, farms, everything—could be turned over to the new bishop to administer as bishops did throughout the world. Thus the Church in Africa would be established, an integral part of the Church Universal, and it would live as long as the world would live, no matter what lay ahead for Africa itself.

It was a tall order. On other continents it had taken centuries to achieve. In Africa, her shores already strongly influenced by European industry and politics and her interior seriously riddled with Islam, there was not time. The White Fathers waiting at Tabora were ready to begin the vital program. Only the heavy rains held them up. It was December, 1878, before they were able to proceed to their destinations. At last, on December 2, Fathers Livinhac, Girault, Lourdel, Barbot, and Brother Amans headed north toward Uganda. Fathers Deniaud, Delauney, Dromaux, and Augier went west to the shores of Lake Tanganyika. Ahead of them all was terror and death.

XIII

BECAUSE of the death of Father Pascal, who was to be superior of the westbound caravan, leadership of it was given to young Father Toussaint Deniaud. Governor Abdullah ben Massib strongly objected to the caravan. He warned that Marimbo, the powerful chief whose country lay northwest of Tabora, was about to attack the town. The trip would be too dangerous, he said, and he added that he would like to have the rifles belonging to the caravan. Deniaud refused the request. In turn, the Governor refused to help Deniaud obtain porters for the journey. On his own, the priest managed to hire one hundred and thirty men, but within a week twenty of them deserted. Torrential rains deluged the caravan for several days, ruining food and equipment.

The vast swamps created by the rains quickly became disease-ridden, and from trekking through them Father Dromaux developed the *bilharzia* eye infection which almost blinded him. The disease spread among the porters, holding back the caravan even more and, from the misery of it, creating more dissension. Where there were not deep, mucky swamps to struggle across, there were impenetrable forests of eucalyptus-type trees that grew as close as weeds. Hacking through them proved as slow and frustrating as chiseling granite

133

with a pin. The sultan at the village of Uvinza was stubbornly irksome. He made the caravan wait three days before he showed up to discuss the *honga*, and the price he demanded was little short of robbery. He thwarted Deniaud's attempts at compromise by declaring unmovably that unless he got what he wanted, the caravan would not be permitted to pass. At last, Deniaud was forced to pay. On January 5, the caravan entered the wide plains of the Malagarasi River and walked unavoidably into absolute clouds of mosquitoes. It was impossible to rest, either to eat or to sleep, and even when a man tried to walk rapidly, he was devoured by a living shroud of the maddening insects. Persistent rains turned the plains into a lake, and with the spreading swamps came more *bilharzia*. Father Joseph Augier was so seriously blinded that he could not take a step without being led by the hand. Food rotted; it was impossible to fish or hunt. The hungry porters got disgusted and quit, more of them departing every day. People along the route were far from friendly. They had heard that Mirambo was attacking villages to the north, and they were very afraid. To them, any stranger was a potential enemy, and so they gave the caravan no food and no help at all. Because of such tribulations, the White Fathers were overwhelmed when, arriving finally at Ujiji, on January 24, they were received with gushy warmth by Hussan, the Arab administrator of the town.

He could not do enough for them. He put them up in the house where Stanley had stayed years before and assured them there would be no rent. Their travel pressures over, the exhausted priests collapsed. Overnight, all of them came down with fever, and for the next month they were even too weak to stand at an altar and say Mass. Hussan was at the house every day, bringing food and medicine. From things he said, the priests deduced that there was some friction between the Arabs and the Protestant mission station a few miles out of town. The priests realized Hussan might be trying to win them to his side and they decided to have no part whatsoever in the controversy. The missionary at the Protestant station had died of fever a few weeks before the White Fathers arrived, and living at the mission alone was E. C. Hore, a British mariner who had been sent by the government to chart Lake Tanganyika. The common British error of combining both missionary and governmental interest had apparently been made; Arabs and Africans resentful of the government probings quite naturally aimed some of their bitterness at the missionary endeavor. Understandably lonely, Hore called on the White Fathers, and they became friends. From Hore, the priests learned a great deal about the country. To the south, he told them, Portuguese and Arabs were at war to gain control of the area, and this explained why no caravans from that direction were getting through. No mail or supplies had arrived at Ujiji from the south for many weeks. At the north end of the lake, Hore said, was a land called Urundi, and there were many people there. Because they were sporadically hostile, no missionaries had settled among them, but in the lake area between Urundi and Ujiji there were several quite friendly tribes, and, Hore said, if one worked his way north slowly and cautiously, there was every likelihood that he could make enough good contacts to help him progress safely and enter Urundi without arousing too much animosity among the people. The idea appealed to the White Fathers. Their original plan was to settle for a while at Ujiji, then spread out, breaking ground for those who would follow after them and build the actual missions. They decided to give serious thought to a northward trip as soon as they had finished their annual retreat.

On the first day of the retreat, Hussan came to the house, in a mood so ingratiating that Father Deniaud sensed it was going to cost him something.

"The house," Hussan began. "It's a very nice house, isn't it? Is everything all right with it? Are you satisfied with all I've done for you?"

"Yes," replied Deniaud. "We're very satisfied."

"I'm so glad. It's cost me a lot, you know. I mean, I'm not sure I'd do so much for anybody else."

"How much *honga* do you want?" Deniaud asked bluntly.

"Well, not *honga* exactly," said Hussan. "I wouldn't call it that. *Honga* sounds so tribal, and after all I have to pay it myself, you know, when my own caravans come through. But the point is there haven't been any caravans lately, as you well know, and I'm having trouble staying in business myself."

"I realize that," the priest said. "How much?"

"Well," said Hussan, "you've been here almost two months, and in view of all I've done to the house, I think fifty cubits of cloth would be fair."

"That's a lot," said Deniaud.

"Not really. I know you've got it, and much more. And," Hussan was suddenly helpless, "you know I need it. I'll have to get it from someone, and I wouldn't want to ask you to move so that I could rent this house to somebody else."

"All right."

"And after that," Hussan hurried on, "I figure fifteen cubits a month for the rent."

"But you said we wouldn't have to pay any rent," Deniaud reminded him.

"That was so long ago; I didn't know then that my caravans wouldn't be getting through."

Father Deniaud sighed. "All right. We'll discuss it later. I'm not supposed to be talking to anyone today, anyway."

"Oh, really? Why? What's wrong?"

"Nothing is wrong," said the priest. "We're all on retreat now, that's all."

"What's retreat?"

"Once a year," Deniaud explained, "all White Fathers enter an eight-day period of silence during which we pray and meditate."

"Oh, that's fine," Hussan said heartily. "Prayer is good. Then I won't bother you any more during the next week."

"Thank you."

"Tell me, how many times a day do you pray?"

"Seven."

"That's excellent," said Hussan. "I pray five times. Where are your prayers?"

"In this book," Deniaud said, holding up his breviary. "I pray seven times each day in this book, and I also recite other prayers I know by heart."

"To whom do you pray?"

"Allah."

"Good. And how do you pray?"

The priest knelt, made the sign of the cross upon himself, put his palms together, lowered his head, and closed his eyes.

136

"That's very interesting," Hussan said admiringly. "What other books do you have?"

"The Gospels," said Deniaud, "and several other books—psalms, Moses, Daniel, Solomon."

"Really?" Hussan was happily surprised. "I have the entire Bible. I was wondering: would you eat a goat that had been killed without having its throat cut?"

"Yes, if it wasn't diseased."

"Oh, I would never do that," Hussan said. "You really couldn't say that such a goat was pure."

"It's all in the way you look at it," said the priest.

"I suppose so." Then: "In France, do people buy slaves?"

"No."

"Why?"

"Because," Deniaud said, "in France all men are born free and they work for what they want or what they want to be."

"I don't think I'd like that at all," Hussan said, then, waving, he turned and walked away. Watching him, Deniaud wondered how many others there were in Africa and how many more to come who, like Hussan, shuddered at the idea of free Africans, and he wondered, too, what the cost of such an attitude would eventually be.

February ended; March and April passed. It was mid-May before the priests could make their first journey northward. Deniaud and Dromaux hired two large pirogues, filled them with supplies, and, with crews, started up Lake Tanganyika. They were amazed by the beauty they saw. Magnificent mountains rose steeply from the beaches. Waterfalls burst out of mountain sides, dropped perhaps a hundred feet, then disappeared behind tree tops—sudden silver strips midair in a rush of green. Neat villages nestled in foothills, a single pillar of purple smoke rising—strangely too real, like a toy display. Further north, the mountains moved inland, making room for banana forests and plateaus of lean palms. Broad rivers swept into the lake, stretching bright fingers of icy clear mountain water into the heaviness of the jungle sea. The lake was full of hippos and crocodile, the crocs scurrying away from the paddlings of the oarsmen, the hippos on the beaches, lifting high their huge heads and looking like fat and curious old women. At times, crowds came to the shores when the priests landed for the night. They were the

137

first white men most of the people had seen, and some of them were afraid. To others, the sight was a big laugh. Cautiously they approached, nervous grins on their faces, until they were close enough to touch the priests; then, their fears gone, they examined them as if they were for sale, caressing their smooth, soft hair, pointing excitedly at their blue eyes, studying their skin with intense interest to determine why it was white, frisking them with the unembarrassed intention of finding out whether these strange, bearded, long-robed creatures, apparently human beings, were either men or women. All the people, even the most suspicious, proved to be friendly. Using the crew as translators, they asked the priests many questions, bringing them gifts of fruit and meat and trinkets before they left in the morning.

Deniaud and Dromaux continued up the lake to Magala, forty miles from the northern tip. By the time they started back for Ujiji, they were convinced that they would have no serious troubles in establishing a mission in Urundi. Their first nights home, they enchanted Delauney and Augier with reports of their experiences. They had been gone only a month, yet so fervent was their enthusiasm for the north that it took them almost that long to relate all they had seen and learned. Hore came to listen, backing up their stories with observations of his own. The White Fathers decided they must move to Urundi as soon as possible. Deniaud realized he should send news of his decision to the other sector of the original caravan, now on its way to Uganda, and to Lavigerie so that, as he had demanded, he would be kept informed of all movements and experiences. However, the letters which Deniaud had written during the months at Ujiji had all been returned. Because of the spreading wars to the south and east, caravans could not get through. He felt, nevertheless, that it was important to keep moving, as Lavigerie had instructed, and Hore agreed to send through the letters as soon as the way was clear. Meantime, he was sure that the other White Fathers were on their way, and that they had picked up news of the first group which they could send back to Algiers.

This was exactly what was happening. The second caravan of eight priests, two brothers, and five laymen was already on its way from Marseilles, and the third caravan of six priests and eight laymen was forming in Algiers. The laymen were former Papal Zouaves from France, Belgium, Holland, and Great Britain who, trained in leadership, had volunteered to accompany the caravans to maintain order among the porters and to protect the missionaries from tribal attacks until they had settled at their stations long enough to assure their peaceful intentions to the people. The need for such men had been expressed by Livinhac in one of his first reports to Lavigerie, who had recruited them easily among young European Catholics who, without desiring to enter the religious life, wanted to find some way to serve the Church. For a while, Lavigerie thought of establishing in Central Africa a kingdom for Catholics, ruled by a Catholic monarch who governed on Christian principles, defended by a Catholic army. He hoped to use the Zouaves to train that army. Thus Catholics could live as a unit without fears of persecution. His plans were well along until the Berlin conference, which chopped Africa up into political zones of influence, and so he abandoned it. The Zouaves nevertheless accompanied the caravans; several of them subsequently joined the society as lay brothers, and they, with others who had gone to North Africa to help Lavigerie's agriculture program among Arabs, formed the nucleus which since has grown into the five-hundred-man team, skilled in all crafts, men who, in Africa and throughout the world, assist the priests by performing the vitally important manual chores.

Confident of reinforcements, Father Deniaud made plans to move his group northward by stages to Urundi. Hore suggested that since the Protestant mission was on an excellent cove, the priests ought to embark from there. Deniaud agreed. On July 10, he told Hussan that he could have his house back.

"Why?" Hussan demanded. "Haven't I been good to you? Haven't I been a friend? What's wrong? Is the rent too high? Just what do you want?"

"You have been a good friend," Deniaud consoled him. "And there is nothing wrong. We simply want to move on."

"But why move on?" the Arab persisted. "This certainly is the nicest spot you're going to find on the lake."

"I'm sure," said Deniaud, "but we aren't concerned about nice places."

"I suppose," Hussan tested, "that you've written the Sultan of Zanzibar all sorts of complaints about me."

"I haven't written the Sultan at all," assured the priest. "And even if I did, I'd have no complaints."

"All right, then," said Hussan, "but I still can't understand why you want to leave. What's up north that you're after?"

"Souls."

"Haven't the people here got souls?"

"Yes," said Deniaud, "and there'll be more White Fathers along soon to take care of them."

"More priests coming?" Hussan said, relieved. "Oh, then everything's fine. Well, have a good trip. And if you need anything, let me know. I'll take good care of you."

Hussan took good care of the priests a few days later when he sold them some boats: the bottoms fell through the first time the priests stepped into them.

Arguments for new boats or at least the repair of the old ones got nowhere; Hussan insisted they were in good shape when he sold them and that he was not responsible to what happened to them afterwards. Repairing the boats themselves, hiring porters and a crew, and buying supplies took two weeks, and it was July 23 before the priests said good-by to Hore and began their lake trip north. A few days later they landed at Kigoma, in the kingdom of the Bikari, some sixty miles south of the Urundi border. They were warmly welcomed and the people seemed friendly enough, but it soon became apparent that Islam was so solidly entrenched that it would be futile to spend too much time there. The priests continued toward Urundi. It was late August when they reached Rumonge, some seventy-five miles south of the present city of Usumbura. Two tribes lived in the area: the Wabikari along the lake shores and a branch of the Bahima up in the hills. The White Fathers settled first among the Wabikari, and though the tribe was known to be hostile, there was no trouble. They acquired land from the chief and began to farm it; they opened a clinic, and every morning scores of people came to be treated; they bought young slaves from passing caravans and raised them. Things were going quite well.

Word came that new White Fathers' caravans were arriving in the south. Father Deniaud received instructions to return to Ujiji

nd meet one of them. The caravan was to be divided: a priest, a
brother, and a Zouave would go to Urundi, and the remainder would
cross the lake and set up a mission on the western shores at Mas-
anze, in what is now the Belgian Congo. Deniaud almost missed
the caravan: it had made a wrong turn and reached Lake Tanganyika far south of Ujiji. Learning this, Deniaud rushed south after
it. He learned that the priest who had been assigned to him had
just died of fever. Two other priests and a Zouave had also died of
the same disease during the journey, and a brother had been stabbed
to death by a highwayman. The caravan was in low spirits, but
Deniaud's enthusiasm for conversion prospects among the pagans
did much to lift them. He stayed with the caravan until it had acquired boats for the lake crossing, then, with Brother Jerome and
Zouave Leopold d'Hoop, he returned to Urundi.

The mission at Rumonge continued to thrive, but when, the following spring, the torrential rains struck the mission suffered greatly.
Situated in the lowlands, it was directly in the path of the floods
sweeping down from the mountains. The entire farm was washed
away and buildings crumbled. To rebuild on the same spot would
have been a waste of time. Also, the priests had discerned during
their safaris into the hills a more encouraging eagerness among the
Bahima to become Christians than had been demonstrated by the
Wabikari. With this and the need for a better location in mind,
Father Deniaud asked the Bahima chief if it would be possible for
the priests to build their new mission in his area. The chief full-
heartedly approved, and the White Fathers made the move. The
move greatly annoyed the Wabikari, but only because they disliked
losing the services of the clinic.

"Don't worry," Deniaud assured them. "One of the fathers will
come to you a couple of days a week to take care of your sick, and
one week a month a priest will live here to help you in any way he
can. After all, we will only be a few miles away, and you can always
send for us in case of an emergency."

But the Wabikari were not satisfied. If anything, they considered
the priests' departure an insult, and though the missionaries continued to visit the tribe, they sensed a resentment which instead of
dimming grew with time. The new mission flourished. Passing
months brought more and more of the Bahima into the catechu-

menate, the crops produced amazing harvests, and the ransomed slaves were happy, grateful, and co-operative.

On a May night, 1881, a band of Wabikari stole into the mission and kidnapped a small boy. By morning, everyone knew what had happened. The White Fathers sent word to the Wabikari that they wanted the boy back, but the tribe refused. The priests learned that an Arab slave caravan was approaching from the north and they feared the Wabikari would sell the boy.

"If they get away with this," the Zouave d'Hoop warned the priests, "they won't hesitate to take more children when the next caravan comes through."

"How can we stop them?" Father Augier asked.

"By fighting."

Deniaud said: "I don't want any fighting. Besides, what would we fight with? These Bahima aren't fighters, and anyway they're too afraid of the Wabikari even to try."

"Then let's at least threaten a fight," d'Hoop said. "Maybe we can scare them into giving the boy back."

"If you think it'll do any good," Deniaud conceded.

Next morning, carefully worded rumors began to move down the hill to the Wabikari on the beach: unless the boy was returned the Bahima would attack.

The trick backfired. On the afternoon of May 4, the entire Wabikari went up the hill, penetrated the Bahima territory, and marched to the mission. They formed a large semicircle some thirty yards from the priests' house, pushed the boy into the middle of it, and called to the missionaries to come and get him if they wanted him. Deniaud, Augier, and D'Hoop stepped from the house. They thought the Wabikari wanted to talk and they took a few paces toward them.

Dozens of lances arched through the air at the three men. Augier fell first—one lance through his chest, another through his left shoulder. A lance split d'Hoop's face open, and he dropped next to Augier. Eight lances ripped into Deniaud's body. He stumbled forward to give absolution to Augier and d'Hoop, then collapsed on top of them.

Father Dromaux and Brother Jerome heard the shouts and screams and ran from the house. The sight of them startled the Wabikari. Shouting war cries, the Africans turned and fled. Dromaux rushed to the fallen men. Deniaud was already dead; the other two died within minutes.

That night, after the three men had been buried, the chief of the Bahima went to the mission and told Dromaux: "I must ask you to leave. The Wabikari will not stop now until you are all dead, and then they will start on us if we do anything to protect you."

Dromaux said: "If my brothers were willing to die here, then I must be willing to die, too."

The chief shook his head sadly. "If you will not think of yourself, Father, then think of us. We will suffer, too, you know."

Dromaux was aware of this. He turned to Brother Jerome and asked him what he wanted to do. "We'd better go," Jerome said. "If we stay here, we will only be the cause of trouble for the people. Let's go, Father, but someday let us come back."

Late that night, several Bahima led Dromaux and Jerome down backpaths to the lake and took them across to the White Fathers' mission at Massanze. Two nights later, the boats went back to Rumonge to pick up the ransomed children, and the White Fathers were not able to return to their mission for almost fifty years.

Father Dromaux wrote Lavigerie about the massacre and the letter reached Algiers months later. It could not have arrived at a more desolate hour. Since the murder of the first three White Fathers who had started for Timbuktu in 1872, Lavigerie had ordered his men to abandon such plans until passage across the Sahara was made safer. The French government's fury over what it considered the imprudence of the original caravan gradually subsided, and the North Africa missions which had been closed were, after a few years, reopened. Despite Lavigerie's orders for the priests to stay put, those at missions along the Sahara fringe were understandably restless. Their work among the Arabs was progessing admirably. More and more White Fathers were becoming available, with most of them going off to Central Africa. Even so, there was an increasing number arriving at outposts in the north, and the more experienced men were anxious to get moving across the desert. They wrote Lavigerie repeatedly for permission to try, but he always refused. Father Louis Richard, now stationed at Ghadames, wrote Lavigerie: "Our work is going so well here that we do not have enough to keep us busy. May I investigate the possibility of organizing a new caravan to Timbuktu?"

Lavigerie approved the investigation, but that was all. Richard read more into the approval than Lavigerie intended. Overzealous as he was, it was easy for him to convince himself after a cursory study that he could reach his destination if, instead of making one long dash for it, he advanced in short hops, staying at principal oases as long as necessary to learn what might be waiting ahead. On December 18, Richard, accompanied by Fathers Gaspard Morat and Alexis Pouplard and five guides, left Ghadames for Ghat, four hundred and fifty miles away. Three days out of Ghadames, the priests were attacked by their guides and killed.

Again the government stepped in, and again all missions south of Algiers were closed. Priests who seemed to take too long leaving their outposts were literally carted away by French troops. Infuriated officials at Algiers and Paris wrote Lavigerie letters of blunt condemnation, blaming him for all that had happened, assuring him that never again would the White Fathers be permitted to go among the Arabs as long as the French government had anything to say about it.

Crushed by the deaths at Ghadames, then completely shattered by the news from Urundi, Lavigerie accepted the accusations without defense. Though he had warned his men that they might have martyrdom in their futures, the massacres and the many deaths caused by disease were far more than he dared imagine. He rushed word to the Central Africa caravans: "Stop everything. If your lives are in the slightest danger where you are, leave immediately. Do nothing until I decide what is to become of you."

XIV

LAVIGERIE's orders for immediate retreat reached the northbound sector of the first Equatorial caravan at an hour when it was already in flight. In just a few months in Uganda, the priests who had gone north witnessed the vilest intrigue and the most vicious cruelty. Their lives and the lives of many new Christians were gravely in danger. Hundreds had already died, and for the priests to remain in Uganda any longer would have been an invitation to incredible bloodshed. At the root of the terror was madness, a madness born in paganism and nurtured in the worst depravity. And there was fear of all kinds —fear of European powers steadily penetrating the interior, fear of Christianity's threat to sorcerers, to Islam, to tribal kings, fear of Catholicity's appeal over Protestantism. Sadly indeed, much of the horror could have been avoided had everyone exerted caution, wisdom, and prudence, but in the panic for power there was only greed, jealousy, deception, and the most shocking evil. The White Fathers found themselves drawn into all of it, victims of the vortex that stirred Uganda to a fury which left an indelible mark on the country. Involvement was something the priests could not foresee and could not escape.

It had all started out optimistically enough. The journey north to

Lake Victoria was made with ease and almost comfort. Once beyond the soggy plains of Tabora, the ground was high and clear. Winds from the huge lake swept across the wide fields, soft enough to be refreshing, strong enough to discourage flies and mosquitoes. The soil was fertile; the many villages were surrounded by rich farms. Caravans had frequently passed through—slave traders, merchants, German and British expeditions, Protestant missionaries. The people were open and friendly.

Among those who had passed through before was Alexander M. Mackay, whose name came to rank among Protestant missionaries with Livingstone and Albert Schweitzer. In the years he spent in Africa, he earned an outstanding reputation as an ardent and diligent worker for his church. In the Lake Victoria area, he expanded on Livingstone's initial foundations, solidifying the Protestant influence among the people. To many, Mackay has remained unequaled among Protestant missionaries to Central Africa. A Scotsman, he was the son of a Free Church of Scotland minister, and he had gone to Africa as a delegate of the Church Missionary Society, a British organization. Raised among severe Calvanists, Mackay was austerely religious. Most of his education, including his religious training, he had received in private tutoring from his father. He was in his mid-teens before he entered a school, but he had been well prepared and was an outstanding student. He took a degree in engineering at Edinburgh and then went to work in Germany. Always in the back of his mind was the desire to become a missionary. He had hopes of working in Madagascar and had even learned the language long before there was any chance of his going there. He applied to several missionary organizations for backing, but all of them refused because he was not an ordained clergyman. Finally the Church Missionary Society accepted him, more because he was a qualified engineer than because he was a qualified missionary. The Society had broad plans for Equatorial Africa and, wisely, wanted roads built and warehouses constructed to ease the journey of its caravans. Also, because of the great lakes in Central Africa, the Society wanted to get a sizable boat into the interior in order to provide freer movement for its missionaries. Getting the boat to the lakes in pieces required engineering skill: Mackay was certainly the man for the job. He had an agreement with the Society that after he got the boat

146

to Lake Victoria, he would be free to pursue his own missionary ambitions.

For a man who intended to spread Christian love among the Africans, Mackay suffered one serious fault: he had a deep and violent hatred for anything that was Roman Catholic. It was evident throughout his life. When he was in Germany, he wrote his sister that none of the young men with whom he studied and worked was in the least religious—with a single exception. "And he," Mackay wrote his sister in despair, "is a Roman Catholic." On his way to Africa, Mackay stopped at Malta, where to fill time he went to examine the architecture of St. John's Catholic Church. His opinions of the building were lost in his vitriolic reaction to a priest he thought had eavesdropped on his conversation with the sacristan. The outburst Mackay recorded in his diary that day was startling to come from the pen of a man who declared himself representative of Christian fraternity. As if addressing the priest, Mackay blasted the man with "Thou disguised Jesuit!" He blamed the priest because the sacristan could not read Latin and for all that might have been wrong with Italy, Spain, Ireland, and Malta. He noted in his diary:

We go to plant Churches of the living God in Central Africa; but we go sowing the good seed, knowing only too well that thy hand will soon come and sow tares among the wheat. The good meal will soon be leavened by thy stealthy hand, till the whole be one vile mass corrupted by thy Mary worship and thy Mass worship!

That an intelligent man who claimed to be religious should know so little about religion was both pathetic and dangerous. The attitude was important to the White Fathers because of the conflict that grew out of it, but they had no idea of Mackay's feelings as they approached Uganda, and they were not ready for him. Though Mackay had arrived on the East African coast months before the White Fathers, his road-building kept him moving back and forth from Bagamoyo to Mpwapwa. He was on the coast when he was stricken with fever, and there was no one to treat him except the White Fathers who had arrived to prepare for their first caravan then on its way from Algiers. By the time the caravan was ready to move inland, Mackay had already gone ahead with his dismantled boat. The boat proved to be a failure. Rain and the sun had warped

147

its planks; it leaked dangerously. Mackay's talents and hard work were unable to save the ship and he abandoned it, crossing to Uganda by canoe. Fifty-five days after leaving Tabora, the White Fathers arrived at the southern shores of Lake Victoria. They learned from the people that Mackay was already in Uganda. All they knew about him was that he was an English Protestant missionary, that the White Fathers had cured him at Bagamoyo, and that he seemed a pleasant enough chap. They looked forward to meeting him as a friend who would welcome them to a strange land.

The king of Uganda was a man named Mutesa. The thirtieth monarch of the country, he had been on the throne twenty-two years when the White Fathers arrived. He was a tall man, magnificently built, handsome, proud, powerful. Only Mirambo in Tanganyika came anywhere near Mutesa in authority or terror, but Mirambo knew better than to challenge him. He had a large standing army, a fleet of thousands of canoes, an impressive hierarchy of battle-hardened chiefs, a closely knit government ruled with a clenched fist. His two chief aides were the Katikiro, a sort of prime minister, and the Kimbugwe, the chief justice. The name went with the job, and the two men who held them during Mutesa's reign were ruthless and corrupt. Moslems had been in the country for several years, and a number of the chiefs had accepted the faith. Those who had not were nevertheless easily swayed by the influence of Moslem wealth. This included the Katikiro and the Kimbugwe. These two held politics and justice firmly in their hands, and simply by the way they presented their opinions they could persuade Mutesa to do almost everything they wanted.

Mutesa had an extravagant evaluation of himself. He knew there was no African power on the continent that would dare question anything he did. But he knew too that the white man was coming more and more to Africa, and this worried him. The Belgians and French were to the west and north of him, the Germans to the south, the British in the east; even the Egyptians were beginning to loom over him in a way he did not like. He was ready to fight any of them—or all, but he was shrewd enough to realize this might not be necessary. The rush of Europeans convinced him that surely there must be a competition among them, and he was prepared to take advantage of it by playing them against each other. From his

148

own experiences at ransacking countries, he deduced the Europeans were interested only in things they could sell elsewhere—human, animal, or mineral, and he was willing to negotiate a treaty with whichever country offered him the best deal. He hinted at this to Stanley when he passed through; to Mackay, whom he accepted as an emissary of the Queen of England; and later to the White Fathers, who were, he thought, agents of France. He indicated to all of them that he was prepared to go to Europe to negotiate with the ruler he chose, provided he would be treated with the dignity he felt he deserved; if the ruler preferred to come to Uganda, that was all right, too. Because of a legend of the land, he was increasingly anxious for the treaty. The legend held that one day a great number of strangers would enter Uganda from the north and overpower the country. As far as Mutesa was concerned, there were already too many strangers in Uganda, and he wanted to negotiate the treaty before the legend materialized and he lost his power to bargain.

Hovering over all were the Moslems from Zanzibar and Arabia. They did everything they could to stall off the treaty because they wanted Mutesa and Uganda as well for themselves.

Aware that Mutesa was apprehensive of white men who arrived in large groups, Father Léon Livinhac decided that it would be a mistake for all five White Fathers in his group to enter Uganda together. As Siméon Lourdel had acquired a fluent knowledge of Kiswahilli, Livinhac appointed him and Brother Amans to make the first entry into the country, effect the necessary contacts and send boats to bring the others and their supplies.

The two missionaries left the southern shores of Lake Victoria in a dugout with a crew of thirteen and supplies for a week. They had no sooner dropped beyond the horizon when a violent storm crashed down on them. They managed to reach shore just as the dugout fell apart. Repairing it took several days and their supplies dwindled. By the time they were ready to resume their trip, they had no food left at all, which meant that every day they had to land and forage for something to eat. They met unfriendly tribes that would not help them, and soon the crew, hungry and weary, refused to go on. Only lavish promises by Lourdel for rich rewards tempted them to continue. Twenty-eight days after starting out, they reached the bay of Entebbe. It was January 17, 1879. The dugout disintegrated a hundred yards from shore, and everyone had to wade to the beach.

Word of the arrival raced the twenty miles to Mutesa's headquarters at Rubaga, a hilltop fortress above what is now the city of Kampala. There was great excitement. The Katikiro suggested that the two strangers be made prisoners until it was certain that no army followed them. Mutesa agreed, then he sent for Mackay and asked what he knew about the newcomers.

From the description he had heard, Mackay recognized the newcomers as Catholic missionaries. "They are evil men," he said. "They will want to preach to your people about a false god. Their ruler is a powerful man in Rome who controls their minds and the thoughts of those who follow them. It would be very unwise for you to let them stay here. They worship cows and statues and make sacrifices. If you permit them to remain, they will lead your people away from you."

Mutesa was understandably disturbed. Arriving at Rubaga, Lourdel and Brother Amans were locked in a small hut and held prisoner for two weeks. Once a day, they were given a wooden plate of steamed bananas, and that was all. Their supplies were examined, and a guard was posted at the lake to watch for others who might be following them. The guard, of course, was a waste of time, and there was nothing among the meager supplies they had managed to salvage that could identify them as enemies. At last, they were brought before Mutesa.

The audience hall, made of bamboo, elephant grass, and mud, was large and dark. After two weeks in a blacked-out hut, a few minutes in the bright sun, then into the dim hall, Lourdel could not see well, and he stood in the middle of the room for several minutes until his eyes focused. He saw that the hall was full of Africans, elegantly dressed, and at the far end, stretched on a couch on a dais, was, he presumed, Mutesa. Moving to him, Lourdel saw a white man seated on the floor near the throne and took him to be Mackay. Lourdel smiled at Mackay, but received no sign of recognition. Brother Amans approached, carrying the gifts for Mutesa. Lourdel presented him with a collection of imitation pearls and a beautiful sword. The king did not even look at them, but studied Lourdel and the brother carefully. Finally he asked: "Who are you and what do you want here?"

"I am a priest of the Church of God," Lourdel replied. "The Catholic Church. I have come here to teach you and your people about my God and to demonstrate the kind of life He requires of those who believe in Him."

"Are there others with you?" Mutesa asked.

"My chief is on the other side of the lake," said Lourdel. "He has sent me ahead to offer you his respects. With your Majesty's permission, he and two of my brothers will come to your country to pay their homage to you."

"You are from the country of France?" said Mutesa.

"Yes." Lourdel deduced Mackay had told Mutesa this, and he added: "Mr. Mackay knows my brothers. They cured him recently when he was sick. He can tell you that we are honorable men who have no ambitions in your country other than to do good and to teach."

Mutesa glanced at Mackay: "Is this true?"

"Not completely," said Mackay, getting up. "I have already told you about these men, Your Majesty. They are idolators, slaves of a cruel ruler in Rome, and their country is not a friend of yours."

Lourdel was amazed. "Mackay, that's not true and you know it," he said.

"It is true," Mackay shot back at him. "You've come here on command of the Pope to destroy everything I'm trying to do."

"I doubt if the Pope even knows you're in Africa," said Lourdel.

Mutesa injected: "Does he know you are here?"

"Not me as a man," said Lourdel, "but he certainly knows my brothers are here, somewhere in Africa."

"And does your country know?" Mutesa asked.

"I suppose the news has reached France," Lourdel conceded, "but I am here as a missionary, not a Frenchman, just as Mackay should be here as a missionary and not an Englishman."

"If these men stay, Your Majesty," threatened Mackay, "then I will have to leave, and when the news gets back to England, you will regret what you have done."

The king did not enjoy the threat. "Go, then," he said. "These men can stay." Mackay sat down sullenly. Mutesa told the Katikiro: "Give them a place to live and send the boats for their chief."

They were given a house just outside the royal compound, and

151

the next day Mutesa sent them a gift of food and banana beer, but there appeared to be no rush to send for Livinhac and the others. Four months passed before Brother Amans led a canoe caravan across the lake to bring Livinhac back. The delay had been carefully calculated to give Lourdel time to disclose any hidden plans he might have that could threaten Mutesa. Aware that he was being watched, Lourdel made a point of staying in the public eye as much as possible. Protocol required him to spend a great deal of time at Mutesa's court, but as often as he could he went out among the people. He had no permission as yet to preach to them, but they had many questions about him, his country, and his religion that he could answer without violating the limited freedom Mutesa had granted him. He visited nearby villages and farms, chatting with people in the joking way they enjoyed. Always he had his medical kit with him, and he gave first aid and medicines with a success that made him somewhat of a hero. He behaved toward the people with a kind of respect they had never known before. Instinctively, they considered him some sort of superior being, as they did Mackay, their chiefs, and the king; but there was a warmth about Lourdel, a gentleness and patience, that melted all the inherent tribal fears and made him irresistible. He would sit for hours with a group of children, teaching them how to hold a pencil and print their names in quivering block letters; or he would talk to the men about farming in France and the advantage of using cow manure as fertilizer, which struck the farmers as too funny to believe, and only his persistent assurances of better crops led them to try it; or he would display such interest in food being cooked by the women that they were too pleased by his praise to realize that in his flattery were instructions to make the food tastier and more nourishing. His appeal with all was in his attitude: he never made anyone feel inferior.

With Mackay, Lourdel decided the best approach was to ignore the man's obvious antagonism, yet do everything to overcome it. The priest sent Mackay gifts of meat and vegetables, which Mackay promptly reciprocated, and whenever Lourdel was near Mackay's house, he stopped in for a brief visit. Lavigerie's instructions for the White Fathers to settle apart from Protestant missions were impractical in view of Mutesa's insistence that both denominations remain at Rubaga. The next best thing, therefore, was to try and get along. Harmony was difficult for two reasons: Mutesa enjoyed putting the two missionaries in debate, and Mackay was determined to get the White Fathers out of the country. Lourdel, on the other hand, couldn't have been less concerned by the presence of Protestantism in the country. If Mackay could turn his Baganda into good Protestants, fine. It was Islam that worried Lourdel, and the oppressive, enslaving paganism. Outside of Mutesa's court, Lourdel never mentioned religion to Mackay, and whenever Mutesa told Mackay to lead the court of chiefs in prayers, Lourdel stepped discreetly aside. Mackay filled his diary with enraged frustrations because Lourdel would not pray with him, but this was something Mackay would never be able to understand because he had absolutely no conception of what the priesthood was, what it meant, what it involved. Infuriated, he did not merely step aside when Lourdel prayed, but stalked indignantly from the room. And in the debates Mutesa demanded, Mackay sometimes became so panicky that he could do nothing but stand there and scream vilifications. The sadness in it all was the impression made on the people: in all the years to follow, the Baganda never got over the idea that Protestants and Catholics were supposed to hate each other. The great wrong Mackay committed in his own time was to provide Mutesa with two foils to use against each other, not only as religions but as nationalities.

Livinhac arrived at Entebbe on June 25. Waiting on the shore were an honor guard and gifts from Mutesa, and when the priest arrived at the White Fathers' house, Mutesa's brother was there with an invitation for him to meet the king the next morning. Livinhac thought things must be going very well. He was a little surprised, therefore, when, next morning, he was kept waiting for an hour in the hot sun before entering the audience hall, and then found Mutesa stretched out nude on his couch. There was a long, embarrassed silence. Livinhac offered his gifts: three swords, some trinkets, and two gold-braid uniforms which Lavigerie had purchased impulsively in Paris and given to the missionaries for just such a purpose. Mutesa glanced at the gifts disinterestedly for several minutes, then managed a half-hearted, "How are you?" The Katikiro announced that the missionaries had requested permission to build a large hut for their work. Mutesa yawned sleepily, scratched himself, and mur-

153

mured offhandedly, "I guess that's all right. I'll send some men to help if I can find some to spare." And then he appeared to fall asleep.

The missionaries were shown out and, puzzled, strolled back to their quarters. Almost immediately men from the palace arrived, leading thirty head of beautiful cattle: a fabulous gift from Mutesa that only a millionaire could top.

Livinhac was bewildered. "Well," he said, "I can't figure it out. What is all this?"

"He just wants you to know that he's the head man around here," explained Lourdel.

"I believe it," Livinhac said, "but he shows it in a strange way."

"He likes doing the unexpected," Lourdel said. "Like being nude this morning. He knew that would shock you."

"It was a bit of a surprise," Livinhac admitted. "We will have to proceed very carefully with a man like this. Does he seem at all interested in our religion?"

"Not much. He asks a lot of questions about Catholicism, but I doubt if he's seriously interested. In Protestantism, either, for that matter. I think he's using us all—Catholics, Protestants, Moslems. Even if he should want to choose one of them, there would be a great deal of opposition. He's head of the local cult of paganism, and I feel a lot of important people around here want him to stay that way."

The Katikiro was one such person. As prime minister, the medicine men, mediums, and pagan priests were responsible to him, and he was thus able to get any answer to prayers he wanted. And the answers he wanted were those that strengthened his position with the king, with the country, and even possibly with the next king. There were several chiefs in the country on whom the gods made little impression. Mutesa, too, was not beyond destroying the temples of gods who did not give him the guidance he preferred. The Katikiro, then, was in a delicate position, for it was necessary for him to know Mutesa's prayers as well as his whims. Too many mistakes could ruin everything. Nevertheless, he had the religion under good control. The Creator, according to local dogma, was called Katonda. Being supreme, good, and almighty, Katonda didn't pay much attention to people; at least he caused them no harm. The people in turn paid little attention to him. But there were other gods, minor gods, who were not so well intentioned. They were frequently angry with people and they had to be appeased with homage and sacrifices. They communicated with people through the dead; for this reason, mediums were important in the country, but they were always mediums the Katikiro appointed. This way the gods produced the problems or solutions that the Katikiro felt met the moment. Medicine men inherited their positions, but they could easily be disposed of if they proved unco-operative. They managed to effect remarkable cures, through their knowledge of herbs and antidotes, but their popularity—and wealth—grew from their fetish business, which they kept up at a good pace by outdating existing fetishes whenever they were in need of funds. The *mwoyo* of the dead—a combination soul and ghost—could cause a great deal of mischief among the living, from which a fetish was the only defense. Medicine men saw to it that *mwoyo* were always busy. Priests were little more than temple attendants and supervisors of sacrifices. It was through them that the gods indicated they wanted to communicate with some living person, and it was for this purpose that the Katikiro used them advantageously.

An urgent use for them arose one day when Mutesa sent word to the White Fathers that he wanted to become a Catholic. "Why?" the Katikiro asked him. "Because you have been ill and they helped you?"

"In part, yes," said Mutesa, "but I have something else in mind."

"You still aren't in good health, are you?" the prime minister persisted.

"No, but I'm much better. Anyway, there's more to it."

"And you think these Christian priests can provide it?"

"That's what I intend to find out."

Lourdel and Livinhac hurried to the palace when they received Mutesa's decision and they could not believe it until they heard the king say calmly: "I have decided yours is the true religion and I will join your church. You have my permission to go out and convert all my people."

Lourdel said: "This is wonderful, Your Majesty. I have been praying for this."

"Yes," Mutesa said, "I imagine you were. Now, I have done something for you and I want you to do something for me. You are my

155

friends; you have proved that often. If you will do this one thing for me, we will be brothers to our graves."

"Name it," said Livinhac.

"My country is in great danger," Mutesa disclosed.

"From whom?"

Mutesa leaned forward and whispered: "The Egyptians! I have learned today that they are sending troops that put them right at my door. I want one of you to go to your country and tell your chief that I am ready to make a treaty with him. I will give him anything he wants, if he just sends me an army."

Lourdel and Livinhac looked at each other sadly, and Lourdel said: "Your Majesty, we are men of God, not of governments. We cannot do what you ask, and even if we tried, nobody would listen to us."

"We are not the men for this task, Your Majesty," Livinhac added. "If you want a treaty with France, then you should get in touch with the French consul at Zanzibar."

"So you will do nothing to help me," Mutesa pouted. "I thought you were my friends."

"We are your friends," Livinhac assured him. "If you want us to write Zanzibar for you, we will do that, but it is all we can do."

"Very well," the king said. "Write. As for joining your church, I will have to think that over now."

The Katikiro was not about to give him too much time to think. Two days later the high priest of Mukasa, the god of healing, arrived from his temple on the island of Bubembe in Lake Victoria. The prime minister took him directly to the king, and the priest said: "You are sick, Your Majesty."

"I know that," Mutesa said.

"You have been sick for two years," said the priest.

"And how do you know this?" Mutesa asked.

"Mukasa has told me."

The king bent forward, interested. "What else has he told you?"

"Mukasa says he has a message for you that he will give you through a medium."

"When?" Mutesa asked. "Where? Am I to go all the way to the temple?"

"No, Your Majesty. A temple must be built here, and then Mukasa will reveal his message that will cure you, but it must be done within seven days."

"Did Mukasa tell you the nature of my sickness?"

"No, Your Majesty. He said only that I was to ask you how long the white men have been here."

"Two years," Mutesa said, and he frowned at the words. "What has that to do with it?"

"I do not know, Your Majesty," said the priest. "I was just told to ask."

Mutesa turned to the Katikiro. "Do what he says. Give him the men to build the temple. We will see what Mukasa has to tell me."

For a week the White Fathers were not permitted to visit Mutesa; they were not even allowed inside the royal compound. They saw the temple going up and they were greatly disturbed. They went to Mackay and asked him what he might know, but he knew nothing. The compound had been closed to him as well.

At dawn of the seventh day, a huge crowd gathered at the new temple. The White Fathers and Mackay were there. Nine cows were brought by the high priest and his four assistants. A gutter had been cut down to the pond which, during the rainy season, was part of the lake. One by one, the cows were brought to the gutter, stretched out on the ground, and their throats were cut. Blood flowed down the gutter, reaching closer to the pond as each cow died. With the last, the blood poured into the pond. The high priest cried out: this was the sign that the god Mukasa was with them and was ready to talk. A puff of smoke rose from the temple. Everyone turned and watched. From the door stepped the medium: she was dressed in hammered-bark cloth, and around her waist hung eighteen white goat tails. She held a branch in her hand from a tree on the island of Bubembe and she beat the ground with it.

"Mukasa speaks!" she called to the people. "Mukasa speaks!" Then her voice dropped to a low pitch, and she said: "I am angry with the king. The white men try to destroy me and all the tribal gods. Yet the king keeps them here. He must kill them, then his sickness will die with them!"

She moaned and wailed and collapsed to the ground. Slave girls picked up her body and carried her back into the temple.

There was a great restlessness among the people, and those who

157

were standing near the White Fathers and Mackay moved away. Mutesa looked over at them. He muttered to the Katikiro: "If the god wants the white men to die, why doesn't he kill them?"

The Katikiro said: "You were the one who permitted them into the country, not Mukasa."

Angered, Mutesa turned and walked hastily back to his palace.

That night, a hundred dervishes encircled the White Fathers' house, dancing, spinning, wailing, and they continued until dawn. No one went near the house for days, not even the children who had been attending the new school or others who had just started catechism lessons. Orphans the priests had taken felt the uneasiness and became afraid. Several of them ran away. At night, the warehouses were robbed and set afire. The sick did not arrive as usual at the clinic for treatment.

"I wonder how long he will make us wait?" wondered Father Livinhac, but no one could answer. Lourdel wanted to go to the royal compound and face Mutesa, but Livinhac considered this asking for murder and would not permit it.

Late one night they heard a soft tap at the door. Brother Amans opened it and saw standing there one of the young pages from the royal court, who had heard Lourdel debate before Mutesa and had asked for catechism lessons when the king finally permitted the priests to teach. He hurried inside and closed the door behind him.

"The others have sent me," he whispered, as if someone outside might hear him. "I am to tell you that the reason we have not come to see you is that we are afraid for you. If the king thinks we have given up your religion, then he may not kill you."

"It was good and very brave of you to come here to tell us that," Livinhac said.

"There is something else," the boy revealed. "Tomorrow, the king is going to make all the people go to the mosque and say the prayers of the Moslems. He says he will kill all of us who refuse."

"Has he become a Moslem?" Lourdel queried.

"He will tomorrow."

"Maybe the Arabs have given him the army he wants," Lourdel said to Livinhac.

"How do the people feel about this?" Livinhac asked the boy.

158

"Most of them are willing to do it," he said, "but those who were studying to be baptized by you do not want to."

"If you refuse," Livinhac said, "you will be killed."

"But you said we should not pray with the Moslems," answered the boy.

"Yes, I did," affirmed Livinhac. "You might be forced to go to the mosque, but you can't be forced to pray."

Lourdel was furious with Mutesa. "What a disgusting thing to do," he said. "Of course we should protect the people, but we ought to do anything we can to stop Mutesa."

"Like what?" Livinhac asked.

"I don't know." Then Lourdel added, "Father, I want permission to go to the royal compound tomorrow."

"Why? What do you want to do?"

"I don't know, but I know I can't sit here any longer. Please let me go."

"All right, but you must do nothing that might cause any trouble."

Early the next morning, Father Lourdel went to the village. The royal compound was closed to him, but he strolled among the people, easily, casually, chatting, chiding, as if nothing were wrong. When the procession hour came and Mutesa went to the compound gate and saw Lourdel, he demanded: "What is he doing here?"

"I don't know," the Katikiro said.

"Does he know what is to happen today?"

"How could he? No one has told him. No one has gone near him. His house is being watched; I would know if anyone went to him."

"Well, hold off everything until he leaves," Mutesa said.

"Why?"

"Because I say so."

But Lourdel did not leave. He idled around the village all day. At last, someone whispered to him: "It will be tomorrow." He was back tomorrow, repeating what appeared to be his harmless visits of the day before. Again, Mutesa did not want him to witness the procession to the mosque. He told the Katikiro: "Tomorrow is the Christian sabbath. The priest should not be here then. We will make the procession tomorrow."

159

So convinced was everyone of this that no one looked for Lourdel the next day, and when he reached the gate to the royal compound, there was no one to stop him from entering. He went into the audience hall where Mutesa was holding court. The sight of Lourdel startled everyone. He went to his usual place and sat down. Mutesa decided he had deferred long enough. Rising, he announced to the assembled chiefs:

"You know that the plague sweeps the country. It is killing my people. It is then necessary to kill the plague. The only way is to pray to Allah. Everyone must pray to Allah. If anyone here in this court does not, Allah will be angry. I command all men to pray with the Arabs. I command you to go to the mosque with me now."

Lourdel jumped to his feet and called: "Your Majesty, I beg you to hear me!"

Angry shouts came from the chiefs. Several of them drew their daggers and rushed to Lourdel. Mutesa ordered them to stop.

Lourdel said: "Mutesa, you are a great king. A great king does not force his people to pray in any special way. God asks for free prayer. If any of your men wish to pray with the Arabs, let them go and do so. But if any man does not wish to do so, I beg you do not force him. That will make God angry."

Indignant chiefs accused Lourdel of trying to tell the king what to do, and again they threatened him. An Arab stepped to Mutesa, demanding: "Are you the king of this country or is this Christian pig? Are you his slave? You should know by now that the white men only want to take over your country and destroy you. They teach their religion to your people to lead them away from you. And they teach lies. Their religion is lies."

Lourdel said: "Your Majesty, the Arabs tell you I am teaching lies. There is only one way to find out whether or not I am. Order wood to be brought and piled up outside this building. Set it afire; let it burn fiercely. I will walk through it with the Gospel of Christ in my hand. Let any Arab here walk through it with the Koran in his hand. The one of us who is not consumed by the flames will certainly be the man sent by God."

A roar of consternation filled the large room. Chiefs shouted that Mutesa should accept the challenge. Bewildered Arabs went into a huddle. One of them at last called out to Mutesa: "Your Majesty,

160

you can't expect one of us to walk through a fire with a sorcerer!"

The Katikiro leaned and whispered excitedly to Mutesa, but Mutesa shook his head. He looked at Lourdel, who smiled back at him, then he turned to the Arabs and asked calmly: "Are you afraid?" There was no answer.

Then Mutesa sat down and waited until the room quieted. He said: "Let every man pray as he wishes."

It looked like a victory for Father Lourdel, but the Katikiro was not the sort of man to let such a victory live too long. The court dismissed, Lourdel hurried to the mission and told the others what he had done. They were both pleased and furious with him.

"Suppose someone had taken you up on it?" Livinhac asked.

"Then I might or might not be here to tell you about it," Lourdel said. "One thing I know, I wasn't in the least afraid. I know as sure as I'm standing here that had any Arab accepted the challenge, I would have come out of it all right."

It seemed, for a few days, that all of the White Fathers were going to be all right. A caravan then arrived from the coast with mail, among which was the letter from Lavigerie, informing the priests of the massacres in Urundi and North Africa and ordering them, if they or their people appeared to be in the slightest danger, to withdraw to a safer place and await further advice. The White Fathers in Uganda did not feel that they were in great danger any longer and were about to write this decision to Lavigerie when suddenly people came running from the village with a horrific tale:

The Katikiro had brought another medium to Mutesa, who told him that she had received a message from his father, King Sano. The dead king had said that if Mutesa would not kill the white men, he should then kill his people who were following them. The number to be killed: ninety-nine. Murdering his own people did not strike Mutesa as the threat to his international relations that the death of the priests would be, so he approved the massacre. Ninety-nine people, known or suspected to be aspirant Christians, were lined against a wall, and their throats were cut.

Now there was no question about what the White Fathers must do. Though they appeared not to be in immediate danger, certainly those who followed them were. For the people's sake, then, the priests would have to get away, at least until the terror was over. They sent word to Mutesa that they were leaving, using the ill health of Father Livinhac as their excuse. Mutesa was both surprised and pleased. The Katikiro offered the priests canoes to transport themselves, their orphans, and their supplies to wherever they wanted to go.

On the day they left, many people went to the lake shore to say good-by, people who had been studying catechism, people who wanted to, people they had secretly baptized in their last hours in the country. There was much weeping, sadness, pleas to accompany the priests, promises to keep the religion alive until the priests returned. The last to step from the crowd was a young man sixteen years old. He was slender of figure, sensitive of face, soft of voice.

He said: "I know why you are leaving and I'm very sorry, but I suppose it's the right thing to do. What hurts most is knowing that my father is responsible for all this. I like you very much, and I promise that I will always let my servants pray as you taught them. Maybe someday things will be different and you can come back. I hope so. Pray for me." He threw his arms around Father Livinhac and burst into tears.

The priest patted the young man's shoulder, comfortingly. "Of course we'll pray for you, Prince Mwanga," Livinhac said. "I'm happy that you feel the way you do. Perhaps someday if you become king, we will be able to come back, and then I know things will be much better."

He was wrong. So wrong.

XV

For three years the White Fathers waited on the opposite shores of Lake Victoria for the moment when they could return to Uganda, knowing that as long as Mutesa remained on the throne, Christianity had small chance of survival in the country. Even Alexander Mackay deemed it advisable to restrain his enthusiasm for Protestant converts. Mutesa's continued interests in a favorable liaison with England saved Mackay from having to close down his mission. Nevertheless, unable to work as freely as he wished, he made several short trips out of the country both in search of a happier environment and to give himself something to do. Mackay, like everyone else in Uganda, had no idea exactly why the White Fathers had left. The priests told no one of their instructions from Lavigerie to move if their lives or the lives of their people were endangered by the fact of their religion. Mackay took the departure as the defeat of Catholicism in Uganda and noted this attitude in his diary with arrogant satisfaction. His opinion was somewhat shared by the Arabs, who lost no time solidifying their own position with the king. The Katikiro kept a long-distance eye on the priests and safeguarded against their return by forbidding baptized and would-be Catholics from holding services of any kind.

The Catholics went underground, and there were some important people among them: Andrew Kaggwa, director of the king's band; Joseph Mukasa, personal servant to the king; Mathias Murumba, a subchief; Matthew Kisule, the king's gunsmith; Charles Lwanga, the country's outstanding athlete and hero. Deprived of their priests and denied public worship, these and many others began meeting secretly. They taught newcomers what they had learned from the White Fathers, they said the Rosary and read the Mass prayers together. From time to time, they slipped a few people out of the country to go visit the priests at their mission across the lake to receive the sacraments and to let the priests know what was going on.

King Mutesa died violently on October 9, 1884, from what has been identified as a cerebral hemorrhage. Whenever the country had been without a king, no matter how briefly, pillage and murder broke out. No king meant no law and order; the people were free to commit any crimes they chose. No king also meant competition among chiefs and politicians to enthrone their own candidate from among the heirs. To prevent the chaos, the death of kings was often kept secret for several days until the inner clique had made its decision for the next ruler. Aware of the mounting tensions, the Katikiro was anxious to make the choice as quickly as possible, and he wanted the choice to be the man who would keep him on as prime minister. The most likely to do that was Prince Mwanga, the third son of Mutesa, who because of what seemed his slim chance of inheriting the throne had been the least trouble of all the sons. True, he had been friendly to the Catholics, but the Katikiro felt this could be controlled. Actually, since the departure of the White Fathers, Mwanga was seen often with the Arabs, and the Katikiro knew that the young prince had adopted many of the homosexual activities practiced by the Moslems. Perhaps, then, the Katikiro felt, Mwanga had lost his sympathy for Christianity. Within a few hours after Mutesa's death, the Katikiro conferred with the chief justice and the head councilor, and they agreed on Mwanga as the heir. Runners were sent to call in all the chiefs, who must be present at the public selection of the next king. The chiefs arrived in the morning with no idea why they had been summoned. Their first inclination came when they saw that the

164

sacred fire, kept burning during a king's reign, had been extinguished and that the keeper of the flames had been killed in order to join Mutesa as his servant in the next world. There was brief consternation, snuffed out by the Katikiro, who quickly called out the army, then, in front of a huge crowd, lined up all the princes. He walked back and forth before the young men, pretending to be in the throes of decision. He stopped at last in front of Mwanga, took his hand, and led him to a platform where he could be seen by the people.

The Katikiro announced: "Mwanga is our king. If anyone wishes to fight him, let him come forward now."

The chiefs were too stunned, too surprised, to accept the traditional challenge to dethrone a new king by defeating him in battle. No one moved.

The Katikiro turned to the line of princes. "Mwanga is your king," he said. "You are nothing but peasants. Step forward and fight him or kneel in obedience."

Bewildered by the suddenness of events, the princes did not think to oppose the Katikiro's choice. After a moment of uncertainty, they dropped to their knees.

A cry went up: "Mwanga is king!"

The sacred fire was lighted. Mwanga's reign began. He was nineteen years old.

The Katikiro thought Mwanga would be an easy king to manage. Mwanga reappointed him the country's prime minister, then approved his choice of two close friends to be chief justice and commander in chief of the army. The Katikiro had hoped to extend his influence further into the royal court, but Mwanga drew the line. He retained Joseph Mukasa as personal servant and head of the royal household, Andrew Kaggwa as leader of the drums, and he appointed Charles Lwanga assistant to Musaka. They were all Catholics: threats to the Katikiro. But most significant was Mwanga's refusal to go through some of the pagan rites of his accession ceremony. There was now little doubt about the influence of Christians, and the Katikiro was greatly disturbed. He was more alarmed when Catholics not only resumed public religious services but also began teaching catechism right in the royal audience hall to the pages and anybody else who cared to listen. The pages—the sons of chiefs who had presented the boys to be servants to the king until manhood—were particularly receptive, especially since Charles Lwanga, their sports hero, was one of their instructors.

Distressed by developments, the Katikiro, backed by Arabs, decided on a test of strength. In front of all the chiefs, he arose one day at court and declared: "Mutesa swore that he would kill all those who prayed with the Frenchmen. But what do we see now? Christians are teaching in the king's own rooms. Christians are destroying the customs of the land. In Mitiyana, a subchief has sent away all his wives, keeping only one as is the Christian custom. Other women who have become Christians are leaving their husbands' houses. Evil things will occur in this country, Your Majesty, unless you stop all this. As your prime minister, I beg you to condemn the Christians before it is too late."

Angered, Mwanga stood. "When Mutesa was king," he said, "he did what he thought best. Now I am king, and I shall do what I think best. The Christians will be left alone. And when the priests return from the south, which they shall do at my request, I will then show you which religion I believe in."

The Katikiro had only one alternative: to kill Mwanga. Plans were made to assassinate the young king during the inaugural ceremonies of the temple to his father, in February, 1885. By tradition, many people would be killed during the ceremonies to provide a retinue for Mutesa on his journey in the next world. At the height of ceremony, a soldier was to stab Mwanga. But the plot never materialized. Mwanga's mother learned of it and warned her son. With the aid of loyal army officers, Mwanga deposed the nineteen chiefs organized against him and ordered them killed. The Katikiro's involvement was also discovered, but he managed to save himself by a histrionic display of remorse, then went on to persuade Mwanga not to execute the rebel chiefs. Mwanga tempered his mercy with a warning: any more evidence of disloyalty and he would replace the Katikiro with Catholic friends he knew he could trust. The prime minister knew Mwanga was referring to Joseph Mukasa and Andrew Kaggwa, and he made up his mind to get rid of both of them as soon as he could.

In April, Mwanga sent a flotilla of canoes across the lake to the White Fathers with an invitation to return to Uganda. Father

Livinhac had gone back to North Africa to be consecrated bishop; Lourdel was in charge.

The reception the priests received awed them. Hundreds of people lined the shores when the canoes were beached. Hundreds more rushed to the road as the priests walked to Rubaga. At points along the route, groups waited to perform their part of the official welcome. There were prayers and gifts, hymn singing, bands, speeches, parades. It was all very wonderful. When Lourdel entered the royal audience hall, Mwanga jumped from his throne and ran across the long room to him and embraced him. There was a big feast and a great deal of talk and all sorts of promises of lifelong friendship and mutual aid. Mwanga gave the priests excellent land, then ordered his men to build a house of sun-baked brick, an accomplishment the priests had earlier introduced. A palisade was built around the mission, assuring privacy and safety from animals and thieves. The priests were very happy.

It did not, however, take them long to discover that Mwanga wasn't all that he appeared. His harem was full; Arabs had taught him hemp smoking and sodomy. Several royal pages were being whipped regularly because they refused to participate in the nightly orgies. Joseph Mukasa and Charles Lwanga had been severely reprimanded for begging the king to exclude the Christian pages from his Moslem entertainment. To protect the boys, the two men sent them off to the mission each night. This incensed Mwanga, but in view of his professed friendship for the priests he could not order the boys to return. The Katikiro took advantage of every incident that piqued Mwanga. Playing on the young king's pride and vanity, he pointed out the Mwanga was the ruler of tribal gods the people were now refusing to worship, that the people were destroying fetishes and amulets they had previously worn for the king's protection. Women, he said, would no longer live in harems and had become uncontrollable. The power of the king himself was in danger. When such complaints failed to infuriate Mwanga sufficiently, the Katikiro had only to allude to the boys who were denying him satisfaction, and this was always enough to make Mwanga explode. He considered the denials the boldest sort of treason, and he warned Joseph Mukasa that unless he stopped hiding the youngsters, they would all be killed. Mukasa was frequently

167

seen sobbing his heart out to Mwanga, pleading that the boys be left alone.

There was already enough death in the country. Kept drunk and doped by the Katikiro, Mwanga lived in a constant stupor. With languid indifference, he approved the murder of anybody the prime minister wanted out of the way, and thus the Katikiro got rid of his own enemies. No day passed but that two or three people were killed at Rubaga. Wives who displeased Mwanga or pages too slow to respond to him were savagely mutilated and left to die. In the next few months, there was an astonishing turnover in the royal harem and the pages' barracks. Other times, Mwanga ordered murders just for the delight of watching death slowly consume someone he felt had lived long enough. Chiefs suffered constant dread, never sure when Mwanga might turn on them, or when the Katikiro would use his influence on the king against them. Though many Christians had been victims of the terror, attacks had not been on the basis of religion. But that was soon to change.

With the consecration of Livinhac as the first Catholic bishop of Equatorial Africa, the Anglicans decided they too should establish a diocese there. The appointment went to James Hannington, who had done missionary work along the coast. Eager to inspect his diocese, Bishop Hannington notified Mackay that he would be visiting Uganda. Mackay was under the impression that the Bishop would come via Tabora, as everyone else had done. However, Hannington was aware of the difficulties of that route, and he made plans to enter Uganda from the north. Learning this, Mackay wrote him immediately, warning him of the Uganda legend that anyone entering the country from the north would come with the intention of conquering the land; anyone attempting such an entry would surely be stopped by violence. His letter arrived too late. Bishop Hannington had already taken off. It was September when he approached the Uganda border. News of him raced to Rubaga. A council of state was called, and the Katikiro urged Mwanga to approve an attack on Hannington's caravan.

"The white men are already in control of lands on the coast," the prime minister said. "This chief arriving at our borders is the first of many who will swarm into our country. If he is not killed, then surely the others will follow him."

168

The chiefs voted in favor of the attack. Mwanga declared: "Let it be done."

A page who had heard the decision hurried to Mackay with the news. Alarmed, Mackay went to Mwanga and pleaded with him to rescind the order. The realization that someone in his court was passing private discussions on to the Christians irritated Mwanga too much to listen to what Mackay was saying. Even the missionary's threat of official retaliation by British forces did not penetrate Mwanga's preoccupied mind. He sent Mackay away, then tried to decide who was the informer. Of all the people in the royal court, the man friendliest to the white men was Joseph Mukasa. Mwanga summoned him, but was told he had gone out for a walk.

"He has probably gone to tell the priests what he has already told Mackay," Mwanga said. "Tell him I want to see him as soon as he returns."

Mukasa had seen the king angry many times, but never had he witnessed such fury as welcomed him when he entered the audience hall. Mwanga's burst of anger almost knocked him over. Stunned, Mukasa lost all prudence, and in defending himself he defended the white men. "If you kill this white man," he told Mwanga, "you will be responsible for it before God."

"You're not talking to one of your page boys now," Mwanga shouted at him. "I am responsible to no one for what I do."

Mwanga twisted Mukasa's words against him. Mukasa said: "Your father never killed a white man." Mwanga challenged: "Are you calling my father a coward?"

"It does not take courage to massacre a small caravan," Mukasa returned.

"Then I am a coward?"

"No, but you are making a great mistake."

"Then I am a fool?"

"No, but you let yourself be swayed by the Katikiro and the chiefs who are his friends."

"You mean I have no mind of my own?"

"You are merely misjudging a man who comes as a friend."

"So I have no mind at all?"

The argument grew until the hall shook from the shouting. People came to the doors and watched. When at last Mukasa was permitted to return to his house, he knew that Mwanga had gone too far to be stopped.

Mukasa went to the Catholic mission to tell Father Lourdel what was about to happen. Since their return to Uganda, the White Fathers had little to do with Mwanga because Mwanga himself was doing very little about being king. Court sessions were infrequent, and though Lourdel attended them, Mwanga was usually too weak from the previous night for anything of note to occur. Having been given permission to pursue mission work, the priests kept busy at it: catechism classes were crowded, the school was full, more and more slaves were purchased from passing caravans. From Catholics working at the palace the priests learned of Mwanga's debaucheries. To confront Mwanga with charges of his immoralities would have been imprudent. The priests could only urge their people to leave the royal compound as soon as they finished their day's work.

But the news about Bishop Hannington was different. Lourdel could not stand by helplessly while another missionary was being murdered. The priest knew that Hannington was already at the northern border, under arrest on orders from Mwanga. Lourdel went to Mwanga to plead for the Bishop's life. To rant or rave or threaten, as Mackay was doing, would only have irritated Mwanga further. Lourdel spoke to him softly, gently, affectionately, assuring him that Hannington was no threat to the country.

Mwanga listened in silence, and from the expression on his face he seemed impressed. At last he said: "Very well, Father, I will countermand my order. But Hannington is not to enter the country. He must go back the way he came."

"I know he will obey you," Lourdel said.

But the order was never given. On October 30, Bishop Hannington, his Goan cook, and the forty Africans in the caravan were murdered. One African, shamming death, escaped.

Lourdel and Mackay stormed Mwanga with protests, and there was a great, sullen resentment among all the Christians. The realization that his people were turning against him incensed Mwanga. He demanded of Mackay: "I insist that you name the man who told you about the decisions made in the privacy of my court."

"All Uganda knew of it within an hour," Mackay replied.

"Then let all Uganda know this," Mwanga said. "You are the next white man I will kill."

Lourdel said: "You have called me your father and your friend, Mwanga, and I have tried to be, but I assure you that if you kill Mr. Mackay, I will leave your country."

Mwanga turned on him. "Do you think that if I killed Mackay I would spare you?" Then he told the Katikiro: "I forbid any of my people to go to the white men's houses. Kill anyone who does."

Mackay stalked from the room. In a soft, shocked voice, Lourdel said: "Well, Your Majesty, I never thought you would ever say anything like that. I remember the day not long ago when on the shores of the lake you put your arms around me and you promised that if you should become king, the people would be free to pray as they wished. You wept, remember, and you asked me to pray for you. I pray for you now, Mwanga. I pray for you now."

The king sank back on his couch, deflated and exhausted. He seemed about to cry again. "Father," he said, "the order is not for you."

"It must not be for Mackay either."

"Why do you care about him? You are French."

"I am not here as a man of France, but as a man of religion. When one religion is persecuted, all religions suffer."

"Nothing will happen to you."

"I am afraid I cannot trust that promise, Your Majesty," Lourdel said. He walked slowly from the room.

With a vacillation that evidenced his own dazed mind, Mwanga within an hour sent Mackay a gift of two cows, then he permitted Joseph Mukasa to retain his position as head of the royal household. He became in a moment like a penitent boy, shameful, sad, silent, moping in the fear that he had been rejected by those he loved and feeling he deserved it. The attitude puzzled his people and worried the Katikiro. A few days later, Mwanga developed an eye infection. Joseph Mukasa suggested that Father Lourdel be asked to treat him.

"No," Mwanga said. "He wouldn't come. He'd let me suffer. He hates me now."

"Permit me to say you are wrong, Your Majesty," Mukasa said. "Father Lourdel doesn't hate you; he couldn't hate anyone. He has stayed away because he thinks you do not want to be his friend, but if you ask him to come now, I'm sure he would be very happy."

"Do you really think so?"

"Oh, yes."

"Would you mind asking him, Joseph? It might seem strange if I did."

Lourdel was at Mwanga's side in a few moments. He said little while he treated the king's eyes, and Mwanga himself was shy and embarrassed. That evening, Lourdel returned for another treatment. Mwanga was much improved, and when Lourdel had finished, the king took his hand and led him away from the others. He became as coy as a girl. "Father, don't ever again say you're going to leave me," he said. "You don't know what it does to me. You are my father and you are my friend. Promise that you'll always be."

"Of course, Your Majesty," Lourdel said. "As long as you want me to be."

Relieved like a child suddenly forgiven, Mwanga turned playful. He put on Lourdel's sun helmet and stood in front of a mirror and made faces. He did a little dance. He took Lourdel outside and insisted that he choose the finest of the king's goats to take home as a gift. He said: "I like you so much, Father, and I have the greatest respect for you."

"That's nice," Lourdel said, somewhat wary. Then he took two opium pills from his medicine kit and said: "Your eyes may still pain you tonight. Take one of these and you'll be able to sleep." And he went away, shaking his head, wondering what kind of man he was dealing with.

In the middle of the night, Lourdel was awakened by Joseph Mukasa: the king had taken a bad turn. Lourdel went to him immediately. The room was full of people. Mwanga told him: "I took one of those pills, as you told me, and I slept all right, but at midnight I woke up, so I took the other one. It gave me great pains in my stomach and now I'm very sick."

"Well, I have something that will fix that fast enough," Lourdel said, and he reached for his medicine kit.

The Katikiro stepped from the crowd. "What are you going to do?"

"Give him some medicine to stop his vomiting."

"You already gave him medicine that made him worse. Do you think more medicine is going to do him any good?"

"Of course," the priest said easily. "I've seen this kind of reaction to opium before."

"How do I know you are not planning to poison the king?" the prime minister asked.

"Wouldn't that be a foolish thing to try in front of this crowd?" Lourdel returned.

"We don't know what you have in those bottles. You could give him something that will kill him tomorrow, or next week."

"Well," said Lourdel, a little impatient, "if the king dies from anything I give him, you have my permission to kill me as well." He spoonfed Mwanga a dose of medicine, then sat back to wait. In half an hour, Mwanga stopped his moaning and indicated that he wanted to go back to sleep. Lourdel returned to the mission.

In the morning, Mwanga felt better, but he had vivid memories of the pains he had suffered the night before, and the thought of them was enough to send the pendulum of his emotions swinging back to discontent and suspicion. In a matter of a few moments he devised in his mind a plot against his life which he firmly believed existed. What a fool he had been to trust Lourdel, to forgive Mukasa! How could he have been so blind to their schemes? Wasn't it obvious how allied they were? Hadn't Mukasa told Lourdel about the plans to kill Hannington? Who had sent for Lourdel last night? Who, indeed, had urged sending the boats to bring Lourdel back to Uganda in the first place? Mukasa, always Mukasa. It was bad enough that Mukasa had dissuaded the pages from complying to whims that were a king's prerogatives, but he had also been directly responsible for those pills which had almost proved fatal. Mukasa had been disobedient, deceptive, and disloyal. What would he try next? Well, there would not be a next time. Lourdel had once said that his Great Chief in North Africa had hoped to establish in Central Africa a Christian kingdom, ruled by a Christian king; who was apparently the prospect for the throne? Mukasa. All right, then, if the young fool thought that becoming a Christian would bring him riches and power, let him discover that it could also bring him torture and death.

Having worked himself into a complete frenzy, Mwanga called an emergency session of his royal court. He stomped into the audience hall, and before the chiefs were able to rise to their feet, he pointed at Mukasa and bellowed: "I order you to be burned alive! What do you say to that?"

There was a burst of confusion among the chiefs; only Mukasa seemed calm, not surprised. "If the king says I am to die, I die," he said.

"You know you deserve it," Mwanga said. "You are a liar, a traitor, an assassin, a deluded Catholic thief who thinks he can steal my throne."

"I am none of those things except one," Mukasa said. "A Catholic."

"If you were nothing else, that would be bad enough."

"So I am to die because of my religion?"

"Your religion is at the root of it."

"Then I die happily for my God, as I would die happily for my king."

"Your conduct hasn't given that impression."

"Your Majesty sees only what he wants to see."

"Well, I see through you," Mwanga said. He turned to the Katikiro. "Burn him!"

Father Lourdel learned the news even before Mukasa reached the prison hut where he was to await the executioner. He hurried to the palace, but both Mwanga and the Katikiro refused to see him. Guards at the prison hut would not let him inside to give Mukasa the last rites of the Church. All day he tried fruitlessly to intercede for Mukasa, but all doors were shut to him. Night came, yet the chief executioner did not appear. Orders to burn Mukasa had reached him at his bush farm, and he was reluctant to obey because he knew Mukasa and liked him. He knew, too, that at times the king changed his mind about executions, and he thought, because of the boyhood friendship between Mukasa and Mwanga, he might do so now. To stall, he sent word to Rubaga that he was away hunting and was not expected back until late but that he would be instructed to go immediately to the palace as soon as he returned. Two of the guards on duty during the night were Catholic and offered to let Mukasa escape, regardless of the danger to themselves.

"Escape from what?" Mukasa asked. "From God? That is where I am going, and I don't want to miss the chance."

"Well, don't you want to get out of that stuffy hut for a while?" they asked.

Symbolic of his towering influence in Africa, a large statue of Cardinal Lavigerie overlooks the sea at Algiers. A similar statue, once in the city of Tunis, is now at Carthage, where Lavigerie is buried.

Author Glenn D. Kittler with Bishop André Perraudin in Ruanda.

Though he is dedicated to meet all the needs of Africa, it is the continent's spiritual welfare which is the White Father's first purpose. He baptizes, he instructs, he hears confessions, he celebrates his Mass in chapels, great churches, in the open air, he bestows the Last Rites, always aware that the future of Africa, no matter how great, would be meaningless without God.

Though a White Father's spiritual work is uppermost, there is much more he must do. In the course of an average day, he supervises the construction of a new building, inspects a school, gives a music lesson, publishes textbooks in a hundred languages, discusses problems over coffee with the local chiefs. Medical aid is an important daily task; working in French West Africa, Father Goarnisson has become a pioneer in the cure of native eye diseases.

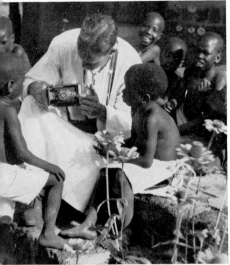

Combating Africa's many diseases is a major problem for the White Fathers, and much of their progress is due to the doctors who go to the missions to help. Aiding in the Gold Coast is Dr. Linn Cooper, of Washington, D.C., who works in the Jirapa mission of Father Remy McCoy, the now legendary "rainmaker." In Tanganyika, Dr. Eleonora Schroeder, of Holland, is at the Sumve mission with Father James Meade, of Brooklyn. Outstanding was Dr. Adrian Atiman (below), freed from slavery by the White Fathers, then trained in medicine at the society's expense. Atiman subsequently received both papal and government honors for his work.

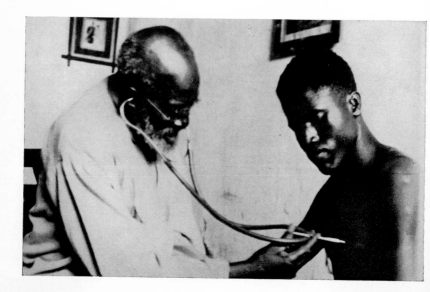

Assigned by the Pope to inspect the African missions during World War II, Francis Cardinal Spellman, of New York, visited the White Fathers in Uganda. Facing him is Father Amédée Goulet, of Springfield, Mass., who became the first American White Father when he joined the society in 1902. He has been in the missions over fifty years.

ust getting where he has to go is
often ordeal enough for a White Father. Trucks and motorcycles break
down or get stuck in the mud; at
times, a path is only wide enough
for a bicycle—and at other times he
must walk or even be carried. In
the Sahara, he can always rely on
the camel. Also in the Sahara, he
may find himself the victim of a surprise snowfall. But wherever he goes,
his African friends are anxious to
travel with him—even youngsters
who just want to go along for the
ide.

A vital and integral part of the White Fathers' society are the men known as "brothers"—men from all over the world who take their many skills to Africa to assist the priests in manual work and to teach the Africans agriculture, building construction, and trades of all kinds. There are three hundred such brothers in Africa, comprising a major influence for the progress of the continent.

The desolate Africa of the Sahara or the merry Africa of a tribal village—both are the domain of the White Father for as long as the continent needs him. Throughout the world, young men, like these Americans, prepare to follow the steps of missionaries who have preceded them for a hundred years, all of them deriving their great strengths and guidance from the dawn hours spent alone in meditation.

Whether she is discussing school instructions with a White Father, explaining the operations of ocean liners to people who have never seen one, or aboard a truck headed for her next assignment, the White Sister fulfills a great need in Africa, ceaselessly at work in the classroom, the hospital, in the fields and the villages.

Superiors of the White Fathers, elected in 1947 to serve ten years, present themselves to Pope Pius XII. On the Pope's right is Bishop Louis Durrieu, the Superior General.

Preparing the African to assume leadership in the Church is one of the primary aims of the White Fathers. Giving the veil to young girls aspiring to become nuns is a triumph surpassed only by receiving the first blessing of a new African priest. A unique event occurred in Central Africa in March, 1956, when Bishop Aloys Bigirumwami, who was completely trained by the White Fathers, became the first African on the continent ever to consecrate a white man— Bishop André Perraudin, a Swiss White Father.

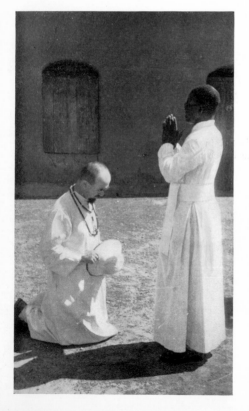

"I'd like to see Father Lourdel."

"Then go to him."

Mukasa remained with Lourdel for an hour, confessing, receiving Communion, assisting at Mass; then he returned to his prison hut as casually as if he were merely reporting for work. It was dawn; the executioner was there waiting for him. The executioner was not in a hurry. He was quite sure the king would feel differently this morning and he did not want the reprieve to arrive too late. Friends of Mukasa's came from the village. The morning grew, and, for his own safety, the executioner felt he had better get on with the task assigned to him. He led Mukasa out of the prison, away from the royal enclosure, through the village and beyond to a knoll a mile away. Mukasa's friends followed at a short distance. At the knoll, the executioner's assistants were waiting, the pyre already built, extra wood piled neatly to one side. The executioner stretched out each preliminary as long as he could, one eye on the village road for the messenger from the king. When at last he saw a boy come running, the executioner sighed with relief and triumph. "You are from the king?" he asked when the boy reached him.

"No. From the Katikiro," the runner said. "He is watching from his quarters and has not seen the smoke rise. He wants to know what is taking you so long."

"He will see the smoke before you can get back to him," the executioner said. He turned to Mukasa. "I am sorry, my friend."

"I am sorry, too," Mukasa said, "but for the king. My death will be a sin upon his soul, but tell him I will pray for God's mercy on him."

"I'll tell him," said the executioner. "I do not want you to suffer this horrible death, Mukasa. Please close your eyes."

Mukasa closed his eyes and made the sign of the cross upon himself. The executioner lifted his broad, sharp sword and as he swung it with experienced skill it made a soft whistle in the air. Mukasa's head fell to the ground with a dull thud and rolled away. He remained standing for an instant, then dropped, blood spurting from his severed neck. The executioner's assistants wrapped him in reeds and put him on the pyre and set flame to it, and in a few moments the smoke rose high enough for the Katikiro to see it a mile away.

King Mwanga laughed when the executioner gave him Joseph Mukasa's message, and he said: "Take one of the pages from the prison and burn him and mix his ashes with Mukasa's. Their ghosts will be confused and will not be able to bother me."

Any possible ramifications from the horrible murder he had ordered did not occur to Mwanga. His only thought was now that Mukasa was out of the way none of the pages would refuse him. An increasing number of the boys had been eluding him. Others had fought and screamed and wept to escape his grip until in disgust he sent them away to prison. Mukasa's death, he thought, would put an end to that. The youngsters would be amenable, if only out of fear of a similar death, and when in time they forgot Mukasa, they would compete for the king's attentions as they had before Mukasa got at them. In thinking this, Mwanga overlooked the presence in the royal court of Charles Lwanga, who, as Mukasa's assistant, was now chief of the pages. Lwanga, for the same reasons as Mukasa, deplored the king's perversion, and he quickly called the Catholic boys together and warned them to expect accelerated demands from Mwanga. The boys promised they would not submit. That night when Mwanga sent for one of the boys who had previously resisted him, it was Charles Lwanga who went to his rooms. Mwanga was surprised to see him, then furious to hear his pleadings in defense of the boy's purity.

"Do you want to burn, too?" Mwanga asked.

"I would prefer it to what you ask of me," said Lwanga.

"Keep on as you are and you'll get your wish," Mwanga warned.

Lwanga kept on. A strange and inexplicable calm came over the pages. They knew that by disobeying the king they were risking their lives, but they did not care. Mwanga had threatened them all, separately and collectively, yet they remained as unmoved as if he had merely frowned at them. One morning during the court audience, he ordered those who prayed with the white men to step to one side. About forty did, and Mwanga told them that they could all consider themselves condemned to death. As soon as they could, they hurried to Father Lourdel and begged to be baptized, which he had kept from them in adherence to Lavigerie's instructions that no one should receive the sacrament without four years' preparation, except in the case of imminent death. On the grounds of the excep-

176

ion, the priests had baptized some before leaving Uganda during Mutesa's reign; under the circumstances, they felt justified of exercising the exception again. Then, with the weird vacillation peculiar to him, Mwanga told the boys that they could pray as they wished, so long as they did not attempt to influence other pages who had not already joined their group.

The emotional extremes of Mwanga puzzled everyone. It was well known that he had killed Mukasa because of the plot he fancied existed between the man and Lourdel, yet Mwanga was openly hurt and pouted like a child when Lourdel stayed away from the royal court for any length of time. Mwanga would one day thrash a reluctant page until he bled, then an hour later chide the youngster affectionately as if he were a naughty son who has misbehaved. He would send two or three freshly butchered antelope to his large harem, then hike into the room while the women feasted, accuse them all of gluttony, and have one of them killed as an example to the others. His dislike for Mackay was a popular fact, but occasionally he would walk arm in arm with the missionary through the village or greet him with profuse warmth in the presence of the White Fathers. He would invite to his palace for a sumptuous banquet the mourning relatives of a chief he had ordered killed a day or two before and display such sincere friendship that he seemed completely unaware of the great sadness he had caused them. In the same conversation in which he complained of a hangover from too much drink and exhaustion from too much vice he would lead Father Lourdel into a serious discussion of purity and the saints. He would for days hang on to the Katikiro's every word as if the older man were Plato himself, then turn around in a flash of temper, denounce the prime minister, and threaten to throw him out of the country. People who liked the king or loathed him were equally bewildered, and they could not decide whether he had lost his conscience, his memory, or his mind.

After a fortnight of outrageous rudeness toward the White Fathers, Mwanga appeared at the mission one day with gifts of chickens and goats. Several of the Catholic pages were there, and he smiled at them and waved and patted the heads of those who were near as if he were their grandfather instead a young man almost their own age. He said to Lourdel: "I understand that Father Livinhac is back."

"Yes," Lourdel said. "He's at the mission on the southern shores of the lake. He's a bishop now."

"So I was told. How wonderful. Is he coming to see me?"

"I doubt it," said Lourdel, "unless you specifically invite him."

Mwanga threw up his hands helplessly. "Of course I invite him. But since when do I have to invite my friends to come and see me? My house is always open to them; everything I have is theirs. Doesn't Bishop Livinhac know that I love him?"

Lourdel: "I believe he had that impression at one time."

"Well," Mwanga said, "it is just as true now. I want to see him. If it's all right with you, I'll send my boats today to fetch him. You can send one of your priests along, if you like, to convince him how badly I want him here, and when he arrives, I'll have a big party at the palace, for him and you and all the Catholics. Do you think he'd like that?"

"Oh, I'm sure."

Mwanga stepped to Lourdel and took his hand. "Father," he said softly, emotionally, "don't be cool to me. It is very lonely being king and I need the friends I have."

"I will be your friend as long as you want me to be," Lourdel said, soberly.

Mwanga smiled happily, nodded with content, then walked away, almost skipping. That day the boats left for the south of the lake and Livinhac came back. But he had to wait a week before Mwanga even acknowledged the traditional gifts of a visitor he had sent to the palace. When he finally saw the king, his reception was cold and impudently brief. There was no party.

The presence of Bishop Livinhac in Uganda stirred Catholic fervor. There were processions and confirmations and baptisms and marriages and pontifical Masses. A thousand people were going to the mission every day for instructions, among them the sister of the king, the son of the Katikiro, and the nephew of the chief justice. The sudden activity annoyed Mwanga, if only because it detracted from the attentions which he felt should be directed toward him. He soon regretted that he had brought Bishop Livinhac to Uganda

178

and he resumed his persistent nagging of anything Catholic, particularly the pages.

Then occurred a series of incidents which pushed Mwanga beyond the point of return. One night there was a great explosion near the beer house where he was drinking with friends which shook the building. Mwanga dashed out, shouting that the British were coming to revenge the murder of Bishop Hannington. It took several hours to calm him down. The explosion had been caused by a fire in the ammunition hut. The next afternoon, a freak African storm burst in a clear sky. There was one crash of thunder, one bolt of lightning. The lightning struck one of the Katikiro's private storehouses just outside the village and set it burning to the ground. Soon afterwards, Mwanga's palace caught fire and burned. Suspicious of the gods, Mwanga had a house built eight miles away and moved there, convinced that the capital itself was doomed. Next, a canoe caravan on the lake overturned, and the crew and the cargo were lost. Two days later the queen mother's palace burned down. The following week, Mwanga's army lost an important battle to hostile neighbors to the west. During the fight, a great warrior who had been a favorite of the king was killed. On top of all that, a letter came from the British consul at Zanzibar, protesting the murder of Bishop Hannington, demanding an explanation, and threatening reprisals. Then the princess who had been studying catechism with the priests was assigned guardian of the temple of a former king and arriving there found the house full of fetishes and amulets, all of which she destroyed. She also chopped to pieces and burned a sacred pagan object her mother had given her for special protection. Anyone else would have been killed for this; the Katikiro worked hard to force Mwanga to punish his half-sister despite the fact that she was a member of the royal family.

Mwanga had many problems. There was to be one more, an incident so trivial that ordinarily Mwanga would not even have lost his temper over it. Under the circumstances, it destroyed him.

He had gone hunting one afternoon with Andrew Kaggwa, the head of the royal drummers, and a few others. The decision had been a hasty one, and no one was officially informed that the king was going away. It was protocol that no matter how briefly the king left his compound he was to be welcomed back formally. When

179

Mwanga returned from hunting, there was no one at the gate to greet him.

Piqued, he asked: "Where is everybody?"

Kaggwa explained: "No one saw you go out, Sire. That is why there is no one here."

"That's a lie," Mwanga said. "They all knew I was away, so they all ran to the white men. They do it all the time. I used to be king around here, but now it looks as if the white men are. Where is Mwafu?"

Mwafu was the Katikiro's son, given to Mwanga as a personal page. Someone said: "I saw him a little while ago with Sebuggawo."

"The Catholic?"

"Yes, Your Majesty."

"Send both to me when you find them."

An hour later, Mwafu and Denis Sebuggawo, both in their teens, stood before the king. Mwanga asked: "Mwafu, where have you been?"

"With Denis."

"And what were you doing?"

"He was teaching me religion."

"You know that is against my orders?"

"Yes, Sire."

"Did your father send you here to learn religion or to serve me?"

"To serve you, Sire."

"You have not done that, have you?"

"As well as my religion permits, Sire."

"Are you already a Catholic?"

"No, but I hope the fathers will baptize me soon."

"You know that you will be displeasing both your own father and me?"

"I'm afraid I must."

Mwanga gripped his chair to control his temper. He turned to Denis. "You are nephew of the prime minister, aren't you?"

"He is the chief of my clan."

"Is it the custom among your people to disobey your chief?"

"No, Sire."

"But you did."

"How, Sire?"

180

"By becoming a Catholic."

"Yes."

"And now you are trying to convert the Katikiro's son."

"He asked me about my religion, Sire, so I've been telling him."

"Despite my orders against exactly that?"

"Yes."

"You know what I do to people who disobey me, don't you?"

"You kill them, Sire."

"Then you are not surprised that I am going to kill you, are you?"
The boy said nothing.

Mwanga said: "When you leave this room, you will go to the executioner and tell him I said you are to be killed. Do you understand?"

The boy nodded, terrified. He turned.

"Just a moment," Mwanga said. "I haven't dismissed you yet." He stood up and took a lance from a nearby guard and broke it over the boy's shoulder. "Now you may go." Then he turned on Mwafu and hit his face with all his strength. The boy slid across the room. Teeth dropped from his mouth. "Go and show your friends what I have done and tell them I have only started."

Then Mwanga told the guards: "Lock the gates. No Christian will get out of here tonight."

On his way to his quarters, Mwanga came upon a young man named Honorat, who, with Charles Lwanga, was a director of the royal household. "You are a Christian, aren't you?" Mwanga asked.

"You know me, Master," Honorat said. "You know I am."

To the guards at his heels Mwanga said curtly: "Castrate him."

Going on, Mwanga glanced into a supply hut and saw another youth. He called: "Aren't you a Christian, too?"

"I have taken the religion of Mr. Mackay," the young man said.

"Come here then."

In his hand Mwanga still held part of the lance he had used on Denis Sebuggawo. He beat the young man in the face with it until blood poured from open wounds, and when he fell to the ground, the king kicked him until he lost consciousness.

In the pages' barracks the Christian boys gathered around Charles Lwanga to hear him relate what they already knew: the king was on a rampage which might mean the death of all of them. "Your only

181

chance," he said, "is to deny your religion."

"I'll never do that." The boy who spoke was Mbaga-Tuzinde nephew of the chief executioner. The others quickly agreed with him

"I hoped you'd say that," Lwanga said. "Then we have decided We will stick together now, no matter what happens. Don't be afraid whatever the king does to us. We would be better off dead than to lose our souls just to please him."

In the morning, there was great activity. All the chiefs had been called to the palace for a special session. The pages were ordered to present themselves to Mwanga for judgment. Executioners holding Denis Sebuggawo postponed their task because they thought he being the Katikiro's nephew, might be reprieved, but when no word came, they took him into the woods and killed him by stabbing him many times with daggers. They left him there. Vultures descended and devoured him.

Lourdel and Mackay were at the palace at dawn, pleading, begging, demanding to see the king, but the guards had been given orders to keep them out. The Katikiro refused to see them, the queen mother, the chief justice, even chiefs whose sons were pages—all ignored the attempts of the two missionaries to save the boys Mackay, unable even in this crisis to control his anti-Catholicism later wrote home: "The Romish Vicar Apostolic of the Nyanza arrived in Uganda a month ago. We asked him and his brethren to aid us in trying to save the lives of some forty Christians who had just been arrested and who were sentenced to death for their faith We hoped that by our making a joint petition to the king, he would less likely refuse to listen to our appeal. But the Romish Bishop refused to interfere, piously adding, *'Dignetur Omnipotens adjuvare credentes et sperantes in Eum'*—in other words, 'Let God help them if He will; we cannot!'" Mackay's "other words" were an extremely loose translation. More accurately: "May the Almighty deign to help these who believe and hope in Him." This was not resignation; it was a prayer, a prayer exclaimed by Catholics in sudden desperation since the first moments of the Church. From it, Catholics took heart, trusting that somehow God would help. There were several ways He could help the pages, and there was one way He did.

Mwanga had made up his mind that the pages should die, and the only hesitance he felt was the fact that they were all the sons and

182

nephews of important men, men who had given them to him not only as a gift during their boyhood but because of the influential futures that could be theirs if they grew up in the king's favor. Killing off some forty of the country's choice youth required a certain boldness. Before he went ahead with it, Mwanga wanted to be sure that there would be no repercussions from the chiefs. When he had all the chiefs together in the audience hall, he presented his case against the pages, naming them, citing their disobedience and disloyalty. Delicately he hinted that the behavior of the boys reflected upon the parents, and he indicated he was most displeased with this and was not quite decided who should receive the punishment.

One chief rose and said: "Your Majesty, when we gave you these boys, they were good boys. If something has happened to them, it must be because of the white men they met at the capital. That could not be considered our fault, and if they have changed, they are not our sons any longer. Kill them, Master, and we will give you new boys."

Other chiefs wildly seconded the idea. Mwanga said: "Then they shall die."

Again he called the pages together and ordered those who prayed with the white men to step aside. Thirty-one of them did; twenty-four of them were Catholics, seven were Protestants. He gave the boys one chance to deny their faith, but they all refused. It was when Mwanga had turned the boys over to the executioners that Father Lourdel managed to break through the guards and get into the audience hall. Before Lourdel could reach the king, the court session was dismissed, and the king, surrounded by a heavy guard, hurried off to his private quarters.

The rest of the day was a fury of confusion. Mwafu, the Katikiro's son, was reprieved, a decision he accepted in a howl of tears and refusals. A Protestant boy was given to a Moslem chief who wanted him, but while being carried off, he fought so wildly that he was immediately beaten to death. Older young men—soldiers, clerks, court officials—were determined to die with the youngsters they were unable to save. Andrew Kaggwa was decapitated in front of the Katikiro's house; Pontain Ngondwe, a famous warrior, was stabbed by lances at the gates of the royal enclosure. Mathias Kalemba, who had been a Catholic leader in the Mengo district, had his arms cut off at the elbow and his legs at the knee. Then arteries and veins were carefully tied so that he would not die too quickly. Bits of flesh were sliced from his body and roasted in front of his eyes. Noah Mawaggali, a county chief, was tied to a tree, and guards spent an hour using him for target practice. A hundred people died that day, because they were Christians, because they were suspected of being Christians, or because someone who disliked them accused them of having once uttered a Christian expression.

The only calm was among the pages. They behaved more as if they were on their way to a picnic. Sixteen miles from the palace was a valley called Namugongo; a jail and an execution site were maintained there. The pages, tied in tight bunches like asparagus, inched the distance in two days. They thought the whole thing was very funny and laughed all the way. During a rest period when the boys were untied, one page approached the guards and said: "I don't see the sense in walking all the way to Namugongo just to be burned. Kill me now and let's get it over with." The guards whipped him with clubs but not fiercely enough, and he cried: "All right, all right! If you won't put your heart into it, let's do it your way." He went back to his place and waited to be tied again to the others.

The guards, the executioners, people along the road were all puzzled by this strange welcome to death. Ordinarily, the boys should be screaming for mercy. Oddly, they seemed impatient to die, not to escape pain but to escape life. They joked about what they knew waited ahead for them, they teased their guards who threatened them with the severest torture, and the only thing that appalled them was the suggestion from anyone that they save themselves by rejecting their religion. Though the boys were indeed young, none of them were children. They had seen death, accidental or by command, often enough to know what it was, how horrible it could be. They had spent two or three years in the royal court among intellectuals, artists, and shrewd politicians, and there was little about the ways of men they had not learned. By the standards of their time, several of them were old enough to marry and have children. Most of them had been Christians a very short time; several had been baptized by Charles Lwanga the night they were arrested. The baptisms, however, had been an outward display of an inner conviction, a conviction strong enough to make the boys impatient o die. From the White Fathers they had learned a new conception of God. He was not Katonda, who had made the world and then abandoned it. He was a God of love, directly interested in each living being, and He had established a moral code with God as its reward. To violate the code risked not only the wrath of God, but the loss of God, and the pages refused that risk even at the price of their lives. Their grasp of this fundamental Christian precept was remarkable, and it was the factor which kept them steadfast in their decision. Anything else—affection or gratitude toward the priests, hero worship for men like Lwanga or Mukasa, boyish pride, the frantic giddiness of the moment—could not have survived the full week the pages waited in prison for their execution. Convinced that adherence to the precept made Heaven theirs, they were eager to get there, and nothing could dissuade them. Twice the chief executioner tried to talk his nephew into rejecting his religion in order to save his own life, but the youngster refused. He was even sent away to relatives, but he returned to Namugongo every day, and at last he told his uncle impatiently: "Please leave me alone. I know what I'm doing."

The number of imprisoned pages rose and fell daily. New ones arrived from the palace, three more were reprieved against their tearful protests, several died in prison from the lack of food, water, or air. All week, Lourdel, Mackay and Livinhac battled ceaselessly to reach the king and plead for the boys' lives. Only Livinhac got to him, but Mwanga would not revoke the death sentence. "But I will kill no more for the time being," he compromised.

On the night of June 2, the drums began, and the boys knew tomorrow was the day. They prayed and sang hymns and tried to sleep, but the executioners—almost a hundred of them had been called in from all corners of the country—had started their preliminaries of drinking and dancing. It was a noisy, sleepless night. Dawn came white hot. When the boys were led out of the dark, musty prison, they blinked in the sudden sunlight and for several moments they could not see. The valley came into focus; the boys saw in front of them the small mountain of wood and reeds which was to be their pyre. Nearby the chief executioner still argued with his nephew, but the boy was adamant. Rather than send the youngster to the flames alive, the chief executioner ordered his aides to club the boy to death first before wrapping him in a shroud of reeds.

One by one the pages stepped forward and permitted themselves to be wrapped in reeds, and then they were placed on the pyre. Charles Lwanga refused to be tied up, arranged his own deathbed and stretched out on it. The guardian of the sacred torch came and applied the flame to the dry, brittle wood at Lwanga's feet. It caught quickly. Flames raced along the logs, encircling Lwanga in a wall of fire. Closing his eyes, he made the sign of the cross, then folded his hands in prayer, his lips moving soundlessly. He gave no indication of being aware that he was on fire.

On signal from the chief executioner, the guardian of the sacred torch went to the huge pyre and put the flame to it. When the pages saw the first smoke rise above them, they began to pray aloud. One of the assistant executioners let loose a high-pitched war cry, and the others joined him in a mad dance around the enormous fire. Leaping and shouting, they continued as the flames soared, stopping only when they became aware of a very strange thing:

There were no screams of pain coming from the burning pages, only the sounds of their prayers, their voices quite normal, growing softer and softer until the last boy died. The executioners could not believe what their ears heard, what their eyes saw. They stood there quietly, stunned, afraid, until the flames finally flickered out.

The White Fathers that morning were under virtual house arrest in order to keep them from going to the pages. Since dawn they had knelt in the chapel, saying the prayers for the dying and, when news came that the fire had been started, the prayers for the dead. It was noon when a man arrived from Namugongo and told them how the boys seemed to have died without feeling the flames that had burned them to ashes.

"This was how God helped them," Bishop Livinhac said, and he led the priests back to the chapel for prayers of thanksgiving for the peaceful deaths. It was while the priests were intent at the prayers that Bishop Livinhac suddenly remembered that this June 3, 1886, was the Feast of the Ascension.

XVI

THE thousands of miles which separated Algiers and Uganda and the months necessary for letters to travel the distance did not in any way diminish the horror of the massacre when news of it finally reached Lavigerie. After reading Bishop Livinhac's report, Lavigerie sank back in his chair and was helpless against the tears that streamed from his eyes. "They are saints, they are saints," he muttered over and over. Desolate with shock, he was useless the rest of the day, and his worried secretary suggested: "Your Grace, let's go to the chapel and pray for the boys." Lavigerie shook his head. "No," he said, "let's go to the chapel and ask these boys to pray for us. They can do more for Africa now than we ever could."

There was much that remained to be done. The greatest job, implanting in the hearts of all Africans the same kind of faith the pages had demonstrated, would require centuries. Whatever else the White Fathers might do for the people, all energies must be slanted toward that end or all the good done would be meaningless. Africa had many needs, and it was within the scope of the White Fathers to meet as many as possible, but always with the intention of bringing the people closer to God. No matter what was done for the African's mind or body, unless his spiritual development progressed as well, then

Africa could only limp to its place in the family of nations—a family which already had enough spiritual paralytics, a family which had already contributed too many of its own spiritual diseases to Africa. To combat the spread of such contagions, Lavigerie found himself continually embroiled in the affairs of two continents. To give Africa a soul, he had constantly to remind Europe that it already had one, and this was a reminder that was not always welcomed. Men in France had risen frequently against kings who threatened their liberties, yet when these same men assumed important political offices, they were reluctant to grant liberties to men of Algeria who wanted nothing more than what the French had. And though one European country after another had gone on record as being opposed to slavery, the African still had a price tag around his neck, for sale in Arab marketplaces throughout the Middle East. Lavigerie was convinced that as long as Africans suffered the indignities—the immorality, indeed—of slavery, Christianity in Africa would be a hypocritical farce. The African would justifiably reject it and would remain a victim of the fears and terrors of paganism. The key to the problem, Lavigerie felt, was therefore in the capitals of Europe.

Every European country that had adventured into Africa either participated in the slave trade or condoned it. In just one century, over four million slaves had entered the United States alone, and this startling number were only the survivors, some ten per cent of those who had started out on the long trek from the Africa interior. At such a rate, it was only a matter of time before the continent would be depopulated. Implicit in the traffic was the explanation why Christianity had practically stood still in Africa for more than a thousand years. During most of that time, the only people to penetrate the continent were Moslems who, as they spread out in search of commerce, established their religion and the slavery it allowed. The Europeans who entered Africa centuries later found, wherever they went, that Moslems had been there before them. With the exception of a few coastal areas, the Moslems had no political or religious competition in Africa until well after the discovery of America. The prize of North America held European interest for almost three hundred years, and Africa's only contribution to the development of the New World was the manpower that arrived in chains. All the slaves had been acquired through deals with Moslems, either

African or Arabic. Besides the slaves destined for the United States, millions more were being transported across the continent—and dying en route—to Egypt, Ethiopia, Arabia, and Asia. Europe's profit-seeking eyes were on those countries as well as on the New World, as future colonies or markets. Either way, the European rulers were not going to do anything to risk their positions in Africa and Asia by denouncing the slave trade openly practiced there, even though all Christian leaders—particularly the Catholic Church—repeatedly and loudly complained against it. Priests going to Africa went as chaplains to European troops or pastors to European settlers, and invariably they were instructed by their homeland governments to leave the native population alone. Even without the orders, the priests would have made little headway: certainly the natives would have been unimpressed by the message of Christianity when one of its basic precepts—the brotherhood of man—was being violated on all sides by Christians themselves. Perhaps the Catholic Church should have been much more forceful in its European spheres of influence, yet after the Protestant Reformation all European countries realized they could ignore the moral protest of the Vatican without losing any of their international stature. To be effective, the Church then had to move its strategy off St. Peter's Hill and into the various countries. Slave traffic was officially banned in England in 1838, in France in 1848, and in the United States in 1865. Since the United States was not materially interested in the colonization of Africa, it was the only nation which applied its new law to its international transactions. Thirty years later, some Frenchmen were still in favor of permitting slave trade in the North African territories, and England was doing nothing to stop the Arab traders in her territories at the Equator. For that matter, neither were Germany or Portugal. Under the political pressures imposed on them by their homelands, Catholic priests in Africa were in the sad predicament of being unable to practice what they were not even allowed to preach. Their effectiveness, therefore, as men of God was greatly restricted. Lavigerie shrugged off the restriction.

To each White Fathers' caravan entering Central Africa, Lavigerie gave orders and money to buy slaves from the traders. Then he gathered together the former Papal Zouaves with the intention of sending them into Africa to form armies among the Africans to fight the Arabs if necessary. There were world-wide repercussions to the plan, particularly from Moslem countries. The Turkish ambassador to France officially complained to the French government, and the Paris newspaper *French Republic* accused Lavigerie of being a fanatic who cried "Charge!" against Mohammedanism and who appealed to secular powers against Islam and asked them to exterminate it under a humanitarian guise. Lavigerie replied to the paper:

I have never during my long life cried "Charge!" at any man under the pretext of religion. I will not begin now, especially when the Church feels every day, more and more and everywhere, the bitterness of the hateful persecution by atheists. I have in particular for the Moslems of good faith only sentiments of paternal benevolence. I am ready not to attack them but to serve them, as I have always done when they needed me. The only thing I wish to exterminate is slavery, which is turning Africa to blood.

Lavigerie was then in his early sixties; arthritis had crippled him severely, and two serious illnesses had almost proved fatal. Twice he asked Pope Leo XIII for permission to resign from his archbishopric, and both times the Pope asked him to stay on. Lavigerie was already the Archbishop of Algiers, and the missionary prefectures of the Sahara and Sudan and of Equatorial Africa were under his jurisdiction; this made him bishop of an area twice the size of the United States. When, in 1882, the French Navy entered the harbor of Tunis and by its presence convinced the Bey of Tunis to turn the country over to French protection, the Pope appointed Lavigerie Bishop of Tunisia as well. That same year, the Pope raised Lavigerie to the cardinalate, then named him to the primacy of Africa, thus making him the ranking prelate of the entire continent. Each time Lavigerie tried to beg off, the Pope assured that he had his reasons for what he was doing.

While Lavigerie awaited the reasons, he continued his campaign to buy slaves. The project kept him perpetually bankrupt. When archaeologists sponsored by Lavigerie discovered third-century sacred vessels in the ruins of St. Cyprian's cathedral at Carthage, Lavigerie immediately sold them to get cash for more slaves. He kept up a flood of letters to France, begging for money, and whenever he could, he went to Paris to make personal appeals to his friends. As full a job as this was, he nevertheless carried on with his duties as the Archbishop of Algiers and Tunis, building churches, colleges, primary schools, hospitals, and orphanages, then tracking down the personnel to run them. He continued guiding the White Fathers and White Sisters through their growing pains and sending them off to the Sahara and Equatorial missions. Too, convinced of the sanctity of the Baganda martyrs, he initiated the complicated preliminaries for their canonization, which eventually took its first step forward when the pages were beatified by Pope Benedict XV on June 6, 1920. Isolated from other leading churchmen, Lavigerie maintained a voluminous correspondence with them. He had been instrumental in making the traditional papal infallibility into official doctrine, an act which did not go down well with some French bishops, and after the deed was done, Lavigerie had to spend a lot of time soothing them back into the friendliness they previously demonstrated by assisting his impoverished archdiocese. Lavigerie was undoubtedly doing the work of ten men, and there is the likelihood that even the ten of them could not have achieved all that he did alone. Certainly he had an abundance of stamina; he had also intelligence, good judgment, and vision; moreover, he had zeal, that impatient determination to cram into every hour so much service to God that each day did not merely come to an end: it burst at the seams.

Early in 1888, Lavigerie received from Leo XIII a request for documentation of slavery in Africa. He replied with a lengthy, detailed report. Four hundred thousand people a year, he said, were being taken from their homes, and scarcely a fourth of them lived to reach their destinations. Those who did not die from hunger, disease, or exhaustion were killed by the slave traders. Any who tried to escape had their arms and legs slit with a sword, and, as an example, others were gathered around to watch the victim bleed to death. The legs of anyone who walked too slowly were beaten with clubs, and anyone who was sullen or rebellious had his tongue cut off or his eyes gouged out. The sick were abandoned at the side of the road; the dead were left where they dropped. The slimming ranks of the caravan were reinforced by new acquisitions as the traders moved eastward to the coast. Mostly, the slaves were captured during attacks on a village, attacks led by Africans in the pay of Arab

191

traders; there were, too, many chiefs who were willing to sell their own people for cash, for guns, for a piece of silk. Arabs could buy three young women for a goat, the average man for fifty cartridges, a child for a packet of tobacco. But when the White Fathers tried to buy the slaves and give them freedom and protection, the price soared so high that buying five or six slaves could bankrupt a mission.

The caravans' destinations were Egypt, Ethiopia, Zanzibar, Arabia, and beyond into the Middle East. The Khedive of Egypt had said: "I prefer white slaves, but if I cannot get them, I'll take black." And he took them by the thousands. Lavigerie put the full guilt for African slavery upon the Moslems. He wrote the Pope:

All Moslems are ready, when they can do it without danger, to buy and sell slaves. Turkey itself prevents slavery only for the sake of appearances, and imperfectly at that. In its African and Asia provinces, the interpretors of the Koran do not condemn slavery. Moslem judges who judge according to the Koran never pronounce sentence against it. I will continue to say aloud what I have seen, heard and touched with my own hands, because it is necessary so that Europe may know of it and finally put a stop to these infamies.

A few weeks after Lavigerie's report reached the Vatican, Leo XIII sent an encyclical to the bishops of Brazil, where slavery, both imported and domestic, was rampant. Much of the encyclical had been taken verbatim from Lavigerie's report. At the end of it, the Pope asked the Brazil bishops to do all they could to bring an end to slavery in their country. It was a long shot, a blast at European countries which the Pope hoped would ricochet from South America. The Church's position in Europe at the moment was too delicate for a direct assault: what would happen next in Brazil would determine action on the continent. The next month, during the silver-jubilee celebration of Leo XIII's reign, Brazil King Pedro II went personally to the Vatican and told the Pope that in response to his encyclical and as evidence of the Brazilians' obedient love for him, slavery as of that day would be forever abolished from the country. The quick action was indeed a triumph for the Pope, and the power of it was felt throughout Europe. Lavigerie was in Rome at the time, and with him were twenty-four children he had ransomed, twelve Africans and twelve Arabs. He presented them to the Pope as evidence of what could be done in Africa to save people from the slave

192

traders. The Pope blessed the children, and he told Lavigerie:

"It is especially on you, my son, that we count for the success of these difficult African works and missions. We know your active and intelligent zeal; we know all that you have done up to now, and we are confident that you will not rest until you have brought your great enterprise to a good end."

That was the go-ahead Lavigerie needed. The next day the Pope provided him with funds to cover his traveling expenses, and he left on a speaking tour of Europe to raise money to buy slaves and to arouse the people against slavery itself. The tour was a sensation; thousands of dollars poured in and were sent immediately to Africa to purchase slaves. The tour finished, Lavigerie started the rounds all over again, this time leaving most of the money he raised in the country itself in order to establish antislavery societies which he hoped would be able to pressure governments into official action against the slave-trading countries. He set up a dozen such committees throughout Europe, and all of them went immediately to work on their governments. So incited were the people by Lavigerie's reports on African slavery that hundreds of men volunteered to go to Africa for him to fight the slave traders and thousands of men offered to join their country's armies if war was the only way the slave traffic could be stopped. Chancellor Otto von Bismarck promised to prohibit slavery in any African zones under German influence and he offered to back Lavigerie as far as he wanted to go. European newspapers carried daily stories about Lavigerie. The Paris *Le Matin,* far from a Catholic paper, said that though Lavigerie was a bishop, he should be followed like a general. The campaign seemed off to a wonderful start.

But there were objectors as well. There were men in Europe who were making money off slavery, directly or indirectly. Lavigerie was a threat to them. Atheism was almost a fad through the continent, and those who adhered to it resented Lavigerie because he was a clergyman. Some Protestant circles worried that the powerful movement led by a cardinal might restore the Catholic Church to its former prominence. Arab organizations, official and unofficial, complained vociferously, denying all the accusations. Companies and government agencies which did business with the Middle East were afraid that the uproar would endanger their positions and turn the

Moslem countries in another direction. All such quarters criticized Lavigerie severely as a rabble-rouser, an ambitious prelate with his eye on the papacy, and a Vatican spy assigned to some sort of denominational sabotage.

Surprisingly rancorous were Protestant missionaries returning from Africa who charged that slaves ransomed by the White Fathers were no better off than they had been before, that they were forced to live on mission property and work for the priests in the fields and at constructions, that they were pressured into becoming Catholics on the threat of being turned out and thus probably recaptured, and that some of them were even bribed into baptism to keep them away from Protestantism. It was a serious accusation to make and one which, uttered, sadly took root, however shallow, and even today has not completely vanished. It amounted to a fraud indictment against the seventy White Fathers then in Central Africa, men who had spent their entire youth preparing for the priesthood, who by now had suffered years of heat and rain and disease and death and murder, and who were, by the nature of their priesthood, morally convinced that anyone who entered the Catholic Church with motives other than the salvation of his soul, and who subsequently received the sacraments shamfully, was thereby guilty of the greatest sacrilege and warranted the deepest hell. To contribute to that sacrilege would be to share its guilt, and rare would be the priest who considered a conversion worth that price. The sadness of the accusation was in its being made by men who otherwise were of the highest intentions, who had suffered as much in Africa as the White Fathers and were willing to go through it again. And the pity of the accusation was that it was proffered as an explanation of the White Fathers' success. As for the treatment of the ransomed children, it would be fitting at this point to detour in order to tell the story of one of them:

Adrian Atiman was never certain of his birthdate; he believed he was born around 1866; he was raised in a village on the Niger banks near Timbuktu. In 1875, he was kidnaped by Taureg and sold to slave traders in Timbuktu for a jug of salt. The Arabs put him in a sack and took him by camel across the Sahara. He had little to eat, and all he was given to drink was camel urine. He was sold twice before he arrived at the slave market in Metlili, where the White Fathers saw him and bought him for the equivalent of seventeen dollars. He was the first Negro boy the priests had purchased in Algeria; the rest had all been Arabs. The priests sent him to Algiers where he met Lavigerie. After a few days of rest and good food at Lavigerie's house, he was put into an orphanage and given an education. In 1881, after being questioned by the White Fathers about what he wanted to do with his life, he and nineteen others were sent to Malta to study medicine at the University of the Hospital Knights of St. John. The next year, after seven years with the White Fathers, he and eleven others were finally baptized—at their own requests and after the usual catechism preparations. When Lavigerie took the ransomed youngsters to present to the Pope in 1888, Adrian Atiman was among them. That summer he finished his training and he was free to go wherever he chose: he chose to join a White Fathers' caravan into Central Africa, first spending a year studying tropical diseases at a Zanzibar hospital run by the Holy Ghost Fathers. At the end of March, 1889, he arrived on the shores of Lake Tanganyika, and he remained there for seventy years. Always he considered himself a man of religion as well as a man of medicine. Often he said: "I am a catechist before all else." Thus as he traveled through the bush to his patients, he treated the soul as well as the body. It is impossible to estimate the number of Africans who became Christians through his influence. His own life was deeply spiritual; those who knew him well suspected he might have become a priest, had he not considered himself too old to begin the long studies. He surprised everyone when he announced his decision to marry a Wabembe princess. He was not in love with her; he openly admitted this, but the Wabembe were a hostile tribe, belligerent toward the missionaries, and Atiman believed that what amounted to an intertribal marriage would bring peace. It brought peace to the community, but not to Atiman's home, for the princess had eyes for every man around, and it was several years before Atiman was able to calm her down to becoming a faithful wife and mother. Their son, Joseph, eventually entered the priesthood. As a doctor, Atiman was to receive a salary, as did all doctors who went to the missions, but the most he ever accepted was fourteen dollars a month during the years he had to support his wife and son. On the death of his wife and the ordination of his son, he refused further salary. He likewise refused payments from the white people he served, as well as from the Belgian government when he treated soldiers during the World War I, fighting in Africa against the Germans. Though he was not a surgeon, he taught himself surgery from medical journals, and there are hundreds of people alive today because of this. Nor was he a research scientist, but because supplies were often slow in arriving from Europe, he made a study of local plants and was thus able to prepare his own medicines from them. In this way, he was able to conquer any number of epidemics that burst out among the people. Time and again he refused important positions with the German, British, and Belgian governments, instead giving his services without charge whenever he was needed. Fees forced upon him by official agencies he gave to the missions. He taught his wife to be his nurse, and he taught the profession to many others. A social problem of the times was the heavy dowry required of prospective husbands, which often made a marriage impossible and turned a young girl into an item for sale to the highest bidder. To counteract this, Atiman became a marriage broker, lowering the dowries of each marriage he handled and even succeeding in doing away with them in many cases. When age made surgery impossible for him, he continued in regular medicine, using his free time to teach catechism. Africans along the Tanganyika shores had so much respect and love for him that they went to him constantly with their problems and he became somewhat of a judge in his area. During the course of his life, he received ten decorations: the French Legion of Honor, three awards from the Belgium government, the *Pro Ecclesia et Pontifice* from Leo XIII, the *Bene Merenti* from Pius XI, and Pius XII made him a commander in the Order of St. Sylvester; among the four decorations from the British government was the Wellcome Medal of the Royal African Society, and the only other medical missionary ever to receive it has been Albert Schweitzer.

Adrian Atiman died in April, 1956, ending a career that made him outstanding in many ways, yet in many other ways he was no different from countless slave boys ransomed by the White Fathers and trained to take their own places in their own society in constructive service to their own people. But the Protestant missionaries who misjudged the White Fathers in 1888 had no way of foreseeing that.

Undaunted by the complaints, Lavigerie concentrated on what he felt would be the strong influence of an aroused people. The antislavery committees he established across the European continent grew into regiments of forceful doorbangers at every palace. Yet Lavigerie also knew that as long as the committees remained nationalistic in structure, if not in attitude, the full effect of a unified Europe against the Arab world would be lost. It was, unfortunately, an era of great nationalism, the age of growing empires, and nations were jealous of their neighbors. Italy was annoyed with France for grabbing off Tunisia where the settler population was Italian five-to-one. The Germans who had lost out completely in North America were not going to let that happen again in Africa. The Spanish and the Portuguese both claimed sizable portions of Africa for themselves. The King of the Belgians had the Congo all to himself, and Britain, at the high point of her colonial expansion, grabbed more than anyone else. There were, of course, fine people throughout Europe who were against slavery, strongly so, and all of the rulers opposed it, and everyone seemed perfectly willing to go along with the ideas of the antislavery committees, but there was a vast distance between the crown and the colony, both literally and figuratively, and within it lay all the troubles. One way to overcome the troubles, Lavigerie felt, was to unite the antislavery committees into one organization which could assure international co-operation and international control, thus safeguarding against the laxity of any single committee toward the shortcomings of its own country. In that was the rub. However high-minded antislavery leaders might be, they were reluctant to join with foreigners who might overrule them, outvote them, or gang up against them at conferences. However much a committee wanted its own country to campaign against slavery, it did not want its national failings pointed out by others. Furthermore, however sincerely rulers themselves felt about the Arab slave traffic, they were hesitant to do anything which might endanger the positions of their industries that did business with the Middle East.

It was a miserable predicament, a delicate predicament, and no field of combat for a man who was afraid of the kings of countries or the kings of industry. Lavigerie was not that kind of man. One of his speaking tours took him to Brussels, and he began an address with:

"I am going to say things many of you won't like, but I am a missionary, a priest, and I must tell the truth." The truth was in-

197

credible. Lavigerie told his audience of the slave traffic in the Belgian Congo and of the forced labor imposed by the King Leopold's own agents, of the mutilations inflicted upon the recalcitrant, of the cruelties toward the sick and the dying. Never before had the people heard such shocking descriptions from the lips of a clergyman. "I tell you these things," he said, "so that you can know what is going on and do something to stop it." At the moment, the best counteractant appeared to be the antislavery committees, and from that single audience twenty-three thousand francs were raised to support the Belgian organization. Lavigerie donated two thousand francs of his own to round out the figure.

Pushing his campaign into the highest circles, Lavigerie proposed to the rulers of Germany and England the idea of patrolling the Red Sea against vessels that were transhipping slaves from Africa across to Arabia, and it was through his efforts that the two countries agreed, on November 3, 1888, to set up a blockade along the East African coast to prohibit the shipments of slaves and arms and assuming the prerogative of inspecting all ships. In announcing the agreement to Parliament, Lord Salisbury credited Lavigerie with the plan. He also said that the French had expressed willingness to join the blockade, but a week later the French denied it. Instead, the French said, they would release a warship from the Indian Ocean fleet to take part in the blockade, with the understanding that this ship alone would have the right to inspect other French vessels. The distrust implied in the French specification weakened the entire vigilance. Soon the German and English were eying each other suspiciously, and before long, the ship inspection was restricted to vessels under five hundred tons. All German and English ships were well over that, and they were thus freed from the watchful inspections of competitors in the rush for anything Africa had to export.

Such unfortunate tactics detracted from what appeared on the surface to be Lavigerie's successful campaign. Convinced that final success would come only from truly international effort, Lavigerie worked toward that end. The idea won wide support among the press. The *Courier* of Brussels, *Tijd* of Holland, and the Catholic papers of France and Italy urged a conference of heads of state under the direction of Pope Leo XIII, identified by them as "the only prince personally disinterested among those who are disputing

Africa's future." Encouraged, the Pope appointed a committee of cardinals to study means by which all of Europe could be marshalled against slavery. Committee reports were sent to all the rulers of Europe, who in turn merely acknowledged them. Only Bismarck replied with praise and support of both the Pope and Lavigerie. From other sources came hints that Europe would never be united on anything, let alone the welfare of Africans thousands of miles away. Determined to prove the doubters wrong, Lavigerie decided to call an international conference of his own antislavery committees, hoping to bring from it a united all-Europe organization that could make itself heard throughout the continent. The next step, in all likelihood, would be a similar union of governments themselves. Lavigerie picked August 4, 1889, and Lucerne as the time and place of the meeting.

The meeting should have been a great success and might have been, but the nature of the human beast was such that he would oppose the second coming of Christ if it interfered with his own plans. There were factions of all nationalities and religions throughout Europe that opposed Lavigerie, because he was Catholic, because he was French, because he was a popular prelate, because he was a close friend of the Pope, because he had founded the White Fathers, because he was a real authority on Africa, and because at some time of his life he had said or done something that somebody didn't like. To such people, the motivation for the conference was secondary to their personal gripes. Lavigerie was well aware that there would be people at the conference who would do all they could to make it fail. There would be others who were not free to act. Because of his personal prestige, Lavigerie had been able, in setting up the national committees, to get prominent personalities to accept chairmanships, but that was when it appeared that the committees would do little more than raise money to buy slaves. The Lucerne conference, on the other hand, had all the earmarks of a semiofficial session at which binding agreements might be made. A few of the chairmen, involved in home politics and big business, were not free to enter such agreements. In order to elude antagonism directed at him personally, Lavigerie made known his plans to withdraw from the conference after making the welcoming address, thus leaving all decisions in the hands of the delegations. Also, to avoid railroading of any kind, there would be no unit vote, each delegate voting as he chose. Eight countries were to be represented at the conference; Holland, Switzerland, and the United States, not having active committees, would be present unofficially.

The first evidence of dirty work came from France. Thirteen of the seventeen French delegates announced at the last moment that they were unable to attend. As reasons they gave an upcoming election, important business conferences, sudden illness, overlooked previous commitments, and unavoidable rush trips to all parts of the world. In each case there was apparent pressure from sources inside and outside France. It was reasonable for Lavigerie to deduce that other delegations, now aware that the conference was intended to be far more than a tea party for philanthropists, would arrive hamstrung by political strings. Furthermore, to go on with the meeting under the circumstances gave France the out of claiming unfair representation in the vote on any agreement unfavorable to her. Already France had displayed her unwillingness to co-operate with other nations on plans which might stir intervention with her own maneuvers. The collapse of the French delegation, besides being a personal slap at Lavigerie, precluded any chance of effective agreements to submit to European officialdom. The day before the scheduled conference, Lavigerie wired all delegations that the meeting was indefinitely postponed.

Criticism raged down at him from all capitals. As reason for the postponement, he cited the depleted French delegation and suggested waiting until France could be fully represented. Other nations accused him, as a Frenchman, of favoring France, asking how he could expect all-Europe unity when he himself was a victim of nationalism. Bismarck announced that in view of his previous support of Lavigerie, he took the postponement as a direct affront against Germany. Rather than reveal the true details and thus expose to public embarrassment members of the French delegation who otherwise had been friendly toward him, Lavigerie let the storm thunder on. At the height of it, Belgian King Leopold II released invitations to the European heads of state to attend a conference on slavery at Brussels the following year. Rather than an effort to follow up on Lavigerie's efforts, this was a gesture to get the subject of slavery out of Lavigerie's hands, once and for all. Up to this moment, all antislavery activity in Europe had been Catholic instigated and Catholic guided, either by the Pope or Lavigerie; nevertheless, there was no Catholic representation as such at the Brussels conference.

Held on the second and third of July, 1890, the Brussels conference was a polite melee of protocol, politics, and the signing of an agreement prepared weeks earlier. The agreement outlawed slavery in all countries under jurisdiction of the signing nations; it expanded the Red Sea blockade to ships of all signing nations, but still limited the inspection to vessels under five hundred tons, and it prohibited the carrying of slaves on ships of other countries flying under the flags of the signing nations. The agreement had no specifications for the release of slaves then in bondage in Africa, it made no attempts to dissolve slavery in Moslem lands, it in no way restricted Moslem "missionaries" who were duping converts into pilgrimages to Mecca, it offered no protection to girls who were being sold like slaves in marriage, and it disregarded the forced labor which was being practiced in Africa by several of the signers. It was, nevertheless, a step forward, and Lavigerie expressed his approval of it.

The agreement was to become effective upon the signing of all nations represented at the conference; Holland King Wilhelm refused to sign. Some sources felt he refused because ships of certain Moslem countries were sailing under the Dutch flag, others thought Holland's business with the Middle East was too brisk to threaten by taking part in the agreement, but there were others who suspected that the refusal had been prearranged in order to squelch the entire antislavery movement. Lavigerie wrote the King several letters, begging him to sign the agreement, but he never received an answer. At last, he went to Brussels for a personal plea, but the King refused to see him. In desperation, he wrote another letter which he asked Princess Wilhelmina to hand to her father:

Sire: Each one of us has to render to God an accounting of our lives. I would not be able to resign myself at an age when I see eternity so close to reproach myself when appearing before God of not having exhausted all means to bring an end to the suffering of slavery. Sire, in the name of Christian honor and the happiness of your daughter, deign to give the order to add without delay Your Majesty's name to those of all the powers to the Conference of Brussels. Pardon my audacity, Sire. It comes entirely from your virtue and goodness so known to your people as well as from the pity which the misery, tears and bloodshed of which I am a witness, has inspired in me.

The King's silence indicated his continued refusal. The Brussels agreement remained worthless, until months later, when the King died. Queen Mother Emma, who became regent of Holland, notified the Pope and Lavigerie on January 4, 1891, that the first sovereign act of her daughter, Princess Wilhelmina, on ascending the throne was to sign the agreement which she knew meant so much to both of them.

Three months after the Brussels conference, Lavigerie finally succeeded in gathering together enough members of his antislavery committees to hold in Paris a conference of his own. By this time, the wind had gone out of the subject, and nothing spectacular was achieved. This was exactly as King Leopold had planned it. Out of the conference came a summary of matters discussed, particularly all the omissions at Brussels. The members took the summary home to their kings, and nothing more was heard of it.

On the last day of the Paris conference, Lavigerie received notice from Pope Leo XIII that, in approval of all he had done, the Holy Father was instructing bishops of countries represented at Paris to take up a special collection each Feast of the Epiphany (January 6) to be used for the ransom of African slaves and the protection of their rights as free men. Of all the talk and discussion, pledges and promises, compromise and deals which came to a head during Lavigerie's two-year campaign against slavery, the collection is the only thing which has survived—that and the record of the man who had done more than all others to free the African.

202

XVII

KING MWANGA's promise that he would kill no more people after the massacre of the royal pages lasted about a week. He had expected sudden obedience and obeisance to follow the murder, but it was not what he got. The entire country went into a state of severe shock. The people were dazed, stunned, lost. Even the chiefs who had so urgently offered their sons to be sacrificed to appease Mwanga were bewildered and unbelieving. Nobody seemed to care about anything any more. People stumbled through their days in squalid lethargy, doing the things they had always done but with a somber indifference. With the dissidents out of the way, Mwanga expected a flash of merriment at the palace, but instead he found his people engulfed by an atmosphere of stuporous unconcern which made them dull and uninteresting. Piqued, he sent others off to be burned or beheaded, and nobody seemed the least disturbed. At the mission, too, there was a change in air. Appalled by what had happened, the priests went days speaking in whispers as if the dead still waited nearby to be buried. There was a certain excitement among the catechumens who came for their instructions because they realized now the dangers in becoming Christians, but it was a sober excitement, a quiet excitement, based more on the dread of what had already happened

203

rather than what might. The country was gray and gloomy and overcast; even the sun seemed to hide itself in shame. Everywhere was a desolate quiet, like slow dawn after a severe storm when people could not decide to start cleaning up the ruins or wait because there might be more. It was incredible that all this could have been brought on by a young man just twenty years old who had in so short a time sunk so deep into the quicksand of evil that he could drag his whole country down with him. Out of the shambles evolved greater discord than ever before, revolutions, and civil war.

Alexander Mackay used the massacres as evidence for the need of stronger British influence in Uganda. In a way, he was right. Certainly a power of some kind was needed to impose peace and order. The only gesture toward unity to rise out of the devastation had come from the Arabs, yet it was a gesture that removed none of the terror in the land. It only made the terror neater. For a year the Arabs tightened their grip on the country by keeping Mwanga drunk and doped, and they were thus able to do whatever they wanted. Arab businesses flourished, slave traffic increased, and the people discovered they were taking orders more from Arabs than from Mwanga. As time passed and the situation grew worse, Christians found themselves provoked to uprisings against the Arabs. But Christian unity was constantly threatened by the idea that Mackay had precipitated, in that whatever was Protestant was British and whatever was Catholic was French: therefore, since Uganda was assumed to be British territory, the Catholics as well as the Moslems ought to get out of the country. Mackay's frantic letters to London created the impression that unless something was done promptly England might well lose Uganda. To prevent it, the Imperial British East African Company was authorized by England. Learning of this, the Baganda Protestants felt in a better position to assert themselves, and they shattered Christian partnership by turning on the Catholics. While not siding with the Moslems, the Protestants nevertheless made life unpleasant for the Catholics, and there was a great deal of friction between the two denominations. The Moslems took advantage of it. On September 10, 1888, they overthrew the government, dethroned Mwanga, and replaced him with his older brother Kiwewa, who was sympathetic toward the Moslem cause. Kiwewa ordered his armies to attack the Christian missions. Buildings were burned, people were killed, and at last all the missionaries were put into fragile canoes and set adrift on the lake. A storm came up and the canoes overturned. Though the missionaries managed to reach shore safely, five of the Christians with them drowned. The White Fathers made their way to their mission on the southern shores of the lake; the Protestants followed Mackay to Usambiro. Then Mwanga himself was exiled to the lake islands, and the Moslems took over the country. Kiwewa, the new king, was ready to espouse Mohammedanism, until he discovered that this involved circumcision, and he was a bit too wary of his new friends to trust them with the deed. He postponed the initiation so long that impatiently the Moslems threw him out and replaced him with his more amenable brother, Kalema.

To the astonishment of the White Fathers, Mwanga appeared at the mission one day in a fit of raging penitence. He wept, he moaned, he begged for forgiveness for all he had done, and he promised to amend his ways. Bishop Livinhac was in an awkward position. He could not, as a priest, doubt Mwanga's sincerity. He had heard enough confessions in his day to know that people were always susceptible to the temptations peculiar to them and that salvation was in the effort to resist; a priest must believe in the ability of the effort to conquer or he could never in clear conscience give absolution: the effort indicated by the act of confession could be his only gauge. Even though Livinhac knew that from the life Mwanga had led the effort in him would be extremely weak, he had to give the king the benefit of the doubt, and so, as Mwanga became a Catholic, Livinhac granted him forgiveness, both in and out of the confessional.

Mwanga remained at the mission several weeks, revealing quite openly his intention of getting his throne back. He knew he still had a certain following among the pagans of Uganda and he felt, now that he had joined sides with them, that he could rely on the support of Christians who had left the country under the reigns of Kiwewa and Kalema. Furthermore, the island to which he had been exiled was the center of lake traffic, and the people there, preferring Mwanga, had offered him their huge fleet of canoes as a navy if he ever decided to recapture his lost kingdom. He needed weapons, and he found them available from an unusual source: Charles Stokes, who had been a lay missionary with Mackay, had given up mission

205

work and gone into business, acquiring supplies of all kinds from merchants on the coast and selling to inland tribes. With the shrewdness typical of the depraved, Mwanga was able to convince the White Fathers that his was now a holy mission—to oust the Moslems from Uganda—and the priests sent word to exiled Baganda Christians that Mwanga could be trusted and should be supported. Both Catholics and Protestants fell in line.

April, 1889, Mwanga led a huge force on Uganda and, through sheer might, regained his throne. He set up a bipartisan government by appointing a Protestant as prime minister and divided other offices between Catholics and Protestants, and he invited missionaries of both denominations to return to the country. On the surface, everything seemed to be going well, but there was a considerable undercurrent which constantly threatened the peace. Despite their union in battle, there was still a distrust, fomented by Mackay, which kept the Catholics and Protestants apart. Mackay did not return to Uganda with the other missionaries, but sent frequent letters of instruction to R. P. Ashe, whom he chose to run the Uganda mission for him. Always he warned Ashe against the Papists he so disliked. Adding to the unrest was the deposed King Kalema, who had enjoyed his short reign and wanted more of it. With Moslem support, he kept his army in continual skirmishes with Mwanga's. Finally, in November, Kalema succeeded in pushing Mwanga out of the country. Back went Mwanga and the missionaries to the islands.

It was at this point that the Imperial British East African Company began to push toward Uganda from the northeast. The Company was actually a combine of British interests, charged by the government to enter the region, exploit its resources, make treaties, and establish the British influence. Backed by private funds, the Company was nevertheless an official agency. It had its own flag and its own small but effective army of Sudanese warriors, but its acts were performed in the name of the Empire. Mackay had urged for just such an organization, insisting that unless at least a quasi-official British influence be imported, the Protestant missions would be destroyed by the Catholic (therefore French) element, and the only bit of England in Central Africa would thereby be lost.

The White Fathers couldn't have cared less who ran the government, as long as it wasn't the Moslems, and when Mwanga, thrown out of his country for the second time, asked Father Lourdel if it would be wise for him to seek British aid in recapturing Uganda again for himself, the priest not only agreed but even wrote the letter to Captain F. J. Jackson, head of the Company's expedition, requesting assistance. Jackson replied that he was ready to assist Mwanga, provided the king would sign a treaty establishing the British influence in Uganda, that he would hoist the Company flag and would grant the Company certain prerogatives in the future government. The specifications amounted to the conquest of Kalema in order to surrender to the Company. Mwanga refused. However, second thought soothed him, and Mwanga wrote Jackson that he was willing to go along with the stipulations, pending further discussion. He expected the Company army to show up, but instead Jackson sent him merely the Company flag. Indignant to the point of fury, Mwanga reorganized his own forces and, in February, 1890, sent them back against Kalema with such ferocity that the Moslems were destroyed beyond repair.

Having regained his kingdom by himself, Mwanga dismissed his earlier negotiations with the British Company. Up from Tanganyika then came Carl Peters, an adventurer traveling under the auspices of Germany. Peters offered Mwanga a treaty that was considerably more palatable than England's, and Mwanga signed it. News of it brought Jackson rushing into the country, vowing to fight Mwanga, Peters or anybody else who interfered with his own plans. Mwanga asked Lourdel for advice and the priest said: "One way or the other, it looks like you've got a war on your hands. All this is beyond my province as a missionary, but I would say that the Germans are offering you the better treaty." They were, but when Lourdel's opinion reached Jackson he was far from happy. Both Jackson and Peters withdrew to the coast to consult with ambassadors to be assured that, should fighting start, they could both rely on support from their governments. But there was no fighting, at least on this score. With familiar presumption, Germany and England decided the fate of Africa by agreeing that Uganda would be British and Tanganyika would be German, and the people who lived in the two African countries had nothing to say about it. Mwanga was forced to go along with the British, and up went the Company's flag.

There were further changes: both Lourdel in Uganda and Mackay in Tanganyika died of fever within a few weeks of each other, and Bishop Livinhac was recalled to Algiers to become superior general of the White Fathers. The three had been strong and influential men in the development of Uganda. Despite the differences between them, they had a great respect for one another, and there were occasions during the turbulent days of persecution when only their mutual co-operation saved their lives. It was unfortunate that Mackay suffered flashes of prejudice which distorted his views; he had at times been thoughtful and generous toward the White Fathers, as they had been with him, but he could never quite forgive them for being Catholics, for being French; and, because some of his attitude seeped into the people who followed him, Uganda became the victim of a great tragedy from which it never fully recovered.

Because Uganda was suddenly British, it followed logically—in the mind of Protestant missionary Ashe—that the country should then adopt the state religion of England—Anglicanism. Ashe passed his sentiments on to Captain Jackson, and though nothing official was done, it was only a matter of time before notable preferential treatment toward Protestant chiefs began to appear. Significantly, only men of Protestant clans were hired for Company safaris after animal hides and tusks; only Protestants got jobs around the Company fort. Protestant chiefs gradually usurped not only the prerogatives of Catholic chiefs at court, but also their property, and there was no reaction by the Company to the complaints which naturally arose. To top things off, Mwanga himself became a Protestant. The country took sides and got ready for the shooting. The hour was tense and threatening; Jackson realized he could no longer control the growing animosity and notified his superiors. He was withdrawn at the end of 1890 and replaced by Captain Frederick D. Lugard, who had already successfully planted the British flag in other parts of Africa and who, until his death in 1945, was to continue upholding the cause of the Empire in Hong Kong, Nigeria, and the League of Nations.

Lugard's first act was to revoke the appellations used for the two factions—the British party and the French party, declaring that now everybody was British, and he applied the at least more appropriate names of Protestant party and Catholic party. Though this was accurate at the time, it was unfortunate in that it created a permanent division in the country on a religious basis instead of a more purely political separation. Since, however, the people were destined to have little to say about their government for some time to come, there were few actual political differences between opposing sides that mattered too much. Lugard next set up a peculiar hierarchy of authority in the country, ordering that if a man—whether the king, a chief, or a butcher—was a Catholic, his next in line would have to be a Protestant, and vice versa. The alternations would hold in both appointed and inherited positions. If a man changed his religion, he automatically lost his job.

The plan at first gave the impression of stability and peace, but there were many faults in it. It established that a man's progress depended not on how much he knew but how he prayed. It turned religion from a matter of conviction to a matter of convenience. It presented a future of flipflop Christianity, according to which denomination offered the best profit. It prohibited a man from following the dictates of his conscience in favor of the demands of his purse. It reduced religion and all it included—honesty, purity, justice —to the level of a bait for the ambitious. Moreover, it was so completely contrary to the principles of mission work that any missionary in the least apostolic should have purpled at the cold-minded suggestion that the precepts of truth he most certainly felt he represented should be apportioned without regard to their validity or the inclinations of the man who accepted them. Oddly enough, the Protestant missionaries were ready to adopt the project without a murmur.

But the White Fathers exploded. Bishop John Joseph Hirth, who replaced Livinhac as the Central Africa prelate, went to Lugard and told him that forcing a man to become a Catholic or preventing him from becoming one was wrong and sacrilegious. Lugard couldn't grasp this, and he took Hirth's complaints to be mere opposition to the Company. Try as he claimed he did to be impartial, it was understandable that he wasn't. He knew that Catholic chiefs were acquiring weapons from Charles Stokes, and so he supplied the Protestants. And more, the Company, so preoccupied with internal conflicts that it was unable to pursue the commerce which was supposed to be its prime concern, soon felt the pinches of bankruptcy and was on the verge of being forced out of business: the thirty thousand British pounds necessary to keep the Company solvent—and in Uganda—came through the auspices of the Protestant missionary society.

In time, Uganda found itself divided into two standing armies, both well armed. Well-meaning Christians on both sides were taking their rifles to church with them. Shooting incidents became increasingly frequent. Hirth sent the full details to Cardinal Lavigerie, who in turn sent them on to Cardinal Manning, then the leading Catholic prelate of England, and he also sent Livinhac to London to discuss the problem with the Colonial Office. Lavigerie suggested that an English Catholic be named head of the Company in Uganda, believing that when the Africans saw that an Englishman could be a Catholic, they would lose the strange association of ideas which was causing so much trouble in the country. If not this, Lavigerie suggested to the Colonial officials, then at least order Lugard to discontinue his unique hierarchy and give complete freedom of religion to everyone. The Colonial Office did nothing.

The first serious outburst between the two sects sprang from an unimportant but complex incident. Mongolaba, a Catholic, had a rifle stolen from him by a Protestant. Following the law of the land, he went to the king, identified the thief, and demanded the return of his rifle. Mwanga ordered this to be done. Then a Catholic stole a rifle from the prime minister, who in turn announced that when he got his rifle back, he would see to it that Mongolaba got his. Several days passed with no action by anybody. The trouble started when Mongolaba, impatient, went to the home of the Protestant who had stolen his rifle, found it, and took it. The Protestant collected several of his friends, and, all armed, they went to Mongolaba's house and forced their way in. Shooting started; one Protestant was killed and the others scattered. According to Uganda law, the guilt was with the Protestants all down the line. Mongolaba's mistake was in going to get his rifle; custom prescribed that the thief, identified, should have returned it voluntarily. There was a lengthy delay before the trial, and during it tempers continued to rise on all sides. One day several Catholics were walking through the woods toward the royal court when they were ambushed. With that, the war broke out.

It lasted for months, with periods of fierce fighting. In one battle, the Catholics had routed the Protestants and were chasing them across the fields. The Protestants retreated in the direction of the hill on which Lugard's fort was located. Reaching there, the Protestants skirted the hill, but the Catholics, seeking to encircle the Protestants, ran into the clearing. Lugard saw them from the fort, and opened his Maxim machine guns on them. Dozens were killed. In another fight, the Protestants won the advantage and, after breaking up the Catholic forces, advanced on a mission and set fire to the buildings. One building, of brick, was safe, and the White Fathers were trapped in it. The Protestants settled a few yards from the front door to wait for the priests to come out. Instead, a Catholic crawled out a rear window and went to the fort to get help. Lugard sent his own men to disperse the Protestants and escort the priests to the fort. Sometime later, peace briefly restored, the Protestants attacked again, chasing the White Fathers southward, clear into Tanganyika. When Lugard finally let the priests back into the country, he sent them to their mission at Villa Maria, in the southern province of Buddu, told them to stay there and ordered that they could not do any work at all outside the restricted area.

Neither France, Italy, nor Germany was particularly Catholic-minded at this time, but as letters began to reach Europe from the White Fathers with reports of how they were being treated, the three countries made gentle and unofficial inquiries in London as to just what in the world was going on down in Africa. The Colonial Office asked Lugard for a report; knowing that one of the inquiries had come from France irked him. He put the entire blame for the uprisings on the Catholics, accusing the Frenchmen of obstinancy because their country had not gained the power in Uganda. Besides the fact that France had not even tried for power there, the idea itself couldn't have been farther from the White Fathers' minds. As gracefully as possible, the Colonial Office filed the report, transferred Lugard to Hong Kong, disbanded the Company, lowered its flag, and ran up the Union Jack. An investigation was made, which took many months, and though the final report did not completely clear the Catholic faction, the White Fathers were once again given free range, freedom of religion was assured for everyone, and the government paid the White Fathers ten thousand pounds for damages done to mission properties. King Mwanga, not too pleased by authorities assumed by the English whom he had joined in body and soul, made an attempt to regain his full powers, but was escorted in chains to

211

an island where he resumed his life of rampant vice and died at the age of thirty-four. Livinhac still felt that the Baganda should be shown that there were such things as English Catholics and he arranged with Cardinal Vaughan and the Colonial Office to have several Mill Hill Fathers—British missionaries—appointed to Uganda and given excellent missions in the thick of the population.

The Mill Hill Fathers achieved their purpose—and far more. Nevertheless, the seeds of denominational differences had been planted in the people's minds, and this was something that would take much longer to overcome. The colonial government, overzealous to prove its impartiality, doled out jobs, appointments, authority, and favors with fanatical fairness. Men found themselves in posts for which they hadn't the slightest ability or interest, but the balance had to be maintained. Thus, instead of letting the conflict die with time, it was inadvertently kept alive.

Both Protestant and Catholic missions flourished. They built schools, and the government, aware of its duty to its young, allocated funds to pay for the cost of education. Again, the allocation was fair, but calculated fairness required a certain vigilance which could become wearisome, and in the course of the years a certain disbalance gradually appeared. It sprang mostly from the arrival of Protestant groups other than the Church of England, small groups, British, European, American, which either couldn't afford schools or did not have the staffs. As time went on, fewer and fewer Protestant missions had their own schools, and more and more youngsters entered government schools. There was nothing wrong in that. However, there grew apparent in time a financial leniency toward both government and Protestant schools which was not shared with the Catholics. The predicament became obvious enough for Catholic laymen to detect and resent.

It was a resentment that never quite died. Agitating it through the years was the steady ascendance of Protestants to all positions of authority, either by appointment or by elections, and the Catholics eventually found themselves almost completely on the outside. Much of this was their own fault. Feeling discriminated against, they pouted themselves out of the political picture, and when the time came that the people had their own legislative council, there were no Catholics with sufficient political experience to campaign successfully. Also, the priests, wary from past adventures with Uganda governments, were reluctant to nudge Catholics into political activities of any kind. Moreover, inherent in the Protestant mind was the traditional suspicion of Catholics in high places, and nothing more dimmed a man's political chances than his being Catholic. It was inevitable therefore that the Catholics should eventually unite, and this was a bad thing. It served only to emphasize the religious factions of the country, neglecting the possibility that a Catholic and a Protestant could still see eye-to-eye politically. The Catholic unity failed to produce a Catholic force simply because too many Catholics had become resigned to second-class citizenship and did not vote for anybody, let alone their own candidates. It was this resignation which finally, in 1955, led the Catholic bishops of Uganda to issue a pastoral letter to the laity, stressing the right and the responsibility of all citizens to vote and take active part in the government of their country. Immediately the Protestants condemned the letter as an hierarchal attempt to push Catholics into control, and the 1956 session of the predominantly Protestant legislative council took into consideration a law which would prohibit the solicitation of votes on a denominational basis.

The advantage in such a law would be that it could work both ways, but the pity of it was that it should be necessary at all. It might not have been—and all the war and bitterness would have been avoided—had Alexander Mackay and England realized sixty years before that it was not the flag in the sky that would make the African a peaceful Christian; it would be the faith in his heart. And yet there were other places on the continent where the African was not permitted to have even that.

XVIII

THERE was still Timbuktu.

And the city seemed as far away as ever. Elsewhere in Africa the White Fathers steadily gained ground, but Timbuktu remained locked off, isolated. Six priests had died trying to reach Timbuktu in a race across the desert. For more to try from that direction would have been foolhardy, but not to try at all would detract from the sacrifice of those who had failed. Further, the very purpose of the White Fathers required that they reach Timbuktu, someday, somehow. There were supposed to be some sixteen million people in the area. Moslems who had migrated from Morocco in the eleventh century had turned the city into somewhat of a second Mecca, winning four million converts. Certainly the many pagans remaining and the heavy slave traffic that must be stopped would provide plenty of work for the White Fathers while they pursued their parallel mission of overcoming the Moslem anti-Christian antagonism.

There were obstacles other than hostile Arabs to prevent further attempts directly across the Sahara. There were the heat, the lack of water, the distance itself, the great cost of organizing an effectively large caravan. And there was the protection the priests would need.

214

During Lavigerie's antislavery campaign in Europe, some twelve hundred men had volunteered for the army of laymen he felt necessary to guard caravans. As a start, he accepted twelve of them. They waited in North Africa for two years for the opportunity to escort a caravan, but continually some insurmountable problem arose to interfere. Finally, under the pressure of objections to the "army" by European countries, Lavigerie disbanded the men and offered to pay their way home. Seven of them stayed on and entered the religious life as the first lay brothers of the society. As such, Lavigerie would not let them bear arms, which meant that once again any caravan going south would have to rely on Arabs for protection, and Arabs were no protection at all.

Just when everything seemed hopeless, reports reached Algiers that French troops, entering from the West Coast, had penetrated to Timbuktu and captured the city. It had been a bold and unexpected thrust inland, made possible by transporting two sizable dismantled aluminum boats overland to the Niger. The mere fact of the conquest indicated that certainly army outposts had been established along the route. Once before the army had permitted White Fathers to use its posts as oases; it might be willing to do so again. The French government itself was strongly anticleric, but the Army was not. Requests to follow the Army's route should have gone though the official government channels, but rather than risk a negative answer from Paris, the White Fathers appealed directly to the army. The reply was a quick yes; there were soldiers in the Sudan who had not attended Mass for months and they would most welcome a priest.

Late in 1894, four White Fathers, with Father Auguste Hacquard as superior, left Algiers by boat for St. Louis on the Senegal coast. Hacquard was the perfect man for the trip. He was young, bright, affable; he had been in the Army and still had friends in the military; he would get on well with commanders along the way. He had also a quick mind for languages. Already he had translated spiritual books into the dialects of the north; with several new dialects to be learned in the Sudan a man with such a gift would be important and helpful.

At St. Louis, the priest learned from the Holy Ghost Fathers something of what awaited them. There were two great obstacles ahead:

Islam and the French government. In ten years, the Holy Ghost Fathers had been unable to make much headway against either, therefore limiting themselves for the most part to Catholic Frenchmen in the immediate area. That was the way the government wanted it, had in fact ordered it. All that France seemed to want was the land itself, otherwise maintaining the status quo. Moslem justice was still the law of the land. No schools had been built, no hospitals, no orphanages, nothing had been done about slavery. And certainly the Moslems couldn't be expected to fret about such things. In Timbuktu, the Holy Ghost Fathers had learned, there was a Moslem school, but only for the rich. Despite the wealth of the city, all the money was in the hands of a few people. Thousands lived in the worst poverty. They lived, too, in the bleakest immorality. Even Islam itself had decayed. Ordinarily, to be a Moslem one had only to wash in sand and water, declare that there was but one God and Mohammed was His prophet, then give up pork and alcohol and kneel toward Mecca five times a day. Yet this would not survive untainted in Timbuktu. Surrounded by paganism, Islam had adopted many of its customs. Moslems were resorting to human sacrifices, to sorcery, to revering sacred forests. Koran verses were being capsuled and worn as fetishes. Ramadan, the Moslem month of strict fasting, had been cut down to three days, spaced a week apart. Laxness had resulted in so many heretic groups that nobody was too sure exactly what Islam was. Whatever it was, the French government was for it. Arabic was the only written language in the land—though few could write, and the government urged all Frenchmen to learn Arabic and speak it. This, oddly enough, was in line with Lavigerie's instructions to his priests, but not for the same reason. It was one thing to become somewhat like Arabs in order to win their respect, but it was quite another to base the imitation on an attempt to blind them to their own squalor.

Prepared for the worst, the White Fathers began the twenty-five-hundred-mile trip to Timbuktu. They left St. Louis on January 16, 1895, up the Senegal River by boat to Kayes, five hundred miles away. Arriving in a month, they rested a week, then went by army narrow-gauge railroad to Bafoulabé, a hundred miles further inland. There they hired a hundred and fifty porters for the seven-hundred-mile walk to Bamako on the Niger. It was a walk that they had to make at night; days were too unbearably hot. Up at two in the morning, they spent an hour at their prayers before starting out. By ten o'clock, the sun was already broiling above them and they had to stop. Tents offered little protection; as often as they could they stayed at native villages, paying to get into the darkness of mud huts. All day the priests were occupied, keeping the caravan well organized, writing reports to be sent back to Algiers as guidance to future caravans, compromising with tribes on payments for safe passage through, taking care of the sick they met on the way. Late afternoons, they cooked a meal, then went to bed. To be able to see where they were going on their night treks, the porters carried burning torches: a fiery train inching across a black horizon.

Waiting at Bamako were the Army's two aluminum boats, which took the priests farther inland as far as Koulikoro, headquarters of the Niger fleet. Two White Fathers remained there to make arrangements for the caravans that would follow after them; Hacquard and another priest went on by flat boat.

It was five o'clock in the afternoon of May 21, when, having left the river, Hacquard entered the plains of Timbuktu and saw the city rising before him. He stopped and looked at it. Here was the goal six men had died trying to reach. Here was the mystery city, so hidden that for centuries no one was sure where it was. Here was the symbol of all that the White Fathers wanted to overcome. To be the first priest to look upon the city was somewhat like being the first man to look upon the world. There was something unreal and threatening about it: Casbah in the desert. Purple smoke of evening fires rose in thin clouds over the city; even the severe sun could not pierce it. Oil lamps, strangely cold and unfriendly, sputtered in high windows. From a forest of minarets came the wails of muezzins. The city gave off a certain music, subdued and discordant, heavy, depressive.

The French commandant welcomed the White Fathers with relief. "I don't know what your plans are for the Arabs," he said, "but I know my own men should keep you busy enough. Timbuktu seems to have got into the blood, like a slowly fatal disease."

The city had fallen easily to the French. The rich, apparently aware that resistance was futile, had quickly demonstrated a friendliness that was too effusive and saccharine to trust. Troops, with little

217

to do, had relaxed into a lethargy which made them easy prey for Timbuktu con-men and vice. The commandant said: "People will come to you readily enough—don't worry about that, but it will be only for what they think they can get out of you. Just because you are busy don't think you are successful; such delusion has a high price in Timbuktu. Remember, this part of Africa is the white man's grave."

The priests were busy right off. They took a small square clay house near the marketplace and enlarged it by adding tiny rooms. From the first morning, the house was crowded with the sick who came for treatment and the curious who came to pry. Beggars arrived in batallions, children hovered in swarms, pedders appeared to barter everything from wool to women. There were days when the priests did not even have time to say their prayers.

Slavery had always been the Sudan's biggest business. The French Army had taken on the duty of destroying it, but effectiveness varied from town to town. Commandants wearied by heat and rain and monotony let the slave trade continue openly. The Timbuktu commandant, bolstered by the White Fathers, did all he could to control it, and one way was to require all departing Arab caravans to submit a roster of personnel to be checked again upon its return. This worked to some extent, but more than anything else it simply moved slave trading out of the city and into the bush.

The year that followed was busy and productive. The four priests who were first to enter the Sudan spent a great deal of time rushing east and west along the Niger, acquiring land for missions, arranging for hospitals and schools, making initial contact with the many tribes. More White Fathers arrived, then White Sisters and the brothers. The Sudan was one big wasteland, in natural resources as well as spiritual, and there was more than enough work for everybody. A major task was finding materials with which to build; there were miles and miles without a tree. This was a chore for the brothers who, with their skill of building mansions out of mud, soon erected a network of neat clay-brick schools and chapels. Crowds came to stare in wonder. Yet in the wonder was a certain stubborn apathy which kept the schools and the chapels empty. Though most of the Sudanese were pagan, the heavy hand of Islam had reached far out from Timbuktu and clamped the people's minds shut against

the influences intended for their own betterment. They learned in
time to go to the mission dispensaries when they were sick, but they
saw no reason why their children should go to school. Just as they
seemed immune to all efforts to inject into their lives the slimmest
progress, so did they lack the slightest curiosity about the religion
which had brought these men and women to the Sudan. As on the
northern fringes of the Sahara, the White Fathers put aside the
hopes for converts and concentrated on acts of charity and social
improvement. In return they got blank-eyed stares of indifference.
The priests, the nuns, the brothers worked harder, determined to
break through the inertia which Islam had diffused over the land.

Like the rest of Africa, the Sudan had its diseases. Within two
years, three priests and a brother died of infections and fevers.
Bishop Anatole Toulotte, Lavigerie's coadjutor appointed to govern
the Sudan, was able to withstand the climate and the tensions just
eighteen months before he was forced to resign his post and return
to France. Father Hacquard was consecrated bishop to replace him.
White Fathers and White Sisters in Central Africa, once they had
settled down and began regular doses of quinine, thrived and were
able to remain on the job for years. But there seemed to be something
in the Sudan—the merciless heat, the rain, the unlimited emptiness
of the land itself—that attacked like a depressant fungus even the
most zealous missionaries, and it was often a matter of only a few
years, sometimes just a few months, before this priest or that nun
would have to start the long, weary, disheartening trek home,
defeated by the Sudan they inexplicably loved. As some measure of
survival, Hacquard ordered all missionaries to spend one hour a day
alone, reading or writing or, better still, just sleeping, and another
hour in the evening for group recreation. Pressed for time though
everyone was, it was wiser to invest the two hours in recuperation
than to tackle the work at the cost of the man.

There were many setbacks. On April 4, 1901, while bathing in
the Niger, Bishop Hacquard drowned. Two boys swimming nearby
saw him go down fast, the victim of either cramps or a crocodile. He
was never found. The next year, the anticleric French government
in Paris let loose a rage against the Church that roared into every
corner of the empire. In France, schools and hospitals were con-
fiscated and various religious orders were forced out of the country.

In Africa, missions and orphanges were closed. Army officers who had been friendly with the White Fathers performed their sad duties with the greatest reluctance. One lieutenant said "Father, I've got orders to close your orphanage, but I realize there's no way I can force the children to leave. I'm going to lock the door and take the key, but your windows still work, don't they?" Another officer, upon closing a mission, immediately asked to go to confession, but the priests assured him that he personally was free of guilt. In other cases, the orders were obeyed only by putting a lock on an unused shed. But with missions near government agents the situation was far worse. Even greatly needed clinics were shut down simply because they were run by nuns. The Sudanese, both Moslem and pagan, saw what was happening, and in areas where the enforcement was not so strict the people nevertheless stayed away in order to win favor with the French government. Europeans, too, civilian and military, left the Church because it seemed wise. Just what the government hoped to achieve by the persecution escaped explanation. In France, there were schools, hospitals, and orphanages other than Catholic where people might go, but in the missions, particularly in the Sudan, there was nothing but what the White Fathers and White Sisters had provided. Millions of people therefore suffered because a fistful of Paris anti-Catholics found themselves in positions where they could effectively release their personal hates. Proof of the error occurred in the Sudan in the next four years. Epidemic and pestilence erupted; in Wagadugu alone, fifty thousand people died in a year from famine. Disease and death were everywhere. Had the missionaries been permitted to continue their import of medicines, the total would not have been so great. Nor would the cost of peace itself have been so great. As in Algeria, the French tried to rule the Sudan with an uncompromising clenched fist, and the result was similar chaos. There were constant uprisings. Again, the French ignored pleas from the White Fathers for tolerance, they were deaf to suggestions that from the start a program should be followed which would train the Sudanese for gradual advancement toward self-government and a voluntary alliance with France. That the White Fathers should even think of such a thing incited the colonial government to greater severity against the missions. It was therefore only with the utmost difficulty that the priests were able to dissuade their few converts from violence against the government, promising that as long as the White Fathers were in the country they would work to gain increasing freedoms for the people. The day came when the French learned the wisdom of the missionaries' efforts. In 1908, two thousand Moslems at Wagadugu announced, on the eve of an Islam feast, that they were going to attack all Europeans in the area and kill them. The commander of the French fort had nowhere near enough men to withstand the assault. Frantic, he went to the White Fathers and asked: "Do you think any of your African converts will help us?"

"They might," the superior of the mostly inactive mission said. "They know this kind of attack is wrong."

"Yes, but can you trust your Christians?" the commander asked. The priest said: "Yes."

"To how many can I give rifles?"

"To as many as can shoot," the priest said, then added pointedly: "It's a pity we haven't got more."

The attack came and it lasted a week, ending principally because the Moslem marabout who had instigated it was killed in the fighting. The priest told the French officer: "Now, unless you want more of this sort of thing, I suggest you let the missionaries go and take care of the Moslems who have been wounded. Then, if you will permit us to work freely with all the people, I think I can assure you that nothing more like this will happen."

The officer agreed—temporarily, and during the next few months he watched the missionaries closely. The attitude of the people around Wagadugu changed so noticeably that it could almost be picked up and measured. Finally, the commander went to the White Fathers and said: "I want you to know that from now on you are free to work as you please, no matter what orders I receive from Paris."

The experience, expensive though it was, opened Wagadugu to what would have been the inevitable rewards of good missionary work. Schools were opened and the children came. Each generation of them stayed longer at their books, learning more and more, growing better equipped to advance their community, developing it far ahead of the rest of the Sudan. Eager to do more, the young people were ready, therefore, when there arrived in Wagadugu a young priest who was about to put the town on Africa's medical map. Father Jean Goarnisson had wanted to be a priest all his life, but his father demanded that his son become a doctor. Obediently, Jean went to medical school. On the day he received his degree, he told his father: "I have done what you wanted me to do. Now I will do what I want."

Within twenty-four hours, he was on his way to Maison Carrée to join the White Fathers to begin the long studies for the priesthood. He was ordained in 1929, then returned to France for a year to study tropical diseases. His next stop was Wagadugu. There was a great deal of sleeping sickness in the area, and at the same time a great deal of blindness. As he treated both, Goarnisson tried to discover if there was any link between them. Research meant months of studying hundreds of cases, and his first observation was that people who survived sleeping sickness without receiving injections of the drug then being used did not subsequently go blind. The trouble seemed to be with the drug. Already, Father Goarnisson had a full schedule, and the research he felt he must do on the drug meant he would have to find someway to get to cut down on his other tasks. Assisting him at surgery were two White Sisters, both experienced graduate nurses. It occurred to the priest-doctor that if he could train the nuns to do most of the minor surgery, he would then have time to pursue his research. They began. More and more each day, he put the scalpels in their hands rather than in his own, directing their movements as they worked. In two months, the nuns were handling the minor cases themselves. But they in turn discovered that the more time they spent at surgery, the less time they had in the wards where they were also needed. The only solution to that, Goarnisson realized, would be to teach Africans to do the ward work. With that, he set up a nursing school. He soon learned that to teach properly he needed a textbook, so he wrote one. At first he had just two or three pupils, then ten, then fifteen, then dozens of them every year. Before long, all hospitals in West Africa were drawing on Father Goarnisson's school for these important additions to their staffs.

Meanwhile, his research fell neatly into place. He found that the poison in the drug which killed the infection would attack the optic nerves after a certain dosage. To work, the dosage could not be decreased; therefore the poison ingredient would have to be changed. He notified the European manufacturer of what he was doing, and rather than wait for someone else to attempt the job, he started on it himself, experimenting with a score of poisons before he came upon one that would kill the infection effectively without injuring the optic nerves. His success saved not only the vision but also the lives of thousands at Wagadugu and throughout Africa.

There was much eye disease in the country. Goarnisson spent a considerable part of each day removing cataracts, developing from repetition and study a technique that was faster and better than that being used anywhere else. Other doctors in French West Africa heard of it and sent their patients to him. Goarnisson ended with more cases then he could perform. Then he thought of the nurses he had graduated. He went first to the marketplace and bought all the cow and sheep eyes he could find, instructing the butchers to send him their full supply every day. Gathering his graduates, he announced that he was going to teach them how to remove cataracts. Several of them shuddered at the idea; he dismissed them and started his instructions with those more willing. Within six weeks, he had two skilled "surgeons." By the end of a year, he had a dozen.

There remained still another cause of blindness Goarnisson could not explain. Every day, children and adults arrived at the hospital, their vision dimmed to varying degrees. All the priest could do was treat the condition, but he knew he would make no progress until he found out what was causing it. Because most of the cases came from the same area, he thought perhaps diet had something to do with it, but a careful study of the people's eating habits assured him this was the wrong track. The number of people infected showed clearly that the disease must have a carrier, and he began to hunt for it. The pattern of contagion soon ruled out the possibility that the disease was spread by human contact. There was only one realm left: insects. Goarnisson asked some boys to bring him a collection of bugs.

"Bugs?" they asked, surprised.

"Yes. As many as you can of everything that crawls, jumps, or flies."

In a few days, Goarnisson's laboratory resembled an insect zoo.

223

The room hummed with the low protest of tiny animals that found themselves in jars and cages. Goarnisson spent weeks studying each one of them, dead and alive, and at last he found on the feet of a species of small flies a flaky substance which when mixed with the liquid normally protecting the eye effected a chemical action which burned into eye tissue. He sent the boys out for more flies, repeating the test hundreds of times until he was sure. From his own observations, he knew that Africans, so used to flies, would ignore the insects as they crawled over faces, to the corners of mouths, nostrils, eyes. First he initiated a program of fly control, practically an impossibility in Africa, and then he produced a counteractant to the infection. Because Africa has always been more the insect's world than man's or beast's, the flies are still there. But nobody is afraid of them any more.

For all he has done to advance medicine in Africa, Father Goarnisson has been heralded by fellow scientists everywhere. His books on tropical diseases are bibles to men who have come after him. Most important to him, however, is the small red-brick building on the mission ground where each year he turns out thirty to fifty well-trained nurses. Also, scores of young men who worked with him during the past twenty-five years have, with his guidance and assistance, gone on into medicine. Curing the sick has been, of course, vital, but teaching the African to cure himself—and his people— has proved even more valuable. No medical missionary to Africa has done more toward that end than Father Goarnisson.

Other sections of the Sudan might have progressed as far in parallel fields had the early missionaries there been granted the same freedoms that were permitted at Wagadugu after the Moslem insurrection. But such was not the case. Adhering to orders from Paris, other commandants did all they could to destroy the missionary influence. Prospective converts were ridiculed for wearing the religious medals given them when they applied for catechism lessons. Catechumens who had given up polygamy were granted special funds to buy wives. In some areas, the people had been turned so firmly against the missionaries that they would not even give the priests water for their horses.

Prevented from doing their work, the priests looked around for another location where they might occupy themselves con-

224

structively until the French persecution died. They were just about to write to Algiers for advice when, one morning in 1904, the British delegate at Dakar arrived in Wagadugu. His name was Cromier, and he told the White Fathers:

"I know what's been happening in the Sudan, and I'm very sorry, for you and for France. Maybe I can do something for you. Would you be interested in sending some men into the Gold Coast?"

They were indeed. With actions curtailed in the Sudan, the men could easily be spared, and the nearness of the Gold Coast, just south of French territory, would make a caravan relatively inexpensive. The priests wrote immediately to Algiers and Rome for the necessary permission. It arrived at the beginning of the following rainy season, which meant another four-month wait, and there was further delay before the caravan could be assembled. It was near the end of 1905 before the priests began moving south.

There were already Catholic missionaries at work in Accra, the Gold Coast capital on the sea, and Protestants had moved northward into Ashanti country, but the Northern Territories, which touched on French West Africa, had been left alone. The people were poor, backward, and unfriendly. Their soil was bad, and their spirits were worse. They resented the people of Ashanti, who were powerful because of their rich mines and plantations, and they loathed the people at Accra, who from their associations with the British and the business advantages of being on the coast had become sophisticated and worldly. The Accrans and the Ashantis looked down on the people of the Northern Territories as being ignorant and primitive. The people of the north were mostly of the Mossi and Dagarti tribes. Either strongly pagan or Moslem, they were impoverished farmers who occasionally found it necessary to suffer the humiliation of going to the Ashantis for employment during lean years. They were poor relations, they knew it, and they hated it. Through treaties, England had taken over the country in 1874. Gradually the British government permeated northward into the Territories and district commissioners were appointed. It was rough duty; the men soon began to look upon assignment to the Northern Territories as some sort of punishment. Those who remained there too long grew as unfriendly and hostile as the Africans.

It was that sort of man who was stationed at Navrongo when the

225

White Fathers arrived in 1906. Superior of the caravan was Father Oscar Morin, who, after a brief chat with the district commissioner, decided it would be a good idea to build the first mission some distance from town.

The D.C. objected. "I'm not the one who invited you into my district," he said, "but as long as you're here, I'll have to keep an eye on you. Build your mission in town."

The priests acquired acreage at the edge of the village and constructed a small school, a small clinic, a small house, and a small chapel, all made of reeds and mud and looking like crude toys. Their first contacts with the people were failures. Nobody wanted anything to do with them. All their expectations, aroused by the original invitation to go to the Gold Coast faded with crushing speed. Letters from superiors at Maison Carrée told of the fabulous successes in Central Africa and the men at Navrongo wondered if they were on the same continent. Their progress was so slow it was practically unnoticeable. Polygamy was rampant among both pagans and Moslems. Even when a man expressed an interest in Christianity, he backed off as soon as he learned it meant giving up all of his wives but one.

The D.C. said: "I don't know why you fellows are so dead set against polygamy. Solomon was a good Christian, and he had a lot of wives."

"Solomon was dead a thousand years before Christ was born," the priests told him and went dismally back to their work.

If people came to the mission at all, it was only when they were sick. They could be friendly enough when they wanted to be, and they were basically a fine people, but they displayed little interest in any religion, save for the fetishes they wore to protect themselves from devils. The chiefs were strong-minded and stubborn, warning people that those who became too friendly with the White Fathers would suffer for it. The influence of the priests, therefore, was limited almost exclusively to medicine. They opened outstations in the Navrongo bush, but it was the clinic, not the church, that attracted people.

World War I brought mission work to a standstill, and starting after it was practically starting anew. By 1929, however, the outstation at Jirapa in the Lawra country had become quite busy, and Morin, now a bishop, felt it was time for something more permanent

226

in the way of a hospital. He sent Father Remy McCoy, a Canadian, to make preparations for the hospital and meanwhile open the first new mission in twenty-five years.

Father McCoy had plenty of time to prepare for the hospital because there was little to occupy him at the chapel. There was a greater restlessness among the people than ever before, and the principal reason for it was a drought that had hung on for crucial weeks. Crops dried up, cattle died, fruit trees were bare. The country, already poor, could not survive a complete crop failure and subsequent famine, but as the days passed and there was no rain, the doom became more and more apparent. All night, every night, drums beat their monotonous prayer for help, and the cries of the witch doctors went up in futile pleas.

One afternoon, Father McCoy was startled to see approaching the mission the Paramount chief and his entire entourage in full regalia. He went to greet them. The Paramount chief said: "We have no rain."

"Yes, I know," said McCoy.

"Our rainmakers have made sacrifices and the witch doctors have prayed every night," the chief said.

"I've heard," said McCoy, suspicious of what would come next.

"You have told the people you are a man of God," said the chief. "We have tried everything else. Now we want you to pray. Do you think you can bring the rain?"

"I can't, but God can," McCoy said.

"Will He do so if you ask?"

"Yes," the priest said easily.

"Ask."

"You will have to pray with me."

"We will do whatever you say."

Into the chapel he led the chiefs from all over the country, and before he started to pray, he said: "I think you should know what this is all about." He gave them a short talk about Christ and the Church, and they listened attentively because they thought this was part of the miracle they expected from him. Then: "I am going to start to pray now, and you must repeat after me everything that I say."

McCoy faced the altar and knelt. The chiefs behind him knelt, and there was a rustle of furs and hides, bells, fetishes, and amulets

227

as they moved. McCoy began: "Our Father Who art in Heaven. . . ."

The chiefs: "Our Father Who art in Heaven. . . ."

McCoy: "Hallowed be Thy Name. . . ."

"Hallowed be Thy Name. . . ."

They prayed for a half hour, an hour, then another hour. Knees ached, and there were soft groans as the chiefs wiggled for comfort. One chief called out pointedly: "No rain yet."

"We must continue to pray," said McCoy.

They prayed another hour; the chiefs had enough. McCoy knew he could not hold them much longer. He stopped and said: "That is all."

"What do we do now?" asked the Paramount chief.

"We wait for the rain."

"When will it come?"

"When God decides."

Several of the chiefs were unhappy. One said: "If you are a man of God, it should rain right now."

Outside the sky was brittle clear.

The dissatisfied chiefs complained loudly. "This had been a waste of time. You can do no more than our own witch doctors. In fact, you do less. And you have lied. You said it would rain, and the sky is clearer now than when we started all this nonsense."

"Prayer isn't nonsense," McCoy said. "God heard our prayers, believe me, your prayers and my prayers. He will make it rain when He knows it is best for all of you."

A chief said: "Let's give them more time. We don't know how Christian prayers work. But if it does not rain soon, we will know there is nothing to it."

The chiefs left, some of them highly disgruntled. Father McCoy went back to the chapel. He knelt and buried his face in his hands. "God," he whispered, "this is the chance. If you will give these people rain, I know I will be able to give you their souls. Let them see that you heard the prayers they said here, then they will come back to pray again. And through the prayers they will learn to love you. Let it rain, God." He remained kneeling a long time, tense with hope, and then he heard the first crash of thunder. He almost smiled. He said: "Thank you." And he reached for his breviary.

It rained all night and into the next day, the slow, steady, penetrat-

228

ing refreshment the soil so desperately needed. At noon, a half-dozen drenched chiefs were at McCoy's door.

He asked:" Have you come to thank God for the rain?"

"No," one said, "I've come to find out why it has rained in his village"—he pointed to another, —"and not in mine."

"Didn't it rain in your village?" the priest asked. He tried to hide his astonishment.

"Not a drop."

"And," said another chief, "not in mine."

"Or in mine," put in another.

Father McCoy studied one man. "Aren't you the one who said yesterday that the prayers were nonsense?"

"Yes."

"Well, then, what did you expect?"

"I don't understand."

McCoy asked: "Would you expect God to heed prayers from a man who thinks they're just nonsense? You can't love God when you ridicule Him."

The man was annoyed. "How can I love anybody I don't even know?"

"That's why I'm here," said McCoy, "so that you can get to know Him."

Within a few hours, there were a lot of people who, like the chief, wanted to know the God who could make it rain when and where He wished. The whole countryside was talking about the half dozen regions where the fields had remained dry and withered, untouched by the downpour as if a great, invisible hand had held back the rains. People went to the fields and stood there, watching the rain fall just a few feet away; then they went to the mission to see the man who had caused it all.

"I did nothing," Father McCoy told the hundreds who questioned him. "God did it. And if He decided there should be certain places without rain, there was a reason for it."

Every day the crowds were larger. Hour after hour, they sat in huge circles and listened to Father McCoy and his two assistants talk about their God, this worker of wonders who, out of love, helped those who trusted in Him. There were no doubters anywhere in the crowds; they had all seen for themselves. Their convictions grew stronger when they saw that after the impatient chiefs had returned to the chapel for more prayers, the rains then covered their lands, too. In a few days, the mission grounds were jammed with thousands who came not only to see but to learn, and when the priests decided that catechism lessons should begin, there were so many applicants that Father McCoy had to send to Navrongo for help. There were as many as ten thousand people a day at the mission, by actual count. By the end of the year, seven thousand of them were studying catechism. Some of them came from thirty miles away. For their sake, the priests appointed catechists to teach in the distant villages, but still the people made the trip once a week to be present at Mass. The small chapel could not hold the crowds.

"Someday," Father McCoy said, "I hope to be able to build a big church here, and when that time comes, I hope I can rely on all of you to help me."

Next day, when the people came to the mission, they brought bricks and wood for reeds and they greeted Father McCoy with a look that said: "Well, where do you want it?" In three weeks the church now at Jirapa was built by the people themselves.

The Dagarti tribe, some two hundred thousand people, had been split almost in half by the boundaries agreed upon by the Frenceh and English, and when the clansmen at Jirapa began to tell their relatives across the border about what was happening, a gigantic immigration took place. The district commander at Jirapa saw it and was worried; he queried Accra for advice. A study showed that the French Dagarti stayed at Jirapa two or three weeks, went home to take care of their farms for a short time, then returned. As a result, there was a great deal of traffic on the roads and periodic strains on Jirapa to absorb the population surges. Something had to be done. The British authorities in the Gold Coast went to the French authorities at Dakar and suggested that, to assure some sort of stability, the French permit the White Fathers to open missions among the Dagarti on the French side. In effect, Protestants were asking nominal Catholics to let priests do their job; it was almost funny. The French approved.

Immediately the crowds on the French side were as great as they had been at Jirapa. It was originally planned that two priests would spend a few days a month at the new mission, but this soon proved inadequate. To guarantee that they would always have priests among them, the people again built a church, clearing the ground in a day and bringing their own materials for the construction. Within a year, a second mission had to be established.

The White Fathers had no illusions. They knew many of the people came to the missions just to be around in the event of another incident that had all the appearances of a miracle. Once again the White Fathers' rule of four years' preparation for baptism proved its worth. Those who had merely been curious eventually fell away; even so, the missions experienced phenonemal growth. Twice when Dagarti interests seem to lag, incidents occurred to bring on fresh crowds. Two years after the sudden rains, the Jirapa area was besieged by locusts. You had only to turn over a rock to watch them spurt out like geysers. Thousands of farm acres were destroyed. Once again the people went to Father McCoy, and he held a special evening service which attracted so huge a crowd that it flowed out of the church and down the hill to the road. In the morning the locusts were gone: there was no trace of them anywhere. Then, in 1954, another drought baked the district to dust. This time there was no great rush to the church. The chief, Yelpwe, was a Moslem who had become increasingly anti-Christian with the passing years, even to the extent of standing on the church steps and forbidding his people to enter. To make church attendance difficult for Catholics, he ordered everyone to work on Sundays, stipulating that Friday, the Moslem sabbath, would be the day of rest. Restricting the work further, he banned the priests and the catechists from teaching the people in several villages.

The drought continued and the people were restless. One old man said: "In the old days when we needed rain we went to the Christians and prayed and got it. Maybe we shouldn't have turned our backs on the priests after we got what we wanted."

The sentiment grew until Chief Yelpwe could not ignore it. But he still did not want people to go to the mission. Instead he decided to go himself; that way there would be less chance of another emotional rush to the mission in the event of results. He sent word to Father McCoy that he and his elders would be at Jirapa the following Monday. McCoy saw them arrive, stopping under a tree to wait for him, and he went to them.

"Before we start talking about rain," McCoy said, "there's something I want to say to you. I am a missionary, and I'm responsible

231

to God for the people who live around here. It's my duty to do all I can to bring the people to God—give my life if necessary. You, Chief, are the biggest obstacle to my work, and now you come here asking for God to give you rain."

"Are you refusing to pray?" the chief asked.

"No," said McCoy, "but I'm just warning you not to expect any results."

"Why not?"

The priest said: "If you want God to give you something, you must first prove your sincerity in some way."

"How could I do that?" Yelpwe asked.

"You can promise me now that you will let the Christians go to church on Sundays, as they should, and that you will let me talk to the people about God anywhere, any time I choose."

"You ask a lot," said Yelpwe. "Why don't we agree on just one of those conditions?"

"Both," McCoy said firmly.

Yelpwe looked at the seventy elders who were with him. "Does anyone object?" he asked. No one objected. "Very well."

They went into the church and they prayed for an hour and they left. It did not rain Monday, nor Tuesday, nor Wednesday. Wednesday afternoon, McCoy got on his motorcycle for a tour of distant outposts. His route took him through the village of Tampooy where, because of Yelpwe, he had not been permitted to preach for many years. It was market day and the village was crowded; McCoy had to drive slowly. The village elder, who had been at the mission on Monday, saw him and waved him down.

"I was wondering," the elder said, "if we might have done anything wrong. It hasn't rained yet."

"Perhaps God is waiting to see if the agreements will be kept," McCoy said.

"Oh, they'll be kept," the elder assured. "Of course, you'll have to wait until Sunday to see about one of them, and if you would like to preach here today, right now, go ahead. There are plenty of people to listen to you."

McCoy was somewhat surprised and tried not to show it. He got off his motorcycle and said: "All right. I'd like to." He began merely by talking to the elder. A few curious people paused to eavesdrop; McCoy lifted his voice. More came, and in a few

232

moments more than a hundred were gathered around, listening to the first sermon they had ever heard.

But there was still no rain.

On the next Sunday the church was full for the first time in months. Purposely, Father McCoy avoided any mention of rain, though he knew it was in everybody's mind. After Mass, people dallied at the mission as long as they could, eager to be nearby for the rain they fully expected. The sun set and the stars came out. Puzzled and uncertain, the people finally went home, some of them with a long journey ahead of them. It was at nine o'clock, when the priests had finished their night prayers and were going to their rooms, that the first rolls of thunder were heard. At ten, you could not hear your own voice above the rain. By morning, it had settled into a soft, steady drizzle which the earth seemed to drink in with audible sighs.

Naturally, none of these events escaped the attention of the British colonial authorities. The men in the Gold Coast were more like those in Uganda than like the British official at Dakar who had originally asked the White Fathers to go into the Northern Territories. Already in 1930 there was a restlessness for independence in the Gold Coast, and the colonials were therefore suspicious of anyone or anything that drew a crowd. Father McCoy was particularly suspect: his name sounded Irish, and certainly an Irishman would be anti-British. That he was Canadian eluded everybody. He was watched constantly, his every move was recorded. To stymie him, all his requests for government co-operation were refused, and on the weakest grounds, and the only way he could make progress was to threaten action at the top level. Once, McCoy wanted to put up a chapel in a distant village where there were many Christians, but the Moslem chief refused to allow it. To overrule the chief, McCoy needed permission from the colonial government, but the D.C. declined with: "You're interfering with the head man."

McCoy said: "You're interfering with God."

"Well, I can't let you go in," said the man.

"Will you put that in writing?" McCoy asked.

He wouldn't; McCoy went in.

He went into many things. He organized co-ops among farmers, he fought for schools and hospitals, for tsetse fly control, for women's rights. Whenever a government agent refused him with a "I'm sorry, Father, I can't do anything for you," he replied: "You're not doing this for me, but for the people. Do you want to refuse them?"

McCoy—and all the White Fathers, for that matter—became somewhat of a nuisance to the government. A special *dossier* was maintained on McCoy: a diary kept by strangers. And every new government agent who arrived to work in the Gold Coast received a private lecture on the White Fathers, as a warning more than a guide. As demands for self-government increased, the British grew even warier of the White Fathers. Father McCoy, returning to the Gold Coast in 1948 after a visit to Canada, was refused permission to enter. He told the immigration officials: "If I can't go back to my mission, I'll need a letter from you to send to the Pope so he'll know why I'm not doing my job." Any such letter would certainly have found its way to government authorities in London; McCoy was allowed to go back to work.

That the missionaries in the Gold Coast—or anywhere else, for that matter—should appear to be problems to the government was in many ways understandable. Being priests, they had a specific responsibility to do all they could to provide a better way of life for their people. Often the means toward that end fell within the realm of government, and for the government to fulfill its obligations required the spending of money. Colonial officials had not been sent to Africa to deplete the London treasury, but rather to enrich it. The same was true of men from Paris, Brussels, Lisbon or Madrid, and the only way they could do their jobs was to prevent the missionaries from doing theirs. The result at times was regrettable animosity, and there were two effects of it upon the people: either it turned them against the colonial government or it drove them from the Church. Both were great misfortunes, and neither would have been necessary had some government agents not looked upon the White Fathers as some sort of anarchists. McCoy as a Canadian was a British subject, and there were English missionaries in the Gold Coast, as well as French and American. All these men understood what loyalty to one's country meant, but they also understood that country owed a certain loyalty to its people, and when the government, with persistent obstinacy, fell short in its duties, the people— or their spokesmen—had the right to demand redress. This should be as true for Africans as it was for Englishmen. But it was not the colonial policies anywhere in Africa, and in the end it was the governments that suffered.

234

XIX

CARDINAL LAVIGERIE had warned his first missionaries that they would have trouble with governments. Intrinsic to colonialism was the strict control of all influences which might affect the government's own intentions, and certainly religion was one such influence. To imagine that a missionary had only to baptize people and teach them to say prayers detracted from the scopes of religion itself, yet that was all that governments wanted religion to do. For the White Fathers, it was not enough. However, it was not only in Africa that European governments vividly demonstrated their opposition to the influences of religion, and in some instances it was an opposition that verged on undisguised persecution. The time came when Lavigerie found himself a missionary to his own country, and in a way that alarmed the very people who should have supported him must strongly.

By the time Lavigerie had finished his antislavery campaign in Europe, he was a very tired and worn-out man. There were times when his arthritis made even breathing a great pain. A stroke he had suffered in 1884 had paralyzed his right arm and affected his walking. And his spirits were low because, his Paris conference over, he was not sure just what he had accomplished. Certainly he was responsible for the Brussels conference, which at least had made the entire continent slavery-conscious and had brought on some measure of control. His own conference, following Brussels, had been somewhat anticlimactic, but he had the satisfaction of knowing that he had not completely wasted his time. He had, actually, called the bluff of the European rulers who for so long had taken stands against slavery—and then just stood there. Now they had taken the matter out of his hands: from now on whatever happened in Africa regarding slavery in any of its forms would reflect upon the men who had met at Brussels. The White Fathers, of course, would continue buying all the slaves they could afford, which was pitifully few compared to the volume of the traffic. At least the record would show that the priests had never rested in their crusade.

Now Lavigerie wanted to rest. He was sixty-five years old; he had been in Africa thirty years. The continent would never outlive the influences he had had upon it. He was ready now to go back there and die. There was one more deed to be done: he must go to Rome and report to Pope Leo XIII the results of the antislavery work. There would be no question as to whether or not he had succeeded; Rome never looked for immediate success. Whatever the circumstances had forced Lavigerie to leave undone would be done by somebody else, in a few years perhaps, or the next generation, or the next century. Men did not change overnight; God had knocked St. Paul off a horse to make him stop his persecution of the Christians, and even then it took several days for him to catch on to what God wanted of him. The men of Europe had had Christianity for almost two thousand years and still could not learn to live as God wanted. It would take a lot more time, a lot more work, a lot more prayers, and maybe even a few miracles to bring them around. The Church considered it her duty to work ceaselessly toward that end, and, knowing men, she realized it might take all God's time to do the job. Time the Church had; God would provide the right men at the right hour; little by little the job would be done.

When Lavigerie entered the Pope's rooms, he tried to kneel for his blessing and to kiss his ring, but the Pope took him by the shoulders and stopped him. The Pope said: "My son, neither one of us is in shape to do things like that any more. Have a seat."

They talked together about slavery for a long time, with the Pope making mental notes he would later put into a report to be studied by future Popes when they needed the information. The subject covered, the Pope asked: "How is the political situation in France?"

"Not so good," said Lavigerie. "There are still a lot of Catholics who would like to see the monarchy restored to power, and this does not make them very popular in the republic."

"I believe they are wrong," said the Pope. "I think the era of the monarch is ending in Europe. Those who remain any length of time will be very ineffectual."

"Perhaps you are right, but the royalists in France would never admit it."

"I know," the Pope agreed. "And what are they doing? In obstinance, they refuse to have anything to do with the republic, and as a result the government is in the hands of atheists and Freemasons. Believe me, the Church will still suffer a great deal in France."

"Not if the royalists can win back the throne," Lavigerie said.

The Pope shook his head slowly. "Always remember this, my son," he said: "The throne needs the altar, but the altar does not need the throne. Just because France may have a Catholic ruler does not mean it would be what we would like to call a Catholic country. Both of us have had enough experience to recognize the truth in that."

Lavigerie nodded.

"No," said the Pope, "it is not the man on the throne who determines whether or not a country is Catholic, but the people, the way they live, the way they are treated, and the way they treat one another. Look at the United States; certainly she is not a Catholic country, but I think she is the most Christian in the world today. She has still a long way to go, but I believe she is moving in the right direction."

"Would you like to see a United States of Europe?" Lavigerie asked.

The Pope smiled and shrugged his thin shoulders. "Yes, but nobody alive today will live to see that. But there is something we can live to see especially in France."

"What is that, Holy Father?"

The Pope said: "Because most of the influential French Catholics are royalists, they think they are wise in refusing to have anything to do with the republic and in that way it will fall. Well, France has been a republic for several years, I suspect it will remain one, and

237

you can see what is happening to the Church there. If the Catholics expect to have a religion at all and if they want to have anything to say about the way they are governed, I think they'd better embrace the idea of the republic and try to win some high offices in it."

"Do you know what would happen if the French Catholics could hear you talking like this?" asked Lavigerie. "Most of the Church's money from France comes from Catholics who are royalists. If you told them you felt this way, you'd never get another sou out of them."

"I don't intend to tell them," said the Pope. "I have somebody else in mind to do that for me."

"Who?" asked Lavigerie.

"You," said the Pope.

Lavigerie jumped to his feet with surprising agility. "Oh, no, Your Holiness, please don't ask me to do that," he said. "I rely on these people to support the White Fathers, the White Sisters—half of Africa. One word like that out of my mouth and I'll be destroyed."

"Don't you agree that my attitude for France is right?" the Pope asked.

"Yes, of course it's right," Lavigerie conceded. "It's right not only for the Church, but for the people themselves. I agree there'll be more republics, and it's right that all people should have something to say about the way they're governed. But don't you think this idea for France would mean more coming directly from you instead of secondhand from me?"

"I wouldn't want you to express it secondhand," the Pope said. "I want you to make it sound as if you thought it up yourself."

Lavigerie wilted into his chair. "It will be catastrophic."

"I can't do it," the Pope said. "In the first place, I am not French, and this must come from a Frenchman. Secondly, whatever the Pope says is applicable to the whole world, and there are several fine Catholic monarchs in Europe who would think my remarks were aimed at them and they would be very annoyed. I believe in time they will give up their thrones anyway, but right now this is an idea for France. The rest of Europe can follow when it is ready."

"I still wish you wouldn't ask me to do it," Lavigerie said.

"I want you to do it," the Pope said, "but not if you think the

238

repercussions will be as serious as you now expect. Why not think it over and let me know tomorrow what you decide. . . ."

Back at his hotel, Lavigerie related the conversation to Bishop Livinhac who, as superior general of the White Fathers, had been touring Europe for funds and had attended the Paris conference, then accompanied Lavigerie to Rome on the way back to Algiers. Livinhac quickly grasped the dangers of the idea. "A lot of people will be unhappy," he said.

"That's what I told the Holy Father," Lavigerie said.

"Wouldn't it be better to have this done by a bishop in France?" Livinhac suggested. "After all, you'll be off in Africa and you won't be able to reply to the attacks which are definitely going to come."

"But the Pope wants me to do it," Lavigerie said.

"Then what else can you do?" asked Livinhac. "If he thinks it's for the good of the Church, you must obey him. And don't worry about the White Fathers. We'll manage somehow."

Next day Lavigerie returned to the Pope and said: "Despite all the consequences, Holy Father, I'll do what you want."

"That's fine," said the Pope. "I know you're doing this out of obedience, and all I can say is that I will back you up in whatever happens. I leave it to you to choose the time and the place and the method for doing it. One thing is important. Don't bring the Holy See into it in any way, until I think it is right for me to say something."

Lavigerie returned to Algiers at the end of October, 1890. The assignment weighed on him heavily, and he was convinced it would backfire. Certainly it was the right thing to do; the Catholics of France had to learn how to live in a republic, to take their place in it not only as citizens but as voters and officeholders. There were surely many French Catholics who preferred a republic and actually wanted to take part in it but didn't because they had been convinced that the political parties engaged in the republic were comprised of atheists and anticlerics. They were right, and the situation would remain so until something was done about it. To join existing parties required becoming as their members were, but if enough Catholics went into politics all at once, they would exert sufficient influence to inject moral justice into the republic and assure religious equality for everyone. The Pope's idea was undoubtedly worthy, but it would be costly to get across and to sustain until the resentment against it faded.

When and how to express the idea publicly Lavigerie could not decide. He thought of writing a letter to a newspaper, but this would not afford sufficient broadside. He considered going to Paris and giving a lecture, but he had just left Paris and his prompt return after a detour to Rome might hint at exactly what the Pope wanted to avoid. His plans were still unsettled when, early in November, he received notice from the offices of the Algerian government that the French Mediterranean fleet would pay an official call on November 12. Since the Governor General would be in Paris at the time, would Lavigerie, as the leading dignitary, give a reception and luncheon for Admiral Duperré, his staff, and a number of prominent people of the city? As Lavigerie replied that he would, he decided this would be the occasion to proclaim the Pope's idea. He could not have had a better—and worse—audience. High officers of the fleet were royalists by attitude and birth. They had remained in the service partly because the dignity of rank somewhat compensated for the faded dignity of their now meaningless titles, partly because they expected the republic to collapse and they wanted to be on hand to help crush it, and partly because the Navy enabled them to continue family traditions of service to France without soiling themselves in the current siege of government by commoners. Their attachments to the Church grew a great deal from the same sense of tradition. A king of France had been canonized for giving his life during the Holy Crusades, the same King Louis IX who had in fact built the first French Navy. Too, there had been a time when princes of the Church were also princes of the Crown, and though this had been changed for centuries the nobility still liked thinking it retained a certain consanguinity with the hierarchy.

The fleet officers expected to enjoy at Lavigerie's luncheon an excellent meal, good wines, and the customary toasts. To avoid repetition in the toasts and also to alert those who had to make responses, the toasts were usually written up a few days before the event and exchanged between the speakers. The day before Lavigerie's party, an aide of Admiral Duperré arrived at St. Eugène for a copy of the Cardinal's toast.

Lavigerie instructed his secretary: "Tell the lieutenant I haven't written it yet. And don't stand there scowling at me as if I were ordering you to lie. I really haven't written the thing!"

The lieutenant returned again in the afternoon and twice the next morning. To avoid him, Lavigerie went walking with two seminarians; because of his illness, the youngsters held him up and he referred to them as his "little canes." Usually he laughed and joked with the boys, but this morning he was strangely quiet. One of the boys asked: "Aren't you feeling well?"

"No," said Lavigerie. "Not very."

"Maybe you shouldn't be walking today," offered the other boy.

"I wish we could keep walking for the rest of the week," said Lavigerie.

They went on a short distance in silence; then the Cardinal asked: "Tell me, do you look upon me as your father?"

"Oh, yes."

"And do you love me?"

"Of course. Very much."

"If I asked you to do something difficult that could cause you great distress, would you do it?"

"Certainly. Why?"

Lavigerie sighed heavily. "The man I love as my father has asked me to do something difficult, and I'm worried."

"Well," said one boy, "if he loved you, he wouldn't ask you to do anything wrong."

"I know you're right, but I'm still worried," Lavigerie said.

Father Chenivesse, his secretary, came from the house. "Eminence, don't you think you ought to get at your speech? It's eleven o'clock."

"Yes, I suppose I'd better." He turned to the boys. "Thank you for walking with me. Now I want you to go to the chapel and say some prayers for me, and keep those prayers in mind especially during lunch."

Lavigerie wrote his toast in half an hour, then sent for young Father Piquemal. When the priest entered the room, Lavigerie was sunk back in his chair, his eyes shut. He looked up at Piquemal.

The priest: "Are you tired?"

"Very."

"What can I do for you?"

241

"Here." Lavigerie handed him the speech. "Read this." Then: "Do you understand what it says?"

"I think I do," Piquemal said, uncertain. "Let me read it again." Lavigerie waited. At last: "Well?"

"Eminence," said Piquemal, "if French bishops had been talking like this for the past twenty years, we wouldn't be in the mess we are now."

"You're right," said Lavigerie. "People haven't learned yet that the Church can stand without the Scepter. But do you really understand the toast? What about the 'authorized voice'?"

"That's the Pope, isn't it?"

"Yes. Very delicate matter. I can't involve the Pope, and yet I must take refuge under some authority to make people understand that this idea is official. Let me hear you read the toast out loud."

Piquemal began in an angry, vigorous voice.

"No, no, no," Lavigerie interrupted him. "You'd scare everybody out of the house. Sound resigned and obedient."

Piquemal tried it again.

"That isn't resignation," Lavigerie said. "You sound like a weeping puppy. Just read it, that's all."

As Piquemal reached the last words, Lavigerie heard carriages arriving at the front door. He waited a few moments, then went into the salon to greet his guests. It was a long, narrow, high-ceilinged room, painted a mild blue that made it seem larger than it was. Lining one side were slender full-length windows that looked out on the foothills rolling away to the sea. Near the opposite wall was the long luncheon table, ready and waiting. At the far end of the room was a small table for press correspondents who traveled with the fleet and reporters from local papers.

The guests came in: Admiral Duperré and his staff, General Breard, commanding general of Algiers, and his staff, city and national officials, judges, the military, businessmen, Bishop Livinhac, and several White Fathers. They all stood around for a while, uttering the meaningless trivia which intelligent, important people always manage to think up whenever they are brought together for a luncheon, a banquet, or a cocktail party. Then they moved to the table and stood at their places while a band outside played the "Marseillaise," the anthem of the republic, to which everyone inside

242

listened glumly. Eating gave them something to do with their hands and also the opportunity to pause while chewing to think of something to say next, and so everyone was a little more at ease. At last the table was cleared, more wines were brought in, and everybody sat back to listen to the principals toast one another for being such splendid chaps. As host, Lavigerie would be first to speak; as he prepared to get to his feet, he caught a glance from Admiral Duperré which said: "I didn't get your script." Lavigerie stood. The room was quickly quiet. Lavigerie began:

"Sirs, permit me before we separate to drink to the French Navy, so nobly represented among us today. Our Navy recalls memories that are glorious and dear to Algeria. From the very first day, she has contributed to Algeria's growth, and the name of the eminent chief who now commands the Mediterranean fleet, a name great in French history, is like an echo of all the glories of the past and the victories of the future.

"I am therefore happy, Admiral, in the absence of our Governor, detained far from us, to have been able to have you here as the crown of honor for all those who represent the authority of France in Algeria, the heads of our valiant Army, of our administration, and of our magistrature.

"What is especially touching for me is that all have come to this table at the invitation of an old archbishop who, as they, has made Africa his second country, while still trying to serve France. May it please God that this same scene be reproduced in our France, and that the union displayed here by us in the presence of the foreigner around us may soon reign among all the sons of the Mother Country.

"Union, in view of the past which still bleeds and of the future which is always menacing, is at this moment our supreme need. Union is also—may I say—the first wish of the Church and her pastors at all degrees of the hierarchy. Most certainly, the Church does not ask us to dismiss either the memory of France's past glories or the men whose loyalty and services pay tribute both to them and their country, but when the will of the people has been clearly stated, when the form of government they choose has nothing in it contrary to the principles which alone can give life to Christian and civilized nations, and when, in order to save one's country from the pitfalls which threaten it, sincere adhesion to this form of

243

government becomes necessary, then the moment has at last arrived to declare that the period of test and trial is over and all men must unite, despite sacrifices which may arise, to work as one for the future and the salvation of the country.

"That is what I teach around me. That is what I hope to see taught in France by all our clergy, and in speaking thusly I am certain no authorized voice will disavow me.

"Without this patriotic acceptance, nothing is possible indeed, neither for the conservation of order and peace, nor for the salvation of the world from social peril, not to save the religion itself whose ministers we are.

"It would be folly to hope to provide supports for the columns of a building without entering the building itself, and this must be done to prevent those who would destroy everything from accomplishing their foul deed. Those who obstinately remain outside the building, as some still do despite recent evils, succeed only in showing to the world their own ambitions and hates and in sowing in the heart of France itself the discouragement which will be the precursor of the final catastrophe.

"The French Navy, as well as the Army, has given us fine examples of supporting the columns. Whatever has been the sentiment of any of its members, the Navy has never considered that she should break with her ancient traditions or separate herself from the flag of the country, whatever be the form of legitimate government which the flag shelters.

"There you have one of the reasons why the French Navy has remained strong and respected—even in the worst days, and why she can carry her flag in honor wherever she has to uphold the name of France, and wherever—let a missionary cardinal say with gratitude—she protects the Christian mission which we have created."

There was not a sound in the room.

Lavigerie remained standing, awaiting reactions, but there were none.

The toast had been full of allegories, but everyone had grasped them: royalists were being told to put aside their heritage and support the despicable republic by participating in its machinations. It was insulting.

Lavigerie looked at Duperré. "Well, Admiral, are you going to give a toast?"

Duperré was tense with fury. He stood and took his glass in hand. "I drink to Your Eminence's health," he said sternly, "and to the clergy of Algiers." He put down his wine without tasting it and he left the room.

After him went his aides, then the Army, the government officials, the businessmen. Left in the room were the Cardinal, Bishop Livin-hac, and the White Fathers. They looked at one another with despair.

"Well," said Lavigerie, "it is done."

It was done, but far from finished. By nightfall the report was all over Europe. A Vatican aide rushed to Leo XIII, waved a newspaper at him, and cried: "Look what Lavigerie has done!"

The Pope glanced at the headlines and smiled. "Really! Even played the 'Marseillaise'! I didn't say anything to him about going that far."

When the Vatican newspaper *Observatore Romano* asked for an official reaction, the Pope said: "I don't see what evil there would be if all French Catholics imitate the Cardinal."

In France, the royalist press was shocked. The *Gazette de France* admitted that everybody in the office was weeping. Other papers attacked Lavigerie savagely. *L'Autorité* said:

The act of the Cardinal was completely unjustified. The pitiful politician who committed this act has lost while in Africa the exact spirit of France. The toast was the unconditional surrender of Christianity before Free-masonry. The Cardinal now invites us to kiss the feet of our torturers. Fortunately, the prelate only represents himself, only his more or less admitted interests, only his own rancors, his own misevaluations. In short, his declaration is only table talk and a speech after a drink.

The Catholic papers, though royalists, were more reserved. *Le Monde* reminded its readers that just a short time ago they were heralding Lavigerie as a great Frenchman; *La Croix* pointed out that Lavigerie was a man dedicated to the Church and his attitudes should at least be respected; *L'Univers* somehow learned of the Pope's interest in the toast and, regaining its composure, suggested mildly that chances were Lavigerie was right.

Figaro and *Débats,* the two leading republican papers, were surprisingly subdued. They considered the toast the foreshadow of a conservative element in the republic, which they felt was a good thing. "That's the way a bishop should talk," *Figaro* said.

From the radical press, however, came shouts of glee tinged with sarcasm. They grabbed at the "foul deed" reference and warned Catholics against leftist spooks. "Save yourself! Come on in the building and grab a column!"

Letters, telegrams, and cables turned Lavigerie's desk into a mountain of insolence. Wealthy royalists who had given him money told him to forget their address the next time he was broke. Bishops asked if he had gone mad. Cardinals wrote tersely that they were passing on their official complaints to the Pope. Hundreds with an ounce of blueblood, illegitimate though it might be, called Lavigerie a disgrace to France and to the Church. It was impossible for the Cardinal to answer all the complaints, and he didn't even try. To reply through any of the Paris newspapers would only have aroused another hornet's nest; instead, Lavigerie chose an Italian paper to put himself on the record. He said he had acted out of reason and conscience, that he meant merely to urge all Catholics to participate in republic-type politics in order to protect their rights to be heard within the government, that he believed that if groups of all interests were active in the republic it would provide fair government. He said: "If in France the attitude of the present defenders of the republic has made it appear as an impious and sectarian government, their attitude then is not the true essence of the republican form of government, as can be seen in the republics of Ecuador and the United States."

But the royalists were not satisfied; bishops were still seething. The prelates put the pressure on Rome for a clarification of official views. Cardinal Rampolla, Vatican secretary of state, replied: "The sentiment of the Holy See is easy to recognize from its doctrine exposed in its public acts. From these it is evident that the Catholic Church neither in its constitution nor in its dogma has anything which is opposed to any form of government, and as the Church herself treats with states and government for the advancement of religion and the salvation of souls, it is fitting that the faithful when the good of religion requires it take part in public affairs in

246

order to bring justice to constitutions and laws."

This, Rampolla explained, didn't mean the abandonment of royalty, but rather encouraged active Catholic participation in the existing government to preclude the expansion of anticlericism through legal acts in the legitimate legislature. The Church, he said, was concerned with what was just and unjust; a democracy could be unjust, as a dictatorship could be.

This didn't sit any better with the royalist than had the toast. In continued resentment, the royalists threatened to cut off all support of Rome as they had of Algiers. There was even talk of severing the Church in France from the Vatican. Lavigerie was desolate with regret. He blamed himself for choosing the wrong moment to carry out the Pope's idea, he became convinced that his toast had been too forceful and yet too vague. He was so distraught by the repercussions that his health broke. He suffered another stroke, which left him completely paralyzed.

Further, his bills piled up. Judging from previous years, he was able to estimate that his financial loss in the first six months after the toast, in contributions cut off by embittered royalists, amounted to almost a hundred thousand dollars. And there was no evidence of a letup.

But something was happening in France. It was happening slowly, so slowly that two years passed before it crystallized, but one by one the bishops of France began to realize that Lavigerie had been right, that—though they didn't know it—the Pope had been right. Continued anticlericism from the legislature had forced the closing of Catholic institutions, the dissolution of Jesuit establishments, the confiscation of Church properties. The need now was no longer for the return of a royalist-Catholic government, but only some influence within the republic that would overcome the persecution so widely imposed. In opposition to Lavigerie, the bishops had prevented organized Catholic action in the republic, and now they were suffering for it. But there was more the bishops had to learn, something Lavigerie had known for a long time: one Catholic layman in a position of influence could do more for the good of the Church—for the good of all religions—than the protests of the combined hierarchy. The task now was to find such men and encourage them by a public avowal of that fact.

247

On January 20, 1892, five French cardinals and seventy-five bishops signed a declaration which amounted to a public apology to Lavigerie and the approval and support of everything implicit in his toast. At approximately the same time, Pope Leo XIII issued an encyclical to France and to the world defining the spiritual responsibilities as well as the political prerogatives of a citizen of a republic.

Lavigerie sent copies of the encyclical to his priests, adding a note:

There are no injustices, even calumnies, that I have not had to undergo since my toast. My dearest brothers, you have seen what my attitude was. Following the example of St. Cyprian, I have thought it my duty to ignore all the attacks. I have harbored no ill feeling, I have pardoned everyone, simply remembering my responsibility as a bishop and leaving to the Holy Father to wait and choose the moment for him to speak. You have just seen that moment has come. The thoughts and words which I pronounced for years in his name he has deigned to recall in this encyclical, which henceforth by the fidelity with which we will follow it will constitute the object of our hopes—not only for our temporal fatherland, but also for the Church, which is our Eternal Father.

Some men near Lavigerie thought this was a moment for rejoicing, but he quickly dampened any attempts to twist the bishops' declaration or the encyclical into personal triumphs. Immobilized by his illness, he no longer cared about triumphs. He knew he was going to die soon, and his only concern was to see that all his affairs were in order for the next man who would take over his many jobs. Unable to stand, he got permission from the Pope to celebrate Mass sitting down, but the time came when he was even unable to do this. He became bedridden, but he continued working from the small, simple, almost austere bedroom that had been his for some thirty years. Once a day he had himself moved to the window so that he could look out on the basilica of Our Lady of Africa on a distant hill as he said his rosary.

By October he was too weak to work any more and he was unable to see anyone. The days dragged by. He grew impatient for death, and when it would not seem to come, he wondered if he was going to go on for years as an invalid. The thought annoyed him. On November 24, he tried to get out of bed and he fell to the floor in a helpless heap. Two lay brothers lifted him up and obeyed his command to aid him in taking a few steps, but he quickly realized that hope of any activity whatsoever was out of the question. Next morning he suffered another stroke. He could not speak. Bishop Livinhac gave him extreme unction. That evening, priests, nuns, and brothers crowded into the small bedroom to pray. At ten o'clock he entered sieges of severe pain. He spoke only once, to the White Sisters, almost gruffly: a command to pray for him to get him out of Purgatory and into Heaven in a hurry. At midnight he died.

A hundred thousand people—Christians, Jews, Moslems, pagans —moved slowly past his bier during the three days he lay in state in the basilica. Then he was taken to Tunis, where another great crowd came to see him. French ships in the harbors of Tunis, Algiers, and Marseilles lowered their flags to half-mast for a week; military tributes were conducted at bases throughout North Africa. He was buried in the crypt beneath the sanctuary of the cathedral at Carthage, close to the ruins of the cathedral of St. Cyprian, close to the arena where, centuries before, hundreds of martyred Christians had nourished the Faith in Africa with their blood.

Obituaries in Paris newspapers read like tributes to a national hero. One editor summed up the thoughts of all with:

"My God, he was a great man!"

XX

THERE were great men to follow him, men who like him put the trinity of God, the Church, and Africa first in their lives. Like him, too, they flourished more on hard work than on the air itself; they kept going more on prayer than on food. Again like him, if there was a laugh anywhere around, they meant to find it. He had demanded saints for his society of priests, and the saints he got were, like the majority of saints, a little devilish. The severity of the training, the austerity of the life, the hardships, sufferings, the failures, deaths, disease, the tensions and pressures, the volatile successes all comprised so great a burden—mentally, physically, spiritually—upon a man that if he could not from time to time laugh at them and at himself as well, he would go mad. Furthermore, each man was convinced in his heart that everything he attempted was for the good of his special trinity, and in that frame of mind no setback could be so devastating that he would be unable to rise above it, sooner or later. To the White Father, inactivity was a particular kind of sin, and since there was always so much work to be done, there was no reason for the man to be anything but ecstatically happy. It was the kind of happiness that became evident the first day a man decided to join the White Fathers. The

250

decision seemed to clear the road of all doubts and uncertainties for the rest of a man's life. What could there be worth fretting about, except the impatience of not doing well enough at one's studies or one's work? This kind of impatience only incited a man to strive harder. Because of the goal in mind, the efforts served to assure the saintly men Lavigerie wanted. And there could be no such thing as a sad saint.

Arthur Walter Hughes was a reckless example of a holy clown. He became an archbishop of the Church and the papal ambassador to Egypt, and he got more fun out of it than a kid on a roller coaster. At one of the most solemn moments of his life, he took time to quip. He was in Alexandria at the reception of the newly appointed Copt-Catholic Patriarch, a man named Amba Morkos II. During the formal toasts, Hughes rose and said with great dignity: "*Ad multos annos*—or as we'd say in English: 'Forever Amba.'"

Hughes had come from a poor English family and he had very little schooling. As a boy he earned his living as a newspaper copy boy. He had a gnawing crave for knowledge. He often spent hours in a museum or library, and he had a remarkable ability to memorize at sight whatever he saw or read. At fourteen, he launched himself on a study of comparative religion, and a year later he walked into a Catholic parish in London and announced that he was ready to enter the Church. The pastor prepared to give the boy the usual preliminary catechism, but at the first session the priest discovered that Hughes knew more than he did. He was accepted into the Church immediately and then declared that he wanted to become a priest. Such extremes of fervor were not uncommon in converts, and the priest expected Hughes to calm down after a while. Instead, the boy applied for admission to the White Fathers' seminary in Hampshire and was accepted. As a student he had to compete with young men who had years of formal education behind them, and it would have been understandable had he lagged at the bottom of his class. It appeared at first that he would, particularly in Latin and French, both of which he needed for his higher studies. In his other subjects, he was always the leader; within eighteen months he knew Latin and French fluently, so much so that he could pun in both languages, usually with Biblical inferences which startled his much older and mission-weary professors. His faculty for languages was phenomenal. In the early weeks of his study of French, he was seen carrying a grammar into the refectory, and, to tease him, other students asked if he was ready to take a test in it.

"All right," he said. "Pick any subject and I'll talk about it in French for an hour."

Amused, the students groped for a subject, then one of them glanced at the food on the table. He said: "Cheese."

Off Hughes went for the full hour in perfect French, astounding his classmates not only by his skill in the language but his knowledge of cheese. He admitted later that he was merely recalling from memory what he had once read about cheese in an encyclopedia at a time when the topic interested him. Years afterward he similarly astounded an audience of the League of Nations Union in London when he was called upon on short notice to give a talk on slavery. He talked for an hour without notes or pause, his mind again full of facts he had culled from his avid reading.

Hughes went to Uganda in 1933, where he was appointed secretary to the bishop, plus supervisor of schools and a half dozen other jobs. He was a small man with short legs, and because it was therefore difficult for him to stay on a motorcycle, he was permitted to use a car. It was a tiny, beat-up English car, and the sight of it bouncing along the rugged Uganda roads at all hours of the day and night became a landmark of the White Fathers. Part of the mission-school budget came from the government, a small part which varied in its generosity according to the whims of the British agent for schools. One year Hughes submitted an unusually large request, and the agent asked: "Why are you asking so much money from the government? Why, the Catholic Church is the richest organization in the world; you ought to be able to get your money from Rome."

"What are you talking about?" Hughes returned. "The Church was founded on a rock and it's been on the rocks ever since." The joke was enough to break the threatening unpleasantness—and he got his money.

At the outbreak of World War II, the Vicariate of Gulu on the Equatorial Nile in the northern part of the Uganda Protectorate was under the jurisdiction of Italian priests and bishop. The British didn't want any Italians, though they were clergymen, at liberty in the country, so the missionaries were moved away from the area. For that matter, the White Fathers, because of the internationalism of the society, were the only Africa missionaries whose Italian and German members were not made prisoners of war. The removal of the Italians required replacements at Gulu; the White Fathers and African priests were sent in, and Hughes was appointed administrator. Typical of him, he did not look upon the appointment as something temporary, though it was, and he went to work at top speed, building missions, opening schools, expanding hospitals. Four tribal languages were used in the vicariate; Hughes arrived knowing none. He realized, however, the importance of learning the languages not only for the convenience of getting things done but for the respect which his knowing them would indicate to the people. In the vicariate just a few days when he made his first tour of the missions, he wrote a speech in English and had it translated into the four languages all of which he memorized, and he was thus able to speak to the people in their own tongue on his initial encounter with them. The Africans were tremendously impressed and were immediately his loyal supporters. Hughes had a genius for making people friendly and keeping them so. One of the African priests with him was extremely shy, to the point of being antisocial, and the nuns at the convent he had frequently to visit mistook the man's timidity for some kind of aloofness aimed against them. Hughes learned about it. One afternoon he telephoned the convent and, disguising his voice, said he was the hospital administrator, that the priest had been brought in for an emergency appendectomy and would not be able to go to the convent the next day. A few hours later, he telephoned again with the same disguise, said the priest had had a remarkable recovery, that he would after all be able to go to the convent, but that since he was so shy, it would be better if the operation were not mentioned by the nuns. Obediently the nuns avoided the subject when the priest arrived the next morning, but they were so overwhelmed by what they thought was his miraculous recovery that they showered him with such attention and affection that he was literally ripped out of his shyness and got along beautifully with everybody thereafter. On another occasion, Hughes was visited by some nuns who were, he knew, starving themselves so that they would have more food to give to the children at the school they ran. At breakfast, Hughes sent eggs to their quarters, but the nuns refused them, saying that they knew that eggs were hard to come by, that Hughes was working very hard, and that he should keep them for himself. It was one of those delicate moments when the slightest pressure from Hughes would have caused the uncomfortable embarrassment which nuns suffer so easily and lastingly. The nuns were happily surprised when Hughes appeared unexpectedly at their car to say good-by just before they left. When they arrived at their school, they found tied to the car's rear bumper a basket of eggs with a note commanding them to eat the eggs as an act of holy obedience to their superior.

The Italian situation which had existed at Gulu was also true in Cairo. The apostolic delegate to Egypt was Italian, and though he was concerned only with Catholic affairs, the British government felt he should not be there and asked the Vatican to replace him with an Englishman. Again the appointment went to Hughes, and it was a most unwelcomed appointment. It meant he would have to become a bishop, and it also meant that his days as a missionary to Central Africa were over. Hughes would have refused the assignment, but in obedience to the Pope he knew he would have to take it. The British were happy to see him when he arrived in Cairo in late 1942 and offered to arrange an introduction for him with King Farouk. "That would be very nice," Hughes said, "but I don't think I should meet Farouk under British auspices. After all, I'm not here as a representative of the King of England but the Prince of Peace."

Learning this, the Egyptians were delighted. Hughes became a frequent dinner guest of Farouk, enhancing his position even more by learning Arabic and always conversing in it. Farouk even then was an energetic sensualist; if his parties did not always end in orgies, they were nevertheless too raucous for a priest. Only once did Hughes have to complain by asking Farouk to be kind enough to hold off the dancing girls until Hughes left. After that, Farouk's parties when Hughes was present were models of propriety. People wondered what Moslem Farouk and Catholic Hughes had to talk about: Farouk, despite his dissipations, was an intelligent, educated man who, weary of the terrified yes-men who surrounded him, enjoyed the company of someone who was bright and well informed, who joked easily with him and openly disagreed on any point of view he felt was wrong.

There were others who should not have enjoyed Hughes so much, but they did. Egypt had some three million Christians, less than a fourth of whom were Catholics. The others belonged to various rites which had over the centuries broken with Rome mostly for nationalistic reasons. Their spiritual fidelity was to their own patriarchs. Important: though they were severed from Rome, they had true sacraments and true priests. The Church of England, on the other hand, had changed the ritual, thereby losing its apostolic inheritance. After the break-off about a thousand years ago, several of the Oriental Rites in a sense returned to Rome while retaining their own patriarchs and special characteristics, again for reasons of nationalism. The Orthodox Rites remained apart. It has always been the conviction of Rome that sooner or later the separated churches would return. To try to hasten that day, however, could be a mistake, especially in view of enduring nationalistic differences still between the various rites themselves, and so the matter had been left to time, to prayer, to God—and to men like Arthur Walter Hughes.

Hughes was a warm and charming man with an abundance of sincerity. Though he was in Egypt as a representative of the Pope, he attended special religious services in other Catholic churches, whether or not they were allied with the Vatican. His presence always stirred a great deal of comment and wide satisfaction. Simply by being there he was helping to bridge both the gaps between the various rites and Rome. The people were as pleased as the patriarchs. When Hughes was consecrated bishop, his pectoral cross and episcopal ring were gifts from Eastern church groups which ordinarily would have dreaded having so influential a Roman Catholic in the country. He was an attraction wherever he went. Once his train south into Egypt stopped at a wayside station, and he stepped out for fresh air. Word rushed through the region that he was there, and hundreds of people hurried to meet him. Even high-ranking Moslems found him irresistible and were constantly sending gifts and doing favors. And when he attended a party given for him by chaplains of the British Army, he enchanted the Protestant chaplains by going first to them because, he said, he

255

was anxious to meet their wives. This was no pose; he meant it, and that was why everybody liked him.

Evidence of his success occurred in 1947 when Egypt announced it would like to exchange ambassadors with the Vatican, the first Moslem country ever to do so. When considerations began for appointment of the Papal Internuncio, Egypt insisted that Hughes be raised to that office. Now Hughes had enough experience to know that though he was apparently well liked, there were many in Egypt who were uneasy over the sudden popularity of the Catholic Church. There was an axiom among diplomats that one must watch his friends closer than he watched his enemies, and Hughes was well acquainted with it. He was therefore not surprised when he learned that his official pouches mailed to the Vatican were being tampered with. He solved that problem simply by sending in the pouch only chitchat letters about the weather and everybody's health; his official observations regarding the position of the Church in Egypt he put into ordinary envelopes with ordinary stamps and popped them into the corner mail box himself. Buried in the usual heavy postal traffic, the letters arrived in Rome untouched. At one time he discovered that certain prominent Moslems were planning a long-term, slow but steadily increasing program against the Church in Egypt and throughout Africa. Through friends, he acquired a copy of the blueprint with the understanding that he just wanted to read it and would return it in the morning. He sat up all night typing a copy of it. The Moslems found out what had happened and suspected what Hughes had done. To keep him from getting the report to the Vatican, undercover men were assigned to watch his every move. His telephone was tapped, whatever he mailed was intercepted, everybody who left his house was followed in the event that he had given the document to them. Hughes was fully aware of all this and he thought it was a great deal of fun. And he knew what he would eventually have to do. His official position had put him in charge also of Catholic affairs in Palestine. The White Fathers were there, running a seminary for young men destined for the Melkite priesthood. The Melkites were —and are—adherents to the Byzantine Rite which had broken from Rome in the fifth century, but the Melkites subsequently returned. In 1859, the Sultan of Constantinople, a French ally in the

256

Crimean War, offered to France as a gift the Shrine of St. Anne, built on the site of the home of the mother of the Virgin Mary. Friends of Lavigerie in Paris asked him to take it over. At first Lavigerie was hesitant because it meant sending White Fathers away from Africa, for which they were intended. But then he accepted the shrine on the grounds that there were Moslems in Palestine, too, who needed the White Father influence. He had another reason that he didn't tell anybody. The Melkites were in union with Rome; if other Eastern rites were to follow suit, the necessary influence, Lavigerie felt, would come from within the Middle East. It was his intention one day to build a Melkite seminary in Palestine whose graduate priests would be, in effect, an attraction toward Rome. He did not want that influence to be too abrupt, and he felt it was most important first to attract more schismatic Easterners to the Melkite Rite, and the way to do that was to have a lot of outstanding Melkite priests. He knew he would never get permission from Rome to open a seminary right off, so he sent White Fathers to Jerusalem to take care of the shrine and open a high school for Melkite boys. Three years later, the Melkite patriarch visited the school, saw how excellent it was, and said he thought it would be wonderful if the White Fathers could start a seminary for the Melkite priests he so badly needed. A request of this kind to Rome was quickly approved, and the seminary began and has since provided for the Middle East scores of fine young Melkite priests. Many years later the seminary became very important to Archbishop Hughes.

In the midst of all the cloak-and-dagger surveillance of him, the seminary provided Hughes with an excuse to go to Palestine to see how the White Fathers were doing. The Egyptian Moslems correctly suspected that he would use the occasion to get the anti-Catholic report out of the country and they were on the train with Hughes when it pulled out of Cairo. The Archbishop had two pieces of luggage. One was a suitcase of his clothes, and this he kept open on the seat opposite and dug into whenever he needed anything. The other was a small briefcase to which he clung as if it meant his life. He never let it out of his sight, wherever he went on the train. The Egyptians watched anxiously for the first moment they could grab it. Hughes even slept with it in his tight grip, resting his feet on his opened suitcase. The Egyptians did not sleep at all. The train pulled into Jerusalem; Hughes busied himself locking up his suitcase. At the last moment, he pretended to be terribly occupied with finding a porter to carry his suitcase and carelessly put down his briefcase. The Egyptians grabbed it, jumped off the train, ran across the platform, and boarded a train just pulling out for Cairo. Hughes almost waved at them. He opened his suitcase and took out the envelope containing the secret report and mailed it at the first post office he saw. The Cairo-bound Moslems soon discovered that they had only a briefcase of old newspapers.

Though Archbishop Hughes never outgrew the physique of a boy, he did the work of a dozen men. When his regular duties did not keep him busy enough, he took on extra chores and studies. He saw everyone who came to him, day or night, however serious or trivial the matter at hand. He was a prince and ambassador of the Church, and though as such he could have rightly lived in a certain elegance, he rejected anything resembling luxury. If he knew he had a sumptuous banquet to attend, he privately fasted for days before it. His work in Cairo freed him from the rules of the White Fathers, but he nevertheless kept them. He was up at five every morning for his meditation, and whatever his schedule, he took time to join the priests who worked for him in the daily religious exercises. The spiritual depth he had evinced as a young man remained with him all his life. Once, soon after his ordination, an elderly priest served his Mass and told him afterward, "Young man, I want you to say a Hail Mary every day of your life for the grace to say Mass as you did this morning." The same could have been said of his piety the day he died. He had, in 1949, gone back to England for what was supposed to be a rest, but he arrived in London with a long list of chores and favors to be done. Up at five every morning, he was off to the parish church and back by the time his parents awoke and found that he had made their morning tea and brought it to them. Then out he went on the endless round of work. He had been warned by doctors that he had a bad heart, but he never let this deter him from what he felt had to be done. Nevertheless, there were times when he was too exhausted to take another step. Once, visiting a White Fathers' house upcountry, he went to his room for some papers he had been discussing, but did not return. The priests looked for him. He had fallen asleep on the bed, fully dressed, and remained there for thirty hours. The tensions and pressures of his work in Egypt were beginning to tell on him. His family and fellow priests were worried; they insisted that he see a heart specialist, and he reluctantly agreed. Three days before his scheduled appointment, he suffered an attack while driving in London but managed to get home safely. The night preceding the appointment, he had two more attacks, and the second was fatal. It was when his confreres were examining his personal effects that they discovered the extent of his mortifications. Bent on sanctity, he had had hidden away several instruments of penance, used apparently as reminders of vigilance against whatever shortcomings he must have felt were keeping him from a complete union with God. The discovery was a great surprise, and it was further evidence of his determination for piety. His sudden death at forty-seven shocked everyone into a sense of loss; people grew jealous of Heaven. Friends remembering him these days always cap their remarks of his achievements with: "Oh, he was a charmer." That, too, is a trait of saints.

A charmer in quite a different way was Joseph Dupont, who had gone to Africa as a missionary and left it a king. Born in France, Dupont decided at six that he wanted to be a missionary, and nothing else interested him. At that age, he had no idea of the lengthy studies ahead of him; the mere thought of school was agony. He was raised on a farm and had to walk two miles to school, always enough distance to convince himself that he wouldn't be missed if he didn't show up. He was the record truant in the school's history, and when his father finally decided that forcing him to school was a waste of time, his teachers were glad to get rid of him. His father soon found him to be an expensive farm hand. Always lost in daydreams of his future missionary life, he paid little attention to what was going on around him. Equipment broke down at his touch, cattle were left unattended, crops had a way of withering when he walked by. It was not what he did that caused so much trouble; it was simply that he did nothing. Punishments from his father's heavy hand had no effect on him. He let the world go by, awaiting the day when he would take off for some foreign country to fulfill what he considered his destiny. He was in his teens when he suddenly realized that to be a priest required many years of study. In heavy resignation, he decided he might as well get at it and he went to his pastor, announced his ambition, and asked for instructions in Latin.

"You a priest?" the pastor said incredulously. "God help the Church!"

His family was equally doubtful, but Latin lessons kept him off the farm a few hours a day and his father was grateful for that. He was fourteen when he finally entered the minor seminary, and he was put in a class with boys much younger. But instead of being embarrassed, he plodded along disinterestedly at something he knew had to be done. The only time he shone was when the students were allowed to go out hunting; he was an excellent shot. He was twenty when he finished the six-year course, which was equivalent to junior high school, and he was ready to plunge into the next six years when he received his draft notice from the Army. As a seminarian, he was exempt from military service; furthermore, the notice was actually for another Joseph Dupont who lived nearby. The error could have easily have been rectified, but he liked the idea of being in the Army for a while and the rector of the seminary couldn't think of one good reason for dissuading him. He took part in the Franco-Prussian War and the subsequent uprising in France. He returned to the seminary eighteen months later, and the rector, surprised to see him back, ordered him to repeat the last year of minor seminary. Dupont obeyed without a murmur, his only complaint being that he was now far behind a former classmate he had liked—Alexis Pouplard, who later joined the White Fathers and was among the three killed on the second attempt to cross the Sahara.

Dupont was finishing major seminary when he decided to join the White Fathers, but his bishop was against the idea, convinced that the White Fathers wouldn't last long. Dupont waited a few months, then asked again. Annoyed by his persistence, the bishop told him to go ahead. He was delighted to encounter Pouplard at Algiers and he was all set to settle down to a happy life as a missionary. He was therefore somewhat alarmed when, his formal studies finished, he was sent to Paris to study remote subjects like photography, geology, astronomy, and surveying. He had no idea where this fitted into a missionary's life, and he was startled even further when after Paris he was assigned to teach seminarians at Carthage. He was a priest five years before, in 1885, he received his first opportunity to go into the mission field by leading a caravan into the Lower Congo. This was more like it.

The caravan entered from the Atlantic Coast and began its slow trek inland. As in East Africa, there were fever, rebellious porters, heavy rains, wild animals, unfriendly natives, and unco-operative government officials. Dupont thrived on all of it. He was a well-built man, daring, almost arrogant. His scowls and sharp voice brought order among the porters and meekness among the natives. He dismissed the nagging Belgian authorities with a crisp: "You do your job and I'll do mine. If we're both here for the good of the people, we won't have any trouble." He established two small missions and a large one at Uluba, which was to play an important part in his future. He was in the Congo a year when he received notice from Rome that the territory had been turned over to the Holy Ghost Fathers. Superiors of the White Fathers sent word that he was to go to East Africa via Marseilles. He was sorry to give up the work he had started, but as long as he was going to remain in Africa, he didn't mind too much. However, Marseilles did not turn out to be the stop-off he expected: he was assigned to teach in France and remained there four years. He wrote his superiors: "I am developing cloisterphobia and I fear this quiet life will do me serious harm. If you have need for an ass-driver on one of the African caravans, I will be grateful for the job." In June, 1891, he was appointed to head a new caravan to Karema on Lake Tanganyika. As he sailed from Marseilles, he hoped this was the last he would ever see of it.

The caravan from Bagamoyo took seven months to reach its destination. It passed across Tanganyika during one of the country's worst droughts. Rivers were dry; lakes evaporated in a day. Porters deserted every day; others died of thirst in epidemic numbers. Progress was halted for weeks at a time as the priests repeatedly came down with fever. Tribes along the route were frantic, demanding water as payment for safe passage rather than the usual bolts of cloth. By the time the caravan reached Tabora, there had been two complete turnovers among the porters, and the priests who finally succeeded in arriving at Karema were skeletons of their former selves. At Karema at last, Dupont refused to rest. He was given a seven-year-old mission that was on the verge of complete decay, and he worked so ceaselessly to repair it and expand it that the Africans called him Bwana Moto Moto—Father Burning Fire. Despite the distances between tribes, word spread fast about the perpetual-motion priest at Karema, and people traveled miles for a look at him. When he saw them sitting around staring at him, he put them to work. In the matter of a few months his rebuilt mission was at top efficiency. His skill as a hunter also became widely known, and through it he was able to keep the people living near him well supplied with fresh meat. He observed that occasionally the male attendance at chapel or catechism fell off: men were unaccustomed to regularities of any kind and easily became bored. When this happened, he would organize a hunting tribe, take as many as three hundred men with him, and disappear into the bush for a week or two. On such trips, there was little the men could do nights but sit around and listen to him; they returned to their villages knowing all their prayers and several chapters of catechism.

The men liked him a great deal. They began taking their problems to him, and he became somewhat of a judge and he knew how to talk a disobedient wife into behaving herself. He learned one day of the death of a chief far to the south and he knew the terror that would riot the tribe until some man proved himself strong enough to claim the throne. He hurried to the village, stopping first at the office of the nearest German authority to ask who in the tribe seemed best equipped to be chief. Told, he went to the tribe, and his unexpected appearance startled everyone into a brief armistice. He called all the people together and in a short but angry speech he told them that there must be no fighting. Then he asked for the man the German commissioner has suggested for chief and said: "You are the new chief and I will now crown you. Anybody who disagrees will have to deal with me, not with you." Then he put on the young man's head a velvet hat to which he had sewn a religious medal and threw over his shoulders a bright robe fringed with lace. Astonished by Dupont's audacity and impressed by their new chief's regalia, the people heralded the coronation with cheers of approval. Dupont stayed at the village a few days to be sure everything was all right, then he returned to Karema. Weeks later he received a letter from the German commissioner saying: "I don't know what you did, but it was wonderful. I hope you won't mind returning to do it again someday when the occasion arises."

There then existed in what is now Northern Rhodesia a powerful tribe known as the Beni Nganda—the Crocodile Clan, which had migrated centuries before from Uluba in the Lower Congo (now Angola). It was at Uluba that Dupont established his large mission. Tribal legend maintained that when the clan had moved eastward, it was guided by a white man, who from descriptions appears to have been a priest, perhaps one of the Portuguese missionaries from the west coast who probably met the tribe on his inland treks. He died during the journey, and the tribe thought so highly of him that it believed one day another white man would come to take his place and lead the people to power and wealth. The tribe had once had a mighty king—Kiti the Great: Kitimukulu, and all subsequent kings took his name. On arriving in the Ubemba country of Northern Rhodesia, the tribe easily vanquished tribes already there and took over control. The country was divided into three provinces: Ubemba itself, ruled by the Kitimukulu, who by tradition married outside the clan and thus his sons could not succeed him; Mpanda, whose ruler was called Makasa, appointed by the Kitimukulu, often from among his own sons; and Ituna, ruled by a Mwamba, who was also appointed the Kitimukulu most often from among his brothers. Being a member of the clan, the Mwamba could become king. There were many other tribes in the area, subservient to the Crocodile Clan, and all the people were known as Babemba. The country was continually at war—minor tribes against the Crocodile Clan, and provinces of the clan against one another. In the spring of 1895, Dupont was assigned to enter the province of Mpanda, set up a mission, and prepare to expand throughout the country. It was British territory, and despite the tribal legend about a white man who would lead the people to greatness, the clan had already had enough trouble with the English to dislike anybody who resembled them in the least. Makasa, king of the Mpanda province, had met the White Fathers and seemed tolerant toward them, but when the priests announced their desire to construct a mission near the royal enclosure, he balked on the grounds that

Kitimukulu didn't want any more white men in the country. Dupont suspected that the hesitation was more Makasa's own doing. He organized a small caravan and took off for the royal enclosures at Mipini.

He found the gates locked to him. Warriors inside the fence pointed to skulls perched on the posts and said: "If you don't want that to happen to you, you'd better get out of here. Makasa doesn't want you around."

Dupont called back: "Tell Makasa he has bad manners. I am a traveler and it is growing dark. He should let me inside to spend the night."

A messenger ran to Makasa with the report, and the king came to the gate. "All right," he said. "You can come in, but you must be gone at dawn. Kitimukulu is angry because you are in the country, and I don't want any trouble with him."

"What about my men?" Dupont asked.

"They have to stay outside."

"But they are travelers, too. Do you want everybody to know how you treat travelers?"

"Oh, all right!" Makasa exclaimed. "Let them in. But you must all be out of here first thing in the morning."

Dupont was shown to a small hut and ordered to remain in it, but he had no such intentions. He put a chair outdoors in the fading sunlight and sat and read his breviary. Finished, he began to think about finding something to eat when he saw an elderly woman hobble by, her legs swollen by infected wounds. He called to her and told her to wait while he fetched his medical kit. As he treated her, hundreds of others watched entranced. She seemed immediately vastly improved, and for the rest of the night anybody with the slightest ache or pain demanded help from the priest. At dawn he was still hard at work.

Makasa was incensed to find Dupont still there long after dawn, but each hour the priest remained, more people went to Makasa to tell about the wonders he was performing for the sick. It was late afternoon when Makasa sent for Dupont.

"I thought I told you to be out of here by sunrise," he said.

"I would have," assured Dupont, "but your people have kept me busy."

"So I've heard."

"And they seem quite satisfied with what I can do for them."

"I've heard that, too," said Makasa.

"But you were also the one who first said it would be all right for me to come here."

"That was before I knew Kitimukulu would disapprove."

"I am not afraid of Kitimukulu," said Dupont. "Why should you be?"

"He is a very terrible man when he is upset."

Dupont laughed. "You know he is old and sick and when he is not drunk he is drugged."

Makasa said: "He has a lot of fierce warriors."

"So have you."

"Nevertheless, I don't want you here."

Dupont assumed his effective frown. "Well, I am going to stay. Now, with your permission I would like to get back to your sick people."

Makasa, like all chiefs, was impressed by bravery in one man, and he concluded that Dupont must be brave indeed to be able to challenge not only him but Kitimukulu as well. He let the priest stay. Kitimukulu's men were seen probing the area, but when there was no attack, Makasa relaxed. Dupont soon realized that his quarters were too cramped for him to do a good job and he asked for land outside the royal enclosure where he could construct a mission. He was given acreage at Kyambi, across a small creek from the palace, and when he indicated that he might need some help with the construction, the people voluntarily brought the wood and did the work.

The mission was a great success. Its first attraction was its clinic, and even Kitimukulu sent his children there for treatment. The school built next had a hundred pupils its first week, including the sons of Makasa. There being no official objection to proselytizing, the mission soon had scores of catechumens, the number increasing so rapidly that Dupont had to send to Tanganyika for African catechists to help him and the other priests teach. As before, whenever the men seemed disinterested, Dupont took them on hunting trips, using evenings to instruct them. The most significant sanction came when Makasa permitted the closely guarded Babemba women to go to the mission for instructions. Dupont complained that once the women overcame their shyness, they talked more than French women and he was seldom able to get in a word about God. He wrote to Algiers and asked for some White Sisters to take over the chore. Final approbation came from the British: an Arab slave caravan had been intercepted and the British agent sent the children to Father Dupont to raise. Everything seemed to be going very well.

Even so, Dupont did not relax his caution. His presence in Makasa's province added stature to the area, which indicated trouble in that Makasa was the weakest of the three kings of Ubemba, and Kitimukulu and Mwamba were not likely to let him get away with it for too long. Both of the other kings sent gifts to Dupont and invited him into their provinces, but he did not think this the propitious time for taking chances. His attitude was strengthened when he learned that Kitimukulu's men were attacking the weakly manned British outposts and stealing rifles. One day, Kitimukulu asked Makasa, Mwamba and Dupont to meet him for an important conference, but still Dupont distrusted him and discouraged the others from going to the session. Furious, Kitimukulu declared war on both kings, but before he could carry out his plans, he suffered fever which turned into black water and he died. Following tribal tradition, those nearest him were blamed for his death and dozens of people were killed. Again following tradition, the throne, inherited through the maternal branch of the family, finally went to one of his stepbrothers, an ineffectual young man who bothered nobody.

Mwamba, though he did not hold the highest rank, was now the most powerful king in the country. His whims became the unwritten law for all. More and more the British were making their presence felt in Ubemba, and Mwamba was anxious to keep the British from interfering in any way with his own rule. He felt the best way to do this was to make some sort of treaty with them which would assure his own sovereignty. With this in mind, he asked Dupont to come to his province. Dupont knew he would have to go. The future of the country was too uncertain for inactivity on his part. Makasa warned the priest against a trap, indicating as well that he was not too pleased to have the White Fathers go away.

Dupont promised that the Kyambi mission would remain staffed, which it was, and that he considered his trip to Mwamba's kingdom just a visit.

From the start it did not look like a friendly visit. Mwamba's warriors met Dupont's caravan miles from the royal enclosure and grimly accompanied him to the king. When Dupont finally entered the compound, he found a great party in progress. Everybody ignored him. Mwamba was sitting on a tall ant hill and paid no attention to him. For several minutes, Dupont stood at the base of the hill and stared up at the king. When Mwamba continued to look past him, Dupont climbed up the hill and sat down next to Mwamba to watch the dancing. Neither man spoke for half an hour; then Mwamba got up and went away. Dupont ordered his men to erect a tent where he could get relief from the sun and he waited there for Mwamba's next move. There was no word from the king, but the prime minister came and told Dupont that Mwamba had changed his mind and did not want him around.

Dupont said: "The king must have had some reason for asking me here. I will stay until he tells me what it is."

In the morning, Mwamba sent Dupont a gift of two tusks—a sign that he was ready to see him at the royal court. When Dupont entered, the king said: "The British are going to fight me."

"What makes you think so?" Dupont asked.

"They have many warriors and they plan to attack me soon."

"Why should they attack you?"

"They want the land for themselves, and they are also angry because of the rifles that were taken from them by Kitimukulu's men."

Dupont said: "The big kings of Europe have agreed that this land will be under British influence, and I don't think the British want to make trouble by trying to push you off your throne for no reason at all. If you will agree to the British law, I'm sure they will leave everything else as it is. As for the rifles, of course the British want them back. You are the most powerful king in the country, so you can see that this is done."

"How can I be sure that is all they want?" Mwamba asked.

"I will go see them for you, if you wish," Dupont offered.

"I wish it," Mwamba said. "And if the British will make a peace that is good for me, you can stay in my province."

Dupont went to the British and was able to arrange the type of treaty Mwamba wanted. The authorities asked only for the rifles and the understanding that, as evidence of good faith, the clan would be willing to pay a moderate tax. Mwamba was delighted with the agreement. In fact, he was carried away by it. He called all his people together and told them the story they had already heard countless times—the legend of the white man, Lukyale Nganga, who had accompanied the Crocodile Clan from Uluba. Then he turned to Dupont.

"I have heard that you came from Uluba," he said. "Is that true?"

"Yes," Dupont said easily. "I was there just thirteen years ago."

Mwamba was ecstatic. "You hear him?" he shouted to the people. "He is the son of Lukyale Nganga!" The people screamed their joy at the fulfillment of the legend. Mwamba told Dupont: "My country is yours!"

Dupont muttered: "Oh, now, really!" He got to his feet and said: "It is enough, Mwamba, that I am your brother. But this is your country and the people need you at the head of it. I am not a man for government, for business; I am a man of God and I want only to teach your people about Him."

"Then you shall do it!" Mwamba assured loudly.

Like most assurances from chiefs then so worried about their personal futures, the offer was short-lived. Mwamba's moods fluctuated wildly, and Dupont was never certain from one day to the next what was going to happen to him. Mwamba approved the building of a mission, but he was angry when Dupont put up a house instead of a hut. Though Mwamba was happy to have Dupont give medical treatment to his own immediate family, he ordered others who went to the mission for help to be whipped. At one period, Mwamba put Dupont under house arrest for no reason. Again, while denying Dupont the right to teach catechism for weeks at a time, he sent messengers asking why the priest hadn't sent him any gifts lately. The king's demands for gifts grew steadily worse. He kept insisting on rifles, and Dupont explained he had only one with him, which he could not spare. "You have rifles at Kyambi," Mwamba said. "Send for them." The situation at last was so desolate that Dupont had no idea which way to turn. Mwamba decided that problem for him by ordering him out of the province. To attempt to argue the king out of his decision would have been futile; Dupont realized that, and he prepared to leave. His resistance dropped as low as his spirits, and he was an easy fever victim. On the day he was to leave, he could just about walk. Many people came to see him off, and there was a great deal of weeping. Men and women fell to their knees to kiss his *gondoura* as he left the village. Children followed him for miles into the bush. After a few hours he realized that he was too ill to take another step. Then men who had volunteered for his caravan urged him to stop for the night, and one of them gently held Dupont's head in his lap as the priest tried to get some sleep. Late that night a messenger arrived from the village with a letter that had been forwarded from Kyambi. It was from Rome. Dupont had been appointed vicar apostolic of most of Northern Rhodesia and Nyasaland and he was to be consecrated as quickly as possible. It was not happy news, for the great burdens of a bishopric on top of what he considered his failure with Mwamba only made Dupont's future look bleaker. He fell asleep with tears in his eyes.

He was consecrated at Kyambi on August 15, 1897, and for a year he was busy with his many new responsibilities. Always he regretted that Mwamba would not let him back in the province, and no matter what other successes he achieved, the experience in the Ituna area continued to depress him. Nevertheless, he was understandably wary when, in September of the next year, messengers from Mwamba said the king begged for him to return. Dupont asked for proof of friendship; Mwamba sent gifts and a hundred warriors to guarantee safe passage. To play safe, Dupont took along warriors of Makasa's province, but he needed just one look at Mwamba to realize that the man was beyond violence of any kind. The king was very ill, and he knew it.

"I understand," the king said, "that you are now a big chief yourself."

"That has happened to me," Dupont conceded.

"It will take a big chief to do what I want," Mwamba said.

"And what is that?"

"Once I called you the son of Lukyale Nganga and I offered you my country," Mwamba said. "I know I am going to die soon and I want you here to take over my throne."

"You know I can't do that," said Dupont.

"If you refuse, terrible things will happen. You know the custom of my people," Mwamba said. "When I die, those near me will be killed for my death. Many will be murdered. I don't want that to happen, and it won't if you become king."

"I will do all I can to prevent it," Dupont offered, "but I cannot be king."

Mwamba tried to smile. "You will be if I make it my dying wish. That is the law here. You can keep the throne as long as you want, then give it to someone else when the excitement of my death is over. But the kingdom will first be yours. That is my command."

Several nights later, when it was obvious that Mwamba would die in a few hours, the prime minister and other leaders went to Dupont and told him Mwamba had revealed his desire to them, and they asked Dupont to accept. A peaceful transition meant their lives as well as the lives of others; they could have fought to defend themselves, though to do so was to violate custom: death for them was inescapable. To avoid that, Dupont agreed to become king. "But just for a little while," he added.

Bishop Dupont was, by Mwamba's last will, legitimate king of Ituna for three months. Two days after taking over, he wrote the British authorities about what had happened, informing them that he had convinced the people to submit to British rule, and asking the British to help choose as his successor a man whose co-operation could be relied upon. The choice was made, but the Babemba people had never heard of anything like abdication, and even after Dupont relinquished the throne, they still considered him king. Though the new king sat on the throne and did the paper work, it was to Dupont that the people went for mediation of their problems and the administration of justice. The people had good reason to trust in Dupont. On Mwamba's death, there had been brief panic in the province. His wives, his children, his close associates all expected to be killed. Makasa and Kitimukulu, in fact, sent men to Ituna to perform the traditional massacre. It was Dupont who held them off by orders and by threats. The massacre averted, he brought a social justice to the province it had never known before. The wives of Mwamba were by inheritance his. He gave them the freedom to do what they chose. Disagreements between the people and crimes committed by other

270

tribes in the province were resolved by fines instead of the usual execution. Previously, the incurably sick and the dead were put outside to be devoured by hyenas. Dupont put up a clinic for the dying and buried the dead with his own hands until the people learned that burial was the proper thing to do. As king of the strongest province, his influence poured into the other two kingdoms. The entire country was opened to the missionaries, who put up schools and hospitals and churches. With the ascendance of the new king, Dupont returned to Kyambi, but the throne followed him there. The people continued to go to him for help, comfort, and guidance. Though he repeatedly assured them that they now had a king from their own tribe, they merely agreed with him politely and went on taking on all their troubles to him. As evidence of what the people thought of him, they suggested the name for a new mission he opened. They said: "Call it Kilubula—deliverance. That is what you have given us."

There was peace and justice and mercy and charity in the country for the first time in its history. For some reason, the British authorities strongly disapproved, and they let their feelings be known in Rhodesia, in Algiers, in Rome, and in London. Their major complaint: they had no control over the people. Whenever they tried to enforce any laws or taxes through the new king, the people went first to Bishop Dupont to see if it was all right. Dupont spoke to them as a missionary, constantly reminding them of the obedience they owed their real king and the British, and whatever the British wanted was done. It was the detour through Dupont they resented, their lack of understanding of the people that caused them trouble.

Being bishop and quasi-king damaged Dupont's health. He asked Rome for permission to become an ordinary missionary again, but the request was refused. Then he asked to have his large vicariate cut in half, but this, too, was refused. With too much to do, he was unable to resist malaria; rheumatism and damp weather combined to make his legs stiff and unusable. In 1900, he asked his superiors at Maison Carrée for a leave of absence in order to regain his health in better climate. In October of that year he returned to Europe, and it was 1905 before he was able to get back to Africa.

The people picked up where they had left off. No one had forgotten him. Many who heard he was coming back delayed their baptisms after their four-year catechumenate so that they could receive the sacrament from his hands. Thousands were waiting for him when he arrived at Kyambi, all assuming that he would be to them as he had been before. That was what the British were afraid of. The vicariate had grown, both in priests and nuns, brothers and missions. Bishop Dupont occupied himself completely with his mission work. He was now a man of fifty-five; he had returned to Rhodesia against doctors' orders because he was impatient to be back among the people he loved. He fully expected to die among them. But difficulties persisted with government officials who suspected him of meddling in their own sphere. Deliberately he avoided anything resembling the slightest invasion of the political realm, but he could not stop the people from going to him. The government wearied of having discussions with Africans either start with "Lord Bishop Moto-Moto said we should—" and end with "We will see how Lord Bishop Moto-Moto feels about this and come back later." Early in his priesthood, Dupont had told a Belgian official, "If we're both here for the good of the people, we won't have any trouble." Any difference of opinion that arose years later with the British in Rhodesia sprang from the same yardstick. Actually, the British were in an awkward predicament. However aware they were of their responsibilities to the people and whatever they might have tried to achieve, their success was limited because of the results they wanted: submission to empire expansion. The wide influence therefore of a missionary who was not even an Englishman was most unwelcome.

Passing years did not ease the situation. Dupont blamed himself for the difficulty—if indeed there could by any guilt in doing good—and again he asked for permission to resign his position and pass the reins to a younger, less involved man. The suggestion was disapproved. In an effort at compromise, however, it was recommended that the vicariate at last be divided and Dupont take the southern section in Nyasaland. This time Dupont disapproved. He would be a stranger in Nyasaland; in Rhodesia he knew the languages and the people. To put a man his age into new territory was to throw away all the experience he had acquired where it would mean the most. There was only one thing to do: his resignation was accepted, and he was reassigned to North Africa. He left Rhodesia in 1911, knowing he would never see it again, blind to the fact that the sense of failure which haunted him could be chalked up against the unusual short-coming of being too good a missionary.

He suffered the worst frustrations for twenty more years. In France, he took any job he could find to keep him busy; he was a curate in a country parish and a chaplain at French Army camps; in time, old age made him incapable of even this. He moved back to Africa, to Thibar, the White Fathers' property in Tunisia where a large scholasticate was built, and he found some pleasure in spending hours telling future missionaries about his glorious years in Rhodesia. He waited for mail from his former vicariate with excruciating homesickness. He was piqued, as old men can be, by short letters that made him think he was being forgotten. One day a young White Father entered his room and found Dupont on his knees in prayers of tearful gratitude. "Read this," Dupont said, handing the man a letter. It was from a White Sister in Rhodesia who had written immediately after giving a twelve-year-old boy his final catechism examination, which he had passed. She then asked: "What name are you going to take in baptism?" And the boy replied: "You ask my name, Mama? My name is Bwana Josephu Lord Bishop."

"They have not forgotten me," Dupont told the young priest. "My Babemba have not forgotten me."

Dupont wrote his successor in Rhodesia:

"My body is here, but my heart is there. I can never say my prayers at Thibar nor anywhere else over here. As soon as I open my breviary, touch my rosary or go up to the Altar, I find myself in Ubemba among my children, and it is for them that I pray all the time. Neither by day nor by night are my thoughts here; they are journeying through the forests and missions of Ubemba."

He prayed constantly that the Babemba would adhere to the religion he had brought to them, and in 1927 he received the following assurance in a letter from Father Paul Voillard, then Superior General of the White Fathers on an inspection tour of the missions:

In a few moments I am off to Tanganyika but I cannot quit this region where you, the first pioneer of the Gospel, cleared the ground, without telling you of my impressions. They are excellent. The results are wonderful, both in numbers and quality, and I marvel at what I have seen and heard. The seed that you sowed so laboriously and watered with so many tears and so much sweat has been fruitful. There is no doubt that this is due in great part to the prudent, solid, and devoted manner in which the first work was done. I want to thank you for this.

Old Christians have talked to me about you. They reminded me of the eventful days of your conquest of the country for God, days at first so tragic and then so suddenly triumphant. They pointed out to me the spots at Kilubula and Malole where you made so great an impression on the chiefs.

When I told them that we were old friends, that I knew you before you ever came here, and that I should soon be seeing you again, they were moved to tears. They said that with my white hair and beard I am like you, and they begged me to give you their affectionate wishes and thanks.

I myself was very moved by all this and I want to tell you all about it because I know that the heart of the "Apostle of Ubemba" will be filled with joy and with the most legitimate pride.

You may be happy, my lord, with the splendid results of your great labors. One day all these good Babemba will form your crown in Heaven.

The letter meant a great deal to Dupont. He knew, of course, that he had been moved from Rhodesia in the hope that the end of his personal influence upon the people would contribute to an harmonious future with the British. The letter proved that his influence had not ended with his departure, that the only influence he had tried to exert had remained in the hearts of a people who were still trying to get the British out of their hair.

Arthur Walter Hughes and Joseph Dupont were certainly outstanding missionaries, yet they were not rare examples among the White Fathers who went to Africa before them, with them, and after them, but to present the fullest picture would require profiles of five thousand men.

XXI

For a long time the White Fathers' work was held up by a charac-
teristic which would have completely frustrated less dedicated men.
There existed throughout Africa a stubborn reluctance to change.
The very nature of tribal life rooted in the people a refusal to have
anything to do with ideas different from what they were used to. The
immobility had its advantages as far as chiefs were concerned, and
colonial governments were happy with it: people resigned to life
as they found it would not make demands on those who ruled them.
The great wrong in the attitude and the crime of those who nurtured
it was that it kept Africa at a standstill. It was an attitude that had
some of its roots in religion. Paganism involved a dread of anything
that was strange and unexplained; Islam was based on a certain
fatalism which destroyed a man's normal urge to want to improve
himself and the world around him. As a result, Africa remained
centuries behind the rest of mankind. Evidence: until as late as 1900
an astonishing vast majority of Africans had no idea of the principle
of the wheel, had never seen one, had never thought of devising
anything like it that could make their lives easier. The same back-
wardness was apparent in every aspect of living, and the African
suffered because of it. Enlightenment of the African therefore em-

braced far more than just his spiritual life, and when the White Fathers entered the continent, they commenced the great task from all angles. They saw, for instance, that though the African relied greatly on agriculture for his existence, he knew practically nothing about farming and was not only getting far less than the possible yield but was not even getting a proper diet. For this reason, the White Fathers started programs to help the farmer as soon as they entered a new area, whether it was at the Equator, on the Niger, or in the Atlas Mountains.

One of the White Fathers' most successful attempts along these lines still flourishes near the ancient village of Thibar, seventy-five miles south of Tunis. Centuries ago, Thibar was a thriving Roman military post and trading station for wandering Berbers, but the fall of the Romans, subsequent Christian heresies, and the Moslem vandals almost completely destroyed it. What remains is a cross-roads village twelve hundred feet up in the Atlas Mountains. In 1896, Cardinal Lavigerie acquired several hundred acres of swamp just outside the town where he intended to build a mission and an orphanage. After many months of work, the missionaries succeeded in draining two hundred and fifty acres, and on this they began their farm. In recent years, French agronomists and representatives of the U.S. Point Four Plan have visited Thibar, to see for themselves how the White Fathers have managed to develop a model farm in an area that was traditionally wasteland. As planned, the wonders performed at Thibar have overflowed into the surrounding area, creating a fertile oasis which stretches beyond the valley to the properties owned by farmers, French or Arab.

From the beginning, it was the intention of the White Fathers to contribute to the progress of the valley as well as support themselves by what they were able to grow. Fortunately, the priests—and particularly the brothers—who were appointed to Thibar had agriculture backgrounds and they knew how to attack the challenge that faced them.

The Arab of Tunis is primarily a shepherd, but because he has never known much about his cows and sheep and less about what they find to eat in the pastures and on the mountaintops where they roam, he has always lost heavily. Animals that didn't die young were thin and weak; the cows gave little milk and the sheep produced an inferior wool. The meat of both was tough and tasteless. Like the farmers, the White Fathers lost much at first, and they knew they would go on that way unless something was done. A study of the pastures revealed a widespread growth of St.-John's-wort, an herb containing hyparicine which acts upon the blood stream of animals and produces early death. It would have been as impossible to get rid of the herb as it would be to sweep the Sahara clean. The alternative was to breed animals that could resist the herb's effect. The White Fathers imported white-skinned merinos from France and Algerian ewes whose wool was pigmented with black. For ten years starting in 1908, the strains were crossbred, using in particular the black-fleeced animals. By 1918, the flock was transformed, producing lambs that were brown or black. To improve the breed, a ewe of exceptional quality was coupled with her sons of equal quality, and the male offspring of such unions were in turn coupled with their mothers. The product by 1925 was a homogeneous flock of ewes that weighed from a hundred and ten to a hundred and thirty pounds, rams that weighed from a hundred and seventy-five pounds to two hundred. Fleeces weighed from four to seven pounds for ewes and from nine to eleven pounds for rams. The twenty years of work gave Tunisia the finest herds it had ever seen, healthy, big animals which could withstand the noxious effects of St.-John's-wort. As a result, some sixty thousand descendants of the flock now roam the pastures of the country, and the breed is officially recognized in the "Flock Book" as the "Black Race of Thibar."

The cattle raisers of Tunis also had a lot of problems, and the White Fathers went to work on these, too. Cows, like sheep, were victims of St.-John's-wort, but hundreds more of them were being killed by ticks and by the severe climate in the mountains. Again, the White Fathers resorted to special breeding. At first, attempts were made to cross the Arab cow with Sicilian stock, but this was not successful. Hybrids of this match, however, were improved by an admixture of Charollais and Zebu blood. The bulls from the Charollais required constant and costly care and easily fell victim to the piroplasmosis carried by ticks. On the other hand, the cows issued from the Charollais, after crossbreeding with Zebus, gave successful and resistant products. But the cows didn't give much milk, and with the hope of improving their production they were crossed with Zebus and Tarentais. Nothing happened. A Mont-béliardais bull was imported, again without much success, and just when the breeders were about to give up, the bull produced a son of remarkable vigor, resistance, and conformation. He was raised as carefully as a crown prince. Named Bello II, he produced from 1920 to 1926 an outstanding strain which won as much world acclaim as the Thibar sheep. Milk production was fantastic for Tunisia: better than three thousand quarts in three hundred days, averaging a six per cent fat content. Again the Arab farmers lined up to profit from the White Fathers' work. Requests for the breed came from all over the world, and the White Fathers have never been able to keep up with the demand. To accommodate everyone, the farm gave away most of its own stock, keeping just enough to keep the original producers under scientific control.

As important as this work has been, the White Fathers were primarily concerned with their influence on the farmers themselves. The priests knew it would have have been a waste of time to try to go to an Arab's farm, befriend him, and expect him to take lessons in farming from Christians. Not only did the Arab's traditional dislike of Christians stand in the way, but so did his Moslem fatalistic attitude that he was the victim of his environment and couldn't do anything to alleviate conditions. True, the priests had the Arab orphans who in time would move away, taking with them all they had learned on the Thibar farm, but this was not enough. The answer was to hire grown Arabs to work on the farm, improving their knowledge of farming by teaching them their jobs. There was much the Arabs had to learn: fertilization, crop rotation, safeguards against soil erosion. And they had to learn that Christians could be nice to know and not bad at all to work for. In carrying out this plan, the White Fathers made a point of hiring men who came from distant areas, knowing that when they went home after a few years, they would take with them new attitudes as well as new ideas. Though with the passing years the farm has become amazingly mechanized for Tunisia, the White Fathers have consistently refused to adopt any new methods which might cost men their jobs. This at times has proved expensive, but no cost could prove too great in view of the intended goal. Undoubtedly, the goal is being achieved. Arabs anywhere in North Africa can always spot one of their own who has spent any time at Thibar. Not only is he a better farmer, but he is a man of plans, ideas, ambitions, and principles; he has a tolerance toward Christians which is rare and a friendliness toward missions which is practically unheard of in the isolated rural areas.

In July of 1956, the new labor element in Tunisia called a strike of Arabs employed on non-Arab farms, and this included Thibar. The White Fathers were startled and considerably hurt. Then the terms for future employment arrived at Thibar and the Arab farm hands discovered they were already being paid a third more than the strike leaders were demanding. Though the rest of the country remained strike-bound, the men at Thibar went back to work. They were actually getting far more than better pay. They were getting free medical care for their family, free education for their children, and free housing for those who came from distant areas, all benefits in effect for twenty-five years. New houses built in 1956 have four rooms, electricity, and running water, luxuries even the richest Thibar farmers do not have. And adopted early in 1955 was a retirement plan, the only one in Tunisia outside government employment.

When the White Fathers arrived in Central Africa, they found agriculture conditions no better than in the north. The equatorial soil was, for the most part, much better, but because the tribes refused to move to new areas and because they knew nothing of manure fertilization their ground was in poor shape. In Northern Rhodesia, the citemene farm system was used. Boys climbed high trees and stripped them bare, almost to the top. The cut branches were piled in a clearing, about two hundred feet wide, and left there to dry. They were then burned and the ashes were hoed under. The first year, finger millet was grown; the second year, beans or peanuts; the third—if the ground had any strength left—pumpkins or squash. When the soil was exhausted, the tribe moved across the road, gradually ruining the entire area. The abandoned "farm" was worthless for a generation, and it took ten to fifteen years for the trees to regrow. Trees cut down for fire or building were never replaced. There was no food-storage plan in the event of a bad harvest. A crop was no sooner taken in than the tribe began to worry if it could survive to the next season. There was no cattle raising in the area, except for small herds owned by kings. What the tribe could not raise for itself, it stole, or it hunted and fished.

Famine was endemic to the region; there was a great deal of sickness and a high infant mortality rate. The White Fathers knew that only good and plentiful food would save the country from extinction. Within a few years after their first arrival, they introduced wheat and corn and potatoes; they started truck farms; they imported the orange, lemon, sweet banana, pawpaw, strawberry, raspberry, mulberry, grape; they brought cattle, hogs, sheep, even goats, from the Tanganyika coast; they broke the first oxen to the yoke, put the first plow to work, built the first irrigation dams, constructed the first carts. They acclimatized the apple, pear, and peach; they developed larger and better mangoes; they grew the first manioc and giant cassava and they made the first butter and cheese in the country. They planted thousands of trees.

Getting the people to eat the new foods was no chore, but getting them to grow them was quite something else. They looked upon the foods as children look at candy: it was all something the missionaries made and gave them. The only way to make them work at growing their own was to make a game out of it. A missionary would arrive at a village on one of his regular visits, spend an hour or two at catechism, then say:

"All right, now I've got something for you to do. You children get your hoes and break up this plot of ground. You men pile up the broken sod in neat mounds two feet high and three feet across and don't forget to put plenty of grass in. You young fellows look strong; dig me some holes three feet deep and three feet across, fill them half full of grass and cover the grass with loose earth one foot thick. You girls get your jugs and fetch plenty of water. *Allez!* Come on, get going!"

The work done, into the mounds would go cassava sticks; into the deep holes went banana shoots, well watered; the shallow holes received large mango stones, and the rills were strewn with potatoes.

"Now, water them," the priest would say. "Water them every day it doesn't rain. Pull out the weeds and keep the bugs off. If everything isn't growing fine when I come back in a month, it'll be your fault, and off go your heads!"

Had it not been for such scenes fifty years ago, Northern Rhodesia today might well be another Sahara. Until 1923, the country was under the nominal rule of the British South African Corporation, with headquarters at Blantyre. The provinces where the White

Fathers were had been set aside as African reservations; the area had no valuable mines; there was no reason why the Corporation agents should try to do anything more in the district than keep everything quiet. The agricultural progress of the country, therefore, was the direct result of the efforts of the missionaries, and this was equally true in Tanganyika, in Ruanda-Urundi, the French West Africa—wherever the White Fathers went.

As with agriculture, so with schools. The British Corporation for Northern Rhodesia, being a mining and commercial concern, was no more interested in schools than it was in agriculture. Because the missionaries felt that education was as necessary to the progress of the people as full stomachs, the White Fathers started schools shortly after entering the country. Archbishop Hinsley, who had been apostolic delegate to Central Africa, urged the missionaries: "Advance all your projects to the fullest extent, but where it is impossible for you to carry on both the immediate task of evangelization and your educational work, neglect your churches in order to perfect your schools."

The White Fathers never looked upon themselves as teachers, except in the seminaries for their own aspirants for the African clergy: there could be no more important place for them to pass on what they inherited from Lavigerie. But when they first arrived in Northern Rhodesia, as in all the other countries, there was no one else to do the job with the children. The problem right off was that chiefs and parents were not particularly anxious for the children to go to school; the people had lived for centuries without knowing how to read or write: why start now? The attitude ignored the future, and to the White Fathers the future glowed with promise. And the greatest promise of the future was for the educated African who could, when the time came, assume the responsibilities of leadership at every level of authority and in every field of life. The White Fathers knew that time might never come if training the African was delayed too long, and they were impatient to get at the job. However, freedom and an equality with Europeans was something chiefs and parents of fifty years ago could not imagine, and they were apathetic to the priests' eagerness to start educating children. Religion was one thing, thought the African adult, but schooling was quite another matter.

The missionaries decided to get around the objections by announcing that not only must the children memorize their catechism in order to be baptized, but they must prove that they understood it by being able to read and write it. There could be no opposition to this, and so the schools began.

The catechumenate was four years; parents considered this much too long to keep a child at the mission all day, every day. The youngsters were growing, and they were needed to work on the tribal farm. It was thus extremely difficult for the priests to keep the children in school for more than two years, and this plight continued throughout Africa until 1920. The idea of educating girls at all struck parents as ridiculous from the beginning, and the priests had to beg, cajole, and pressure to get the girls into school. The first teachers were actually catechists, older teen-agers who had managed to spend their full four-year catechumenate at school and thus learn more and who subsequently convinced their parents to let them become teachers by bringing home a salary of vegetables, meat, cloth and trinkets. Not only did the catechists relieve the priests of teaching and free them to expand their spiritual work, but the young teachers were also able to move into distant villages, visited only occasionally by the missionary, and there add a fourth "R" to the three they were already teaching.

But the time came when even this was not enough. As the colonial governments themselves took over more authority, they faced the fact that they would have to invest some money in the education of the people they had absorbed into their empires. It was not a fact they faced with happy hearts, but persistent pressures by missionary societies, both Catholic and Protestant, gave the governments no way out.

The educators who went to Africa to set up school systems were invariably professionals of the highest caliber and with the progress of the African uppermost in their minds. They realized the best investment of school funds was in the already existing mission institutions and in the plans for expansion the missions presented. This was the recommendation they took home to their governments. It did not work out that way. Consistently, the men handling the purse strings for Africa's schools were politicians with their own prejudices, their own allegiances, their own whims and moods. They felt, too, that government money should go into government schools, ignoring the irrefutable fact that the missionaries could run schools better and cheaper than the government and with incomparably more successful graduates.

A great deal of money was spent on mission schools, to be sure, mostly by the Belgians, about equally by the French and British, least by the Portuguese, but nowhere near the amount that was needed. And only a percentage of the construction and maintenance cost was granted, as high as eighty per cent in some regions, but as low as forty in others. Bush schools, which made up by far the bulk of primary education, received no financial help at all. There was even discrimination in teachers' salaries. Teachers in mission schools got less than those in government schools; Africans got less than Europeans; priests, nuns, and brothers got less than everybody else. There was, of course, favoritism on a denominational basis: Belgium, a Catholic country, was more lenient with the Catholic missionaries; England favored Protestant and government schools; anticleric France did as little as possible for everybody. In 1954, there was a severe change in the Belgian Congo: the present Freemason government took office in Brussels that year and promptly notified the Catholic missions that allotments to existing schools would be decreased and there would be no funds for new schools. The reason given was economy, but then the government went ahead to show that it had no idea of economy at all. At Bukavu on the Congo shores of Lake Kivu, the government built a boarding school for six hundred and fifty boys at a cost of seven hundred million francs. Ten miles away, the Barnabite Fathers built a similar school for thirty million francs. The salaries of the seventy disciplinarians (not teachers) needed at the government school is five hundred thousand francs a year, which is almost triple the annual salary of the entire teaching staff at the Barnabite school. Both schools are new and it will take several years to compare the caliber of the graduates, but if the past is any measure, there will be no question of the results. In Uganda, for instance, at the high school at Kisubi, founded by the White Fathers and now run by the Brothers of Christian Instruction, graduates in 1956 won twenty of the fifty-six scholarships offered by Makerere College to high schools throughout all of East Africa.

Statistics show that seventy-five per cent of the young men now employed by the Belgian and British governments in Central Africa as office supervisors, clerks, department heads, instructors, and skilled laborers received their training at mission schools. The percentage holds throughout positions of importance in private companies and industries. The mission technical schools in Central Africa are the only places a boy can learn a trade; older men get on-the-job training in mission workshops of all kinds. The mission senior school at Astrida, in Ruanda, is the only place in the area where a boy can train to be an agronomist, a veterinarian, or a medical assistant. The excellent school, founded in the White Fathers' mission and now run by Christian Brothers of Ghent, is the only school in Africa with a hatchery (ten ponds) and a complete farm and arboretum where students can study and experiment with everything that will grow on the continent, plus several things that might. In all, the White Fathers have some fourteen thousand schools with more than a million students. This does not include the eight major seminaries which have given Africa five hundred priests, five of whom have become bishops. Nor does it include the five novitiates where the White Fathers have trained scores of lay brothers and the White Sisters have produced seven hundred African nuns.

Equally impressive has been the exceptional progress made in hospitals and hospital training. Each of the White Fathers' six hundred missions in Africa has at least an out-patient clinic. In each of the thirty-eight dioceses or vicariates under White Fathers' jurisdiction, there is at least one sizable hospital, often two. Particularly fine are the hospitals at Kabgayi in Ruanda, Jirapa in the Gold Coast, Wagadugu in French West Africa, Bukoba, Chala and Sumve in Tanganyika. Important at each hospital is the attention given mothers, who arrive at the hospital a month before delivery and remain two weeks afterwards, receiving vital training in child care which has slashed the infant-mortality rates in those areas. Almost all of the hospitals have nurses' training courses; in the Congo is a school which turns out fifty laboratory technicians a year. Interestingly, there is a large government hospital in the Eastern Congo, which proved to be so unmanageable that the government could no longer tolerate the financial loss. The hospital was about to be closed when somebody thought of calling in the White Sisters to run it. In the first year of their management, the deficit disappeared, and the hospital has remained within its budget ever since.

Undoubtedly, the missions have been the greatest factor in the development of Africa. The contributions made by governments and industry could not have been effected had not the missions first completed the long and difficult preliminaries, and even today those contributions would wither should the efforts of the missions be curtailed in any way. That several governments have not as yet realized this fact is to their discredit. To be sure, there have been missionary societies other than the White Fathers that have played vital roles in the progress of Africa, but using just statistics as a gauge, it is evident that the White Fathers have done most. Yet the full scope of what they have achieved is something that will remain unmeasurable for many, many years.

XXII

For many years there stood in the heart of Tunis a statue of Cardinal Lavigerie in a most evangelical pose. There were mixed feelings about the statue. For one thing, it had been placed with some imprudence just outside the Medina, the Moslem headquarters building, and only a few feet away was the entrance to the Arab Quarter of the city. There stood Lavigerie, bigger than life, one hand high, holding a large cross, the other gripping a Bible. Many an Arab flinched as he hurried past the statue on his way to the Medina or on the way home. On the other hand, there were French in the city who took some delight in the statue. To them, Lavigerie was a hero, a great Frenchman, a pioneer of France in North Africa, and in entertaining such thoughts they either forgot or never knew that Lavigerie repeatedly declared himself an African above a Frenchman, a priest above all else. Then one night in April, 1956, the statue disappeared and there was a great furore. The French protested that this important symbol of their faded authority in Tunisia had been carted away by Moslems with insulting effrontery. The Moslems, who were actually completely innocent, cheered that this towering evidence of French imperialism was out of sight. The newspapers were full of stories for days.

286

The facts were really quite simple. There were just three men involved in the disappearance of the statue: Archbishop Maurice Perrin, Bishop of Tunis and Carthage; Father André Demeerseman, a White Father who had worked in Tunis over thirty years, and Habib Bourguiba, the first president of Tunisia. The idea had been Perrin's. He knew that there were still strong feelings against the French. And he knew that the French in recent years, in search of a standard-bearer, had displayed far more adulation toward the statue than their grandfathers had toward Lavigerie himself. Doing this, especially right in front of the Medina, irked the Arabs. Perrin thought it would be a good idea to move the statue to a less conspicuous place.

He sent for Father Demeerseman. Assuredly, no Frenchman in Tunisia understood the Arab and admired him more than Demeerseman. A short, rather chubby man of fifty-seven, with just a fringe of white hair and a short white beard which gave him a startling resemblance to Santa Claus, he had an intelligence, wit, charm, perception, sympathy, and honesty which both Arabs and Europeans appreciated, respected, and trusted. During the complex negotiations toward self-government, both French and Tunisian leaders consulted with Demeerseman for guidance and advice. To both sides he gave the benefit of his experience, but to neither side did he reveal the plans of the other that had been confided to him.

Archibishop Perrin told Demeerseman his feelings about the statue. Demeerseman agreed that it should be moved, and he suggested that, in order to avoid any kind of a scene whatsoever, it be moved in the still of some quiet night. He agreed to take the plan up with the president.

Habib Bourguiba had been an old friend and an old neighbor of the White Fathers. His house was next door to the White Fathers' house in the Arab Quarter, and at a time during the struggle for independence when it seemed there might be great violence in the city Bourguiba had told his wife: "If anything happens to me, go to the White Fathers and they will help you." Bourguiba is a Moslem and president of a Moslem country, but he has developed from years of friendship with the White Fathers the tolerance which Cardinal Lavigerie always said was latent in the heart of all Moslems; it was because of Bourguiba that the new Tunisian constitution provides freedom of religion in the land.

Bourguiba told Demeerseman: "Very well, if you want to move the statue, I will send you the men and trucks to do the job."

And so in the middle of the night the statue was moved out to Church property at Carthage. Those who did not know the facts were passionate in their objections or approvals, and there was almost another fight because of it. But then the three men primarily concerned revealed the discussions they had had, displaying the understanding and co-operation which Lavigerie himself had predicted a century before.

Actually, the least necessary monument to the memory of Cardinal Lavigerie was the concrete resemblance of him, high on a pedestal. Stretching for thousands of miles southward throughout Africa were much more important monuments, living monuments: the sons of Lavigerie: the White Fathers.

One of them was just ten minutes away from where the statue once stood—Father Demeerseman. There could be many ways to serve Arabs along the lines Lavigerie had recommended, but Demeerseman's was most unique. Years in Tunisia had made him an authority on Arab culture. He had written several books about it, lectured on it—to Arabs, if you please, and was consulted constantly by experts throughout the world. In 1948, the young men of Tunis found in Demeerseman a very special friend. Three of them had been expelled from college for political action, and they had no place to study for their university entrance examinations. They went to Father Demeerseman's house, which is called IBLA—L'Institut des Belles Lettres Arabes, and they asked if they might study there. The youth of Tunis were exceptionally politically active at the time, and in a few days there were five young men studying at IBLA, then ten, then a hundred, and at last two hundred and fifty. They had free access to the excellent library, Demeerseman added class rooms to the building for their use, and the five priests assigned to IBLA went to work as professors. To their assistance in 1955 went Yvon Hamel, a young Canadian who had been on a one-man pilgrimage to Palestine when his funds ran out. He went to the White Fathers for help, discovered their unique school, volunteered to teach, and after a year of it became convinced that his place, too, was with the Arabs.

He has entered the diocesan seminary and will one day be a priest in Tunis.

With such a staff of professors, the expelled students soon found themselves ahead of those who had managed to remain at the college, and when the time came for the examinations, the young men who had been tossed out of school did better than those who stayed there. And they had learned something more. Many of them were from out of town, from the rural sections where feelings against Christians still ran deep. At IBLA, they lost such feelings. Just getting to know the priests was all it took, just getting to know laymen like Hamel. Adhering to Lavigerie's earliest instructions, the IBLA staff never mentioned religion to the students, unless they asked specific questions. The students asked, and asking, they learned, and learning, they lost their inherited antagonisms, and having lost that, they could be friends. That is how Lavigerie said it would be.

These days, it is overwhelming to realize how many of the things Lavigerie predicted subsequently materialized. His phenomenal grasp of the African temperament, whether Moslem or pagan, enabled him to detect trends on the continent long before they even appeared. As both a student and professor of history, he had only to glance backwards into the years to be able to foresee the current problems of Africa. He was a Frenchman and he loved his country, but when he became the Archbishop of Algiers, he declared himself an African, and after that he always thought as an African. As a clergyman, he was primarily interested in the welfare of the Church in Africa. At one time he urged Frenchmen to move to Algeria and Tunisia, and he did so because he wanted the two countries to become not more French but more Catholic. It was understandable that Lavigerie should feel that the Catholic Church would prove to be the best civilizing agent in Africa; he was, after all, a Catholic himself, and he was a historian. He also knew that the act of civilizing a country was like a door that could only be opened from the inside. For this reason, he went to work at the earliest moment, setting up schools, hospitals, and farms where the Moslem could learn methods of self-improvement, and when the White Fathers' caravans headed into the interior, he armed them with instructions to carry on the same programs. There were many in his homeland who opposed him, either because they were anticleric or merely ill informed, and he warned them that unless the Church was allowed to work freely and openly, gradually exerting its influence for good, the people would not rest until they pushed the French into the sea. None of Lavigerie's opponents lived long enough to realize how right he was.

Lavigerie displayed the same vision in the organization of the White Fathers. He knew that as sentiments of the people grew against their European rulers, there would also be strong feelings against the Europeans in Africa. This meant there could be resentment against a priest simply because he was born in the country ruling the colony. To avoid that, Lavigerie built the White Fathers on a truly international foundation. His first priests were French because it was in France that he was best known, but in a few years they were coming from Belgium, Holland, England, Canada, and the United States, until now they come from fifteen different countries, living and working together in mixed groups with friendship and harmony between themselves and with the people. Thus during World War II when missionary societies from Germany or Italy were moved away for the sake of security, the White Fathers were able to continue their projects uninterrupted, and even fill in for those who had to leave. Perhaps Lavigerie could not have foreseen the situation exactly as it occurred, but the unexpected benefit of being an international society upheld the instinctive wisdom of the original idea.

It was also Lavigerie's idea that his missionaries should always remember that they were in Africa for the sake of the African. He was stern in his instructions not to Europeanize the African, believing that in time the African could decide for himself what there might be in Europe he wished to make his own. It was inevitable that many European factors would be attractive to the African, especially the fruits of scientific progress, but Lavigerie wanted these factors to be adjusted to Africa—not the other way around. That there should be many important Europeans in Africa who failed to grasp the subtlety of Lavigerie's idea was no surprise to him, nor to the White Fathers who have followed after him. But the African understood, and that was all that mattered.

One man who has proved to have far more understanding than many people suspected is Kwame Nkrumah, prime minister of the Gold Coast, the first African to become the elected leader of a country that was once a colony. For years it was well known that certain colonial officials in the Gold Coast tried persistently to thwart the influence of the Catholic missions. Long before he rose to prominence, Nkrumah hungered to lead his country to independence, and though he was a Catholic, mission-educated, and for years a mission teacher, he left the Church during his political ascendance and even dabbled in Communism. In time, he described himself as a non-denominational Christian and Marxian Socialist. His friends considered both descriptions a strange contradiction of terms, and many of them felt that Nkrumah had actually removed himself from the Catholic Church because he believed it to be politically expedient. In any event, the attitude spread through the Gold Coast that Nkrumah had become as anti-Catholic as the colonials whose favor he curried while at the same time appearing to oppose them. Africans who admired Nkrumah adopted the sentiments they thought were his, and soon Gold Coast Catholics began to wonder if they were going to be any better off under their own government than they had been under colonial rule. For a long time, Nkrumah did nothing to offset the growing impression, even when he was quoted as saying that he felt the missions had held back his people, particularly in the Northern Territories—where the White Fathers were. Though it was common knowledge that the only schools in the Northern Territories for twenty-five years were those built by the White Fathers, the fact was lost in the sweep of hero worship for the country's liberator. And when the colonial government cut off its partial support of the mission schools, the White Fathers continued their building program on whatever money they could beg from friends abroad.

Though they lived a century apart, Lavigerie's faith in future African leaders like Nkrumah proved to be well placed. Despite rumors of his anti-Catholicism—all denied by his closest friends, Nkrumah appointed five Catholics to his cabinet of ten. Rather than oppose mission schools, he approved early in 1956 a program to build five schools a year for the next seven years in the White Fathers' area. Furthermore, he told J. H. Allassani, then his minister of education, that he believed the mission schools to be the only place the youth of the country could receive the proper moral training. Sometime later, the Catholic missions were criticized in his presence, and Nkrumah said: "I am a product of the missions myself."

Several of Nkrumah's friends believe that he has never really left the Catholic Church; one friend reports making private visits with him to isolated chapels on tours of the hinterlands, and another quotes him as saying: "Once you're a Catholic, you're always a Catholic." But that is a matter for Nkrumah's conscience. Already his unheralded actions have proclaimed his recognition of the contributions made to his country by the missions, and his apparent willingness to support the missions until African staffs are available to take over makes him an admirable model for other leaders now rising throughout the continent.

That is the aim of the White Fathers: to prepare the African staffs to take over. Through the years, the society has developed a most effective technique toward that end.

It would be difficult to discern exactly what makes the White Fathers different from other missionary societies, and yet the other societies have acknowledged the difference. A Salecian Father who is superior of a school adjacent to a White Fathers' mission in the Congo recently said: "I never expected to find, even in the great fraternity of the priesthood, another society of missionaries with whom I could live in such harmony and friendship. I would follow the White Fathers anywhere in Africa. Nobody has done so much for the African, and so well." Similarly, when the Maryknoll Fathers —the American missionary society—settled in Tanganyika not long ago they asked the White Fathers to remain with them five years in order that they might observe the White Fathers' missionary methods.

Actually, there are not such marked differences in the techniques of various societies; all missionaries go into the field as well prepared as possible. But the White Fathers have had a singular advantage: they have had Lavigerie. Somehow during his long preparation for the missions, a White Father becomes another Lavigerie, developing the same love for Africa, the same dedication to hard work, the same devotion to the future of the African people. All of Lavigerie's original ideas for the missions are as applicable today as when he first introduced them—the four-year catechumenate to assure firmer Christians, the rule of three together to strengthen the spiritual solidity of the priests, the concentration on an excellent African clergy to give the Church its roots.

292

With the many influences in Africa today determined to destroy Christianity, the presence of an excellent African clergy becomes all the more essential.

One such influence is Islam, which sees in the growth of Christianity the loss of Africa to the Moslem world; another is the sorcerer, whose importance in a pagan tribe is lessened by each conversion; and another is Communism. Each year, scores of young Africans go off to Prague and Moscow for free university educations they are anxious to have. Since World War II, hundreds of them have returned to Africa, each one a trained Communist agent, each one part of the announced Communist campaign to crush the missions. With Russian funds and equipment, they have gone into newspaper publishing, into teaching and medicine, into law, even into mission work itself as fraudulent clergymen.

The Communist plan for Africa is no secret. What the Communists themselves have not revealed has been discovered by strategically located White Fathers throughout Africa whose job it is to watch for Communist action, however subtle, identify it, and alert Catholic groups. The names of many returned Moscow-trained students are known, as are the infiltrations into government, education, and labor, the disguised Communist publications, the Communist-backed social and cultural organizations, and many of the agents appointed from Europe. That the White Fathers can do little more than alert Catholic groups and try to balance Communist papers with Catholic publications is unfortunately necessary in order to avoid accusations of priests meddling in politics—a delicate matter in Africa as everywhere else. But Communism is more than politics; its convictions regarding morals and atheism put it into the realm of religion, and it is therefore within the sphere of the priests assigned to combat it—a combat which is the strongest force against Communism in Africa today.

In recent years, the Catholic combat to preserve Christianity in Africa has expanded into a unique field outside the sphere of the clergy, yet in co-operation with it. It is the lay-missionary program, which began to unfold in Europe soon after World War I, limited itself to local Catholic actions for several years while it formulated its spiritual distinctiveness, then after World War II entered the mission world with a resounding impact. This, too, was as Lavigerie would

293

have it. When he sent the former Papal Zouaves into Central Africa, he meant them to be primarily lay missionaries. Some of the Zouaves eventually joined the White Fathers as priests or brothers; others remained a few years before returning to Europe; one was killed with White Fathers in Urundi; another—Captain Joubert—lived in the Congo for many years and literally became the chief of the tribe among which he worked with the priests.

The Catholic lay apostolate, now recognized by the Church as a specific religious vocation, grew from what seemed to be a spontaneous desire among young men and women who wanted to work for the Church in the missions but who were not inclined to become priests or nuns. Many admitted that their interests had been stirred by returning missionaries, especially White Fathers, who brought back reports of what had been done and the great task that remained to be done. The laity began to realize the need for its skills in the missions. Women particularly offered to go to the missions as nurses, doctors, and teachers. At the time, Europe, like most of the world, was in the pits of a postwar moral depression, and bishops suggested that the women remain on the continent for a while to urge others to lead more spiritual lives. Such was the beginning of both the Grail and the International Catholic Auxiliary. Another idea was meanwhile growing in labor groups—the Young Christian Workers, dedicated to the promulgation of Christian principles and papal writings among workers and in labor organizations. All three groups grew rapidly. By the late thirties, they had expanded throughout Europe, into Canada and the United States. But it was not until after the Second World War that they finally got to the missions.

Of the three, Grail has become most popular in the United States. There are some seven thousand members working out of seven centers, most of them trained at Grail headquarters near Loveland, Ohio. At some period during their Grail careers, the girls live together, working for a bishop in offices, hospitals, on publications or in social work, the salaries they earn going into a common treasury to support the program. Most of them eventually marry, devoting part of their time to Grail work and encouraging younger girls to join the movement, but about a hundred women have given their lives completely to the work and provide its nucleus. Grail's aim is to urge Catholic women to participate more in Church liturgy—to attend weekday Mass, receive the sacraments, lead better Catholic lives, and as such they have a place in the missions. Twenty-two American girls are now working in Africa, with others in the India, South America, and U.S. South mission fields. They run a hospital at Rubaga, a high school in the Uganda mountains, and they teach at the Catholic university in Southern Rhodesia. Such jobs provide an income for each group as they pursue their spiritual program among African women.

The International Catholic Auxiliaries, though comprised of lay women, has a rule more approaching the life of nuns. After a trial period, members are expected to take a life pledge in the society which includes chastity and poverty. The ICA training period is longer than the Grail; aspirants who do not have a profession are entered into universities near the Chicago headquarters of the organization so that when they eventually go to the missions they will be prepared to perform specific jobs in the program of the advancement of native women.

As yet, the relatively new American branch of the Young Christian Workers has not attempted the mission field, devoting itself to Catholic action at the parish level among young laymen. The organization has members in most of the major unions; they have succeeded in influencing a California factory from aligning itself with a Communist-linked union and have ferreted Communists out of unions in Milwaukee and New York. And when the American YCW is ready to enter the mission field, it need only look to the Holland branch of the organization for examples of what to do.

In March, 1956, six young Dutchmen left their home for two years in the Tanganyika missions, declaring that having given two years of their lives to the governments in military service they felt they should likewise give two years to the Church. Each man is a skilled construction worker and has held excellent jobs in Holland. In Africa, they will build schools and churches for the missions, teaching their trades to Africans while at the task. Unique about the group is their financial arrangements. Bishop James Holmes Siedle, in whose diocese they are working, provides board, room, and pocket money. The YCW provides more pocket money, most of which is banked in Holland to be given to the men on their return. The YCW will also give each man three weeks' salary upon his return. Unions to which the men belong keep them on the records as members in good standing, but they pay no dues during their absence. Employers have agreed to take the men back after their mission work, but if for any reason this is impossible, their unions and the YCW will find them jobs. Should they decide to settle in Africa, Bishop Siedle will locate jobs for them. Meanwhile, Bishop Siedle has six skilled lay missionaries working for him at no major expense to the diocese, which is an important benefit since no missionary bishop can afford all the helpers he needs.

Actually, the missionary bishops have probably been the most surprised by the current surge of lay missionary activity. For years, it was difficult for them even to arouse more than passing interest in their work. These days, the bishops now find themselves devoting an increasing part of their time to correspondence with people who want to go to the missions or at least stir support of the missions at home. Agencies like the Grail movement have been particularly swamped with applicants: the new Grail training center in Brooklyn proved to be too small even before it was opened. Undoubtedly, much of the American interest is the result of the television appearances of Bishop Fulton J. Sheen, who, as national director of the Office of the Propagation of the Faith, heads mission work in the United States. In his present position, he has perhaps done more than anyone in the country to make Catholics mission-minded. Diocesan mission directors have followed his lead in spurring the laity. Monsignor Anthony J. Browers, the Los Angeles director, for instance, will, by the end of 1957, have sent thirty lay missionaries to work with the White Fathers.

Surely there are many reasons for the growing concern among the laity, among them being the realization that there is a place for them in the missions. Yet, despite that need, the Church has not rushed the qualified laymen off to Africa, as at first might seem the sensible thing to do. Instead, applicants are required to go through at least a year of special preparation for the missions, a year spent in deepening their own spiritual lives. This, too, conforms with Lavigerie's insistence that his men strengthen themselves with strong spirituality, without which they could achieve nothing of lasting value. Whatever else the priests or laity might achieve for the African, the spirituality of the African was uppermost in

Lavigerie's mind, and it was this he wanted his men to implant in order to give purpose and direction to everything else. That Lavigerie's instructions were carried out is evident in the permanency of all the White Fathers have initiated.

Certainly another factor in arousing interest in the missions of all denominations has been Dr. Albert Schweitzer, probably the most famous missionary in Africa, and perhaps the most controversial. Some missionaries complain that Schweitzer has received too much adulation for what he has done during his forty years in Africa, that as a result of it he receives more attention and financial support than others who are doing more. To be sure, Schweitzer's hospital at Lambaréné in French Equatorial Africa is undoubtedly the best-known mission on the continent. Yet it is not exactly a mission; it is across the Ogowe River from a Catholic mission and down the river from a thriving French Protestant mission, but it is more specifically a hospital. The only formal place to pray on the property is the Catholic chapel built by patients of the adjacent leper colony. Because of the proximity of actual missions, Schweitzer conducts no formal religious services as such at the hospital, except on important days like Christmas and Easter, otherwise leaving the usual church ceremonies to ministers in Africa for that specific purpose. However, he prays publicly in the dining room and leads hymns there regularly. Schweitzer has made no attempt to lift the African by making him into a doctor, or nurse or even a laboratory technician. All such work is done by a European staff comprised of men and women who desire to work in the missions, specifically to work with Schweitzer. Yet Schweitzer went to Africa fundamentally to provide medical care for the African, and this he has succeeded magnificently in doing. True, others have done the same, but what makes Schweitzer uniquely important to the missions is that he was a celebrity long before he went to the missions. He was a leading theologian, teacher, writer, speaker, and probably the finest organist of his time before he studied medicine with the intention of going to the aid of the African. His fame followed him to Africa, and it was natural that it should. His subsequent writings, plus the great deal of writing about him, have kept his fame alive. Though he appears to overshadow all other missionaries, he has nevertheless inadvertently drawn attention to the entire mission field and thus been a valuable asset to it. The only misfortune is that on his death his hospital is likely to fade away from the lack of his dynamic appeal, an unavoidable risk when the success of a mission depends on the personality of the missionary.

On the other hand, the White Fathers' highly developed concept of mission work advocates minimizing the personality of the missionary so that the station continues to function undisturbed no matter what personnel changes are made. This approach, plus Lavigerie's instructions to the priests to become as much like the African as possible, results in an enduring program which puts the emphasis on the native, his material and spiritual welfare, and particularly his place in the future of the Church. The obvious goal is the secure establishment of the Church and the permanent expansion of Christianity. With these assured, it is inevitable that all the other fruits of Christian life will follow, providing not only a better world for the people of the mission area but for everyone everywhere else. It has been to this goal that the White Fathers have dedicated themselves for a century, and recent evidence of it occurred on Palm Sunday, 1956, when Bishop André Perraudin was consecrated at Kabgayi in the heart of Ruanda. In the idea of the consecration itself there was nothing unique, for in the past seventy-five years many White Fathers have become bishops in Africa. But this time there was something special. The prelate chosen to consecrate Perraudin was Bishop Aloys Bigirumwami, whose diocese was just to the north of Kabgayi, and the distinctive feature was that Bishop Bigirumwami was an African, a product of White Fathers' missions, schools, and seminaries. The event was the first such consecration in the history of Africa; the second in the history of the Church. A friend in Europe wrote Perraudin: "I am impressed that you should have chosen a black man to consecrate you, but I think I can understand. These days, it is the fad."

"No," replied Perraudin. "It is the Faith."

It is the Faith which has made the White Fathers so remarkable a group of men, the Faith which has been the source of their astonishing zeal.

Perhaps the outstanding feature of the Society is that a White Father is more than one man. He is a priest, a teacher, a farmer, a publisher, a counselor, a writer, a doctor, a mediator, a jury, a veterinarian, a Scout master, a contractor, an engineer. He is, as

Cardinal Lavigerie instructed him to be, all things to all men, and to all men a spiritual father channeling his efforts towards spiritual welfare.

Such a man was Father Jean Tabart, who was killed in the Algerian mountains on his way home from the French Army camp. In a way, he was no different from any other White Father, except that in doing what he considered his job he had taken on the additional duties of a chaplain to men who were without a priest. Day after day for more than ten years, he had rushed from his mission at Géryville in an impatient search for the opportunity to serve the people around him. His death at the hands of Algerian insurgents was a grave misfortune and a serious loss, but his Moslem friends had no sooner lowered him into his grave when a new White Father arrived to follow in his footsteps, to spend a lifetime treating the sick, solving family woes, teaching the illiterate, befriending the children, aiding the struggling farmer, each day crammed with acts of charity performed in the love of God and the love of Africa.

It is love, then, that makes the White Father something special; it is love which inspires him to tireless service to the God and the Africa to which he has dedicated his life; and it is a love which is apparently discernible everywhere in the world. In October, 1956, for example, the various missionary societies with training centers in the United States met in Philadelphia for their annual exhibition under the auspices of the Propagation of the Faith. On a rainy afternoon, an elderly Negro woman slowly made her way through the exhibit hall and paused in front of the White Fathers' display. One of the photographs caught her interest and she looked at it a long time. It was of a young White Father on a motorcycle, talking with two African boys. Someone had apparently made a joke, probably one of the boys, and they were all laughing. After a few minutes, the elderly woman smiled, and she said softly:

"Isn't that wonderful? I've never seen so much love in a man's face. The way he looks at those boys, you'd think he was one of us."

With that, Cardinal Lavigerie's dream was fulfilled.

Set in Caledonia
Format by James T. Parker
Manufactured by The Haddon Craftsmen, Inc.
Published by HARPER & BROTHERS, New York

A WHITE FATHERS MAP OF AFRICA

Total Number of White Fathers in Africa: 2,253
Total Number of White Sisters in Africa: 1,200
Number of Mission Stations, White Fathers: 468 }
Number of Mission Stations, African Clergy: 109 } Total 577
Dioceses: 37

SHADED REGIONS INDICATE WHITE FATHERS MISSION AREAS